Decisive Decade

Praise for the Book

Futurology is an inexact discipline, an odd mix of determinates and indeterminates. For this reason, Kiran Karnik's is a bold venture, more so because the typology of 'gazelle' and 'hippo' tends to underplay the diversity of the animal kingdom and its techniques of survival and success. That said, there is no denying the criticality of the nine areas of endeavour on which we, as a people, must focus in the present decade. Priorities would differ; for me, social peace and harmony would impact each of them.
—**M. Hamid Ansari,** former Vice President of India

Kiran Karnik is one of India's rare public intellectuals. Over the years, he has not only shaped our understanding of the important development policy issues facing our country but also led to many successful breakthroughs to meet the difficult challenges with his artful praxis. In *Decisive Decade*, Kiran lucidly illuminates the decisive policy challenges that our beloved country will be facing in the coming decade. Thankfully, he also offers thoughtful proposals for taking actions and achieving what he beautifully describes as the 'gazelle'-like outcomes. I warmly recommend everyone to read this wonderful book, infused so much with hope and wisdom.
—**Vijay Kelkar,** former Finance Secretary

In this unputdownable book, Kiran Karnik combines his amazing insights and uncanny observational powers to show that 2020s will be a make-or-break decade for India. His powerful strategy for shaping the 'desirable future' of India@2030 should inspire every single Indian into action.
—**R.A. Mashelkar,** former Director General, Council of Scientific and Industrial Research (CSIR)

Will the 2020s be India's decade? Will India leverage the Information Age to create or destroy value? Will technology be used to bring peace and prosperity or disharmony and decline? Kiran Karnik's poignant analysis indicates the head and tail winds that the Indian economy will need to navigate and create its destiny in the decade ahead.

—**Kiran Mazumdar-Shaw,** Executive Chairperson, Biocon

Kiran Karnik has been associated with the key organizations that have created modern India, ranging from the Indian Space Research Organization to NASSCOM and the Reserve Bank of India. His varied experience makes him the ideal person to ask and answer the question: What will India be like in 2030? In this extremely readable and interesting book, Karnik argues that it is quite possible India could be a gazelle—sleek, agile, and likeable. Yet he also suggests dystopias where India ends up a hippopotamus—bulky, slow-moving, bad-tempered, and ultimately the nightmare its founding fathers sought to prevent. Everyone who cares about India should read this book so that we can strengthen the better angels of its nature.

—**Raghuram Rajan,** former Governor, RBI

Forecasting the future is never easy but in the hands of Kiran Karnik, not only is it insightful but, I'm pretty confident, it will prove prophetic. There are few people who understand the deeper issues connected with our politics and democracy, our society and our security and the impact of all of this on technology. Kiran Karnik's vision of the future offers us a chance to see what our lives will be like 10 years from now. Astrologers and *jyotshis* might be wrong but not Kiran Karnik.

—**Karan Thapar,** Journalist and Author

In *Decisive Decade*, Kiran Karnik looks ahead to the next twenty years of Indian society. Examining what our country could look like through spheres ranging from technology, jobs, and education to health and democracy, Karnik provides insightful and thoughtful reflections on the paths India could take. Thinking ahead with a hopeful yet realistic strategy for the future is critical for a country that hopes to progress, and Karnik's guide is a valuable resource.

—**Shashi Tharoor,** Author and Member of Parliament

Decisive Decade

India 2030: Gazelle or Hippo

KIRAN KARNIK

RUPA

Published by
Rupa Publications India Pvt. Ltd 2021
7/16, Ansari Road, Daryaganj
New Delhi 110002

Sales Centres:
Allahabad Bengaluru Chennai
Hyderabad Jaipur Kathmandu
Kolkata Mumbai

Copyright © Kiran Karnik 2021

The views and opinions expressed in this book are the author's own and the facts are as reported by him which have been verified to the extent possible, and the publishers are not in any way liable for the same.

All rights reserved.
No part of this publication may be reproduced, transmitted, or stored in a retrieval system, in any form or by any means, electronic, mechanical, photocopying, recording or otherwise, without the prior permission of the publisher.

ISBN: 978-93-90547-47-0

First impression 2021

10 9 8 7 6 5 4 2 3 1

Printed by Nutech Print Services, Faridabad

This book is sold subject to the condition that it shall not, by way of trade or otherwise, be lent, resold, hired out, or otherwise circulated, without the publisher's prior consent, in any form of binding or cover other than that in which it is published.

CONTENTS

Preface	*vii*
Introduction: Twenty Twenties: The Time to Transform	*ix*
1. Democracy and Politics: Ensuring Justice and Freedom	1
2. Security: Maintaining Social Harmony and Peaceful Borders	36
3. Health: Adding Years to Life and Life to Years	65
4. Education: Building a Knowledge Society	88
5. Economy: Eradicating Poverty, Reducing Inequality	123
6. Demography: More Age-Care Homes, Fewer Anganwadis	144
7. Society and Social Dynamics: Challenging the Status Quo	169
8. Jobs and Livelihoods: Will a Machine Steal Your Job?	195
9. Technology: Every Breath You Take: Pervasive Tech	219
Epilogue: India 2030+Creating a Happy Country	246
Index	263

PREFACE

This book had its genesis in an informal conversation over lunch in the office of Rupa Publications. Kapish Mehra, Yamini Chowdhury (Managing Director and Senior Commissioning Editor, respectively, of Rupa), and I were chatting about my last book (Evolution), especially its focus on technology and its role in years to come. The discussion veered to the state of the country and how technology may influence so many aspects of its future. Detecting my passion about the state of the nation, Kapish suggested that my next book must be on a broader canvas, looking at India and where it is headed. He was confident that my perspective would be different and of interest to readers. Within a few days, Yamini followed up with a possible outline, and the seed of this book was sown.

I am grateful to Kapish and Yamini for initiating this book, and their conviction that my viewpoint would be of interest. Yamini has, subsequently, stayed the course, with regular discussions—almost all in e-mode, given the pandemic. I thank her for the many inputs in the formative stages, followed by suggestions and meticulous editing of the manuscript. Her diligence and gentle reminders of deadlines missed (many!) have greatly helped in the production of this book.

I also thank Debangana Banerjee, copy editor, for rigorously re-checking facts, figures and references, and for painstakingly copy editing the manuscript. Remaining errors, if any, are my responsibility.

In the course of writing, I benefited from numerous

discussions and conversations with colleagues and friends, so many of whom have unknowingly helped to shape and hone the thoughts in the book. A few also gave specific inputs or relevant information. I can name many, but in fear of missing out on some, I refrain from mentioning names. I do, though, want to record my gratitude to all these anonymous contributors.

A more direct and major collaborator has been my daughter, Ketaki. Having helped with my three previous books, she has developed the expertise of not just providing the right inputs into whatever I am writing, but also to influence and shape it. Amidst a full-time job and completing her own book, she spent endless hours digging up data and finding the right sources or references for me. Ranging from such assistance to being a frank critic to a why-aren't-you-working boss, she played multiple roles. As in my earlier books, this one too would have taken many more months—and suffered in quality—but for her invaluable partnership.

Finally, an acknowledgement to the big silent contributor, my wife Sunitee. Ever encouraging, prodding gently and not-so-gently about deadlines for the book, she ensured that I stayed on the job. She made sure that I had the time and space for writing: space to spread papers, cuttings, drafts, computer, and other tools of the trade all over the house—including, especially, the dining table (my most productive space!); and time, by exempting me from all household duties. The latter was particularly important during the lockdown, with no household help. I was allowed to escape my not-so-favourite BJP (*bartan, jhadoo, pocha*) duties, and spend time on the book. I owe her much for all this, and much, much more.

And thank you, dear reader, for reaching so far. Do read on...

Kiran Karnik
April 2021

INTRODUCTION

Twenty Twenties: The Time to Transform

One thing about the future was certain, at least till recently: that it would arrive. However, a worldwide nuclear war could kill most of us and make the planet uninhabitable for humans. Alternatively, climate change and runaway global warming could lead to a similar result: an earth on which our species may not survive. In both cases, there would hardly be a future. This book does not foresee such apocalypses, and believes that humans are wise enough to avoid such an end, even if we sometimes seem to be at the very edge of this cliff. It looks at the future with cautious optimism and hope.

Predicting what the future holds is a fraught exercise. One can take the view, as a popular song from yesteryear did, that 'Que sera sera/ Whatever will be will be/ The future's not ours to see/ Whatever's to be will be/ Que sera sera'[1]; that destiny and historical determinism will decide our fate. Yet, much of what we do today, from saving money to goading children into studying, is aimed at trying to create our own future and ensuring a better tomorrow. At a collective level, communities and countries too seek to influence and improve

---

[1] The lyrics by Jay Livingston and Ray Evans were popularized through Doris Day singing it in the Alfred Hitchcock movie, *The Man Who Knew Too Much* (1956).

their future. This book is based on the firm belief that our actions can determine the future. Accordingly, we attempt to look at India's future through the major factors that will shape and define it. The horizon is 2030, thus covering the decade of the 2020s, though we end with a cursory look further ahead: to 2050.

Ten years in the life of a nation is but a blink of an eye. For a country like India, with a history that stretches back some 5,000 years, it is a negligible period. Can one really expect to see any discernible change in such a short period of one decade? On the other hand, the accelerating pace of change means that time scales have been telescoped. Lenin said, 'There are decades where nothing happens; and there are weeks where decades happen'. Technological advancement seems to have brought us to the stage where decades happen in weeks; this, and the speed of technology's penetration into society, means that the extent and pace of change are both high. As technology becomes a part of almost all that we do, its influence and effect are immense. It has a deep and wide impact on our work, leisure and behaviour. While effects on individual behaviour and societal norms are typically slow and long-drawn-out processes, the timeline on this too is changing. The velocity of technology's spread and its ubiquity are shrinking the time required for social change. It is in this context that there are clear possibilities of seeing tangible and substantial changes over the period of a decade. This, then, is the premise of what follows: that there will be considerable and visible change in many aspects of India between 2020 and 2030.

The century began well, with the first ten years recording unprecedented growth rates in the economy. Millions were lifted out of poverty, and the economy grew at an average of

7.36 per cent a year from 2003 to 2010.[2] If the exceptional year of global slowdown (2008) is excluded, the average growth rate increases to 7.97 per cent. India was also unique in terms of successfully weathering the global economic crisis of 2008. This added to its international stature. On the political front, relations with China were stable, with booming trade overriding past suspicions; the US was a strategic partner; our long-time friendship with Russia continued (even if with lesser intensity); Pakistan was getting increasingly isolated diplomatically, with no takers for its propaganda against India and our relationship with other neighbours was cordial. Within the country, there was comparative harmony. India's star was very much on the ascendant.

The hope (indeed, the expectation) was that this would be India's century. Some even felt that it marked the beginning of an Indian millennium. However, from around 2012, things started going downhill. Accusations of corruption and scams bedevilled the government, seemingly paralysing policymaking and affecting governance. This, and some retrograde (and retrospective) tax laws in the Union Budget of 2012–13, put the brakes on economic growth, worsening the impact of a general global economic slowdown. The change of government in 2014 led to initial optimism, but soon the downward trajectory resumed (visibly so, after demonetization in November 2016); if anything, the increasing communal disharmony and the focus on divisive cultural and political issues created greater problems. 'Muscular' policies with regard to Pakistan and in Kashmir may have paid off for the Bharatiya Janata Party (BJP)

---

[2]Annual percentage growth rate of GDP at market prices based on constant local currency. Source: 'GDP Growth (Annual %)—India', *The World Bank*, https://data.worldbank.org/indicator/NY.GDP.MKTP.KD.ZG?locations=IN, accessed on 17 March 2021.

in the 2019 elections (bringing it back to power with even more seats in Parliament), but have not done any good for India in strategic terms. The 2020 border fracas with China took our relationship back by many decades, and is going to require a big increase in military spending (at the cost of pressing social and infrastructure needs). The economic and livelihoods situation suffered a further setback from March 2020 due to the COVID pandemic and consequent lockdowns. In summary, it seems that the years from around 2011–12 may be considered India's lost decade.

The 2020s provide an opportunity to once again emulate the period from around 2000 to 2012. Will we choose the correct path at the crossroads? India can either sink further into a morass of disharmony, social unrest, low economic growth and poverty, or it can begin to build itself up. If the nation can focus on key areas that affect its future (and not on our 'glorious past' or the '70 years of misrule'), we have an opportunity to not only take the country forward in a big way, but also to strengthen the base for crafting a glorious future.

In looking ahead, one approach could be to identify and call out the changes that may be seen in a decade, as compared to 2020. This would, therefore, look at outcomes: the actual impact on our work, leisure, life and the environment around us. It would, in a way, present a scenario of life in 2030. Another approach is to look at a step preceding the outcomes. It would seek to identify key factors that will drive the major changes that we may see in 2030 and track how each of these would evolve over the course of the decade from 2020 to 2030. This requires, first, analysis to determine the factors that would have the maximum influence on individuals and society as the country goes towards 2030, and then prediction of what changes might be seen in each of them between now and 2030.

It is also necessary to understand and project the results of the interplay between these factors, since each of them affects many of the others.

Every facet of all that is around us—and also within us—will affect the future. From all these, picking only a few is a difficult exercise, and the choices can easily be questioned. Yet, there are some that stand out as being major determinants of our future; on these, there is likely to be widespread agreement or even a consensus.

For the purpose of this book, nine such areas have been picked as the major determinants of the 'state of the nation' in 2030. These are:

- Democracy and politics
- Security
- Health
- Education
- Economy
- Demography
- Social change
- Jobs and livelihoods
- Technology

In what follows, each of these have been discussed, beginning with the history and present status, then identifying trends and predicting future directions and finally projecting the likely state in 2030. In a dynamic and rapidly changing world, the uncertainties are many. Predictions are, therefore, risky. Yet, such an exercise is useful because it stirs thought, discussion and debate—not just on where the country may be in 2030, but also on where one would like it to be; not merely on likely futures, but equally on desirable futures. This opens up a dialogue on trends, behaviour and a whole host of cultural, sociopolitical, economic and strategic matters. In addition, by looking at desirable futures, it may stimulate debate on the model of development and on basic assumptions. For example, we have moved from a stated (though only minimally implemented) socialist model of economic development to an unstated—but very visible—capitalist one. At the same time, the assumption that education and economic growth will quickly obliterate or vastly reduce divides (of wealth, caste, religion), seems to have been belied. These issues merit deliberation.

Having covered each of the major 'influencers' separately, there is then an attempt to bring them together to paint a holistic picture of India 2030. Finally, to look at the longer-range perspective, we leap ahead by two more decades, and outline very briefly a scenario of India in 2050: the country as it may be 100 years after its birth as a republic.

Apart from the nine areas covered, one might have liked to add a few others too. Also, the changing context alters impact, making an area seem far more important. For example, health was earlier subsumed in some of the other areas covered. However, following the COVID pandemic, it is clear that health is going to be a major determinant of the future. Countries worldwide have experienced both the health and economic impact of the pandemic. The former is, obviously, important in itself: it determines the quality of life of people. Now, however, 'economic health' has added connotations in recognition of the big role health may play in economic well-being. This multiplies its importance in a poor health–status country like India.

Technology will, without a doubt, be a major element in shaping the future. It is now so widespread and ubiquitous that it influences practically all facets of an individual's life and that of the country. Its ramifications are, therefore, discussed in almost all the other identified key areas. Yet, given its pervasiveness and importance, it merits a separate discussion too, as a distinct, future-shaping factor.

Of the other areas, one could have been India's global positioning. The country has always been an active and important participant in global fora. It plays a key role in various United Nations (UN) bodies and in vital issues like those related to climate change, cybersecurity, outer space and oceans. India's voice has carried a lot of weight in the past as a leader of the non-aligned countries; even today, most developing nations go by its lead. Its standing in the comity of nations is, therefore, exceptional and is a significant part of its self-image (and, importantly, its soft power). However, given the discussion on this in the chapters on security and economy, separate coverage may have resulted in avoidable duplication.

Culture is certainly a factor that shapes the progress and position of countries. In France, it is a proud literary and artistic identity; in Germany and East Asia, it is an image of hard-working people; in Scotland, it is the thrift of people: each one is an important determinant of the country's progress. Despite this, here it is subsumed in other areas—primarily under 'society and social change'.

Amongst other areas that will certainly be of importance are water, environment and energy. Even though the country as a whole is endowed with generous rainfall, there are pockets of water shortage, and droughts are not uncommon. Worldwide, concerns about water availability have even led to predictions of 'water wars'. These fears are enhanced by models of climate change, which forecast water scarcity in some areas and floods in other places. At the same time, more efficient use of water, rainwater harvesting/storage, reforestation and actions to slow climate change should help to counter droughts to some extent.

Climate change and environmental issues are serious and could, in the long run, be amongst the most important ones. Failing collective corrective action at the global level, this could even be species threatening, as was noted at the outset. India may see a far greater frequency of 'extreme climate events', of the type it has been experiencing in recent years. Droughts and floods could get worse, and sea-level rise could inundate many low-lying and coastal areas. Deforestation, mining and the extensive use of highly-polluting coal in India is adding to overall global problems. All these will certainly impact India in many areas, including economy, politics, jobs and social change. It is estimated that just one impact of climate change—extreme heat—poses a $250 billion risk to India's GDP by 2030.[3] Clearly, environmental issues and climate change are of great concern to India. Despite this, the view taken here is that the impact in this decade will not be of a magnitude that warrants attention, considering it is a critical factor shaping India of 2030.

Energy is the basic driver of civilization and progress. It is, therefore, a variable that could affect the future. Worries about the world running out of oil and gas, though, are now dying down as new oil-recovery technologies (for tapping shale oil or for deep-sea drilling), renewable energy (solar and wind, in particular) and new hydrocarbon discoveries give assurance of energy security. In addition, technology may soon provide other options like nuclear fusion and hydrogen fuel. In the

---

[3]This is based on a report released by McKinsey as quoted in the *Times of India* article, 'Extreme Heat Poses $250 Billion Risk to India's GDP by 2030: Report', 28 November 2020.

light of these considerations, neither water nor energy are separately addressed as key variables (though the latter is covered, in part, in the chapter on technology).

The nine areas, each of which has a dedicated chapter, are not independent variables that influence the outcome; each of them is related to some of the others (technology, as noted, influences all the others in one way or another), and there is an overlap too amongst them. Even so, each is important enough to merit separate consideration and discussion.

This book makes no pretence of being an academic study in terms of an in-depth and thorough analysis of each of the areas covered. Such an exercise would require expertise in a variety of disciplines—from anthropology and biology, to science and technology, to zoonotic diseases (to understand the possible genesis of viruses like coronavirus)—and may yet leave gaps in the inter-disciplinary space, besides meriting a separate book for each area. This is, therefore, an attempt at taking a 'non-expert' but holistic and experiential view, drawing more from the reports and experiences of day-to-day life, rather than deep, academic research. Consequently, the approach followed in examining each of the areas is not through a quantitative or rigorous methodology, though this may well have been possible in some cases (demography or economy, for example). Instead, the attempt is to look at the qualitative aspects, use a more descriptive style and avoid the use of figures and tables, let alone equations or quantitative analysis.

In major fields, technology is creating radical changes—or on the cusp of doing so—resulting in discontinuities. This includes areas like social dynamics, in which a now-commonplace device like the mobile phone is triggering or vastly amplifying social change. Experience indicates that trend projections, or even sophisticated quantitative methods, have difficulty in dealing with discontinuities. Therefore, it may be meaningful to rely more on analysis, descriptions or scenarios, and less on quantitative techniques. A judicious combination of the two is ideal, though it may not be possible to arrive at a mix that is just right. The effort here is to use the approach that is suitable for the particular context and area, and then combine the objective and quantitative with the subjective, somewhat fuzzy—but often more insightful—qualitative aspects.

This method of using some data—definite figures—but relying equally, if not more, on qualitative analysis, is particularly appropriate for India. It has been observed by many an astute commentator that whatever one says about India is true—but so is the opposite.[4] India is indeed a country of great contrasts, even contradictions, and both data and anecdotal observations can be misleading. A recent book[5] summarizes this well when it says: 'India is … an inscrutable place. There is the everyday country of the senses, and then the country made of numbers—the analysts country. One is overwhelming, the other is confounding. It's a rare day when their stories line up.'

Different kinds of data on India may occasionally contradict each other, and there is even greater likelihood of data being contrary to observed (or felt) reality. This makes it imperative for the writer to choose a point of view, especially

---

[4] Amartya Sen, in his article in *The Economist* dated 18 November 2005 says: "The frustrating thing about India," I was told by one of my teachers, the great Cambridge economist Joan Robinson, "is that whatever you can rightly say about India, the opposite is also true." https://www.economist.com/news/2005/11/18/contrary-india, accessed on 17 March 2021.

[5] *Bridgital Nation: Solving Technology's People Problem*, N. Chandrasekaran and Roopa Purushothaman, Penguin Allen Lane, 2019.

in a book that is projecting possible outcomes a decade from now. Here, the analysis is set within the framework of optimism. One could, with some validity, adopt an opposite and pessimistic frame. There are enough facts and cues to be picked up that would justify a downhill scenario of gloom and doom. However, despite ups and downs, India has, on more than one occasion, demonstrated resilience, an ability to overcome difficult circumstances and come out stronger and better. Here, we count on this innate characteristic, and take a stance that one might consider 'cautiously optimistic'. The main intention, though, is not to project a rosy view, but to outline the contours of a possible future, a 'strawman', which can be discussed, critiqued, improved upon and reconstructed, with many differing views and perspectives contributing to it. India deserves this: a vision of the future based on the synthesis of informed and varying viewpoints, with diverse perspectives being harmonized to convergent action for common good.

This decade, the 2020s, will set the course for India, just as the ten years from 1950 laid out the path for the country in the 20th century, through the enunciation of values and the creation of key institutions. It is the make-or-break decade for India, a time for transformation—indeed, the decisive decade. Globally, its size, leadership and 'positioning' as being independent from the two major power blocks, propelled it to leadership of the 'non-aligned' countries. This made India a powerful moral force in the geopolitical world. The coming years from 2020 to 2030 are when we will go through a reiteration or a re-set of many vital parameters. With changing power equations and the virtual demise of non-alignment, the country will have to reposition itself. Various options exist, but we pick two. To summarize them through an analogy, by 2030 India could be viewed as a gazelle: sleek, agile, fast-moving and likeable. Or it could end up like a hippopotamus: large, but bulky, slow-moving and—worse—aggressive. What will we be?

1

DEMOCRACY AND POLITICS

Ensuring Justice and Freedom

Democracy has a long history, going back at least a couple of thousand years. The term is derived from the Greek word 'dēmokratiā', which was coined from 'dēmos' (people) and 'kratos' (rule) in the middle of the 5th century BCE to denote the political systems then existing in some Greek city-states, notably Athens.[1] Therefore, it means, literally, rule by the people.

During the Classical period (corresponding roughly to the 5th and 4th centuries BCE), Greece was of course not a country in the modern sense but a collection of several hundred independent city-states, each with its surrounding countryside. Although it is tempting to assume that democracy was created in one particular place and time—most often identified as Greece about the year 500 BCE—evidence suggests that democratic government, in a broad sense, existed in several areas of the world well before the turn of the 5th century. For example, studies of non-literate tribal societies suggest that democratic government existed among many tribal groups

---

[1]From 'Democracy', *Encyclopaedia Britannica*, https://www.britannica.com/topic/democracy/Democratic-institutions, accessed on 17 March 2021.

during the thousands of years when human beings survived by hunting and gathering. To these early humans, democracy, such as it was practised, might well have seemed the most 'natural' political system.

One of the earliest instances of democracy, predating Greece, was found in republics in ancient India, which were established sometime before the 6th century BCE, and prior to the birth of Gautam Buddha.[2] These republics were known as Mahajanapadas, and among these states, Vaishali (in what is now Bihar, India) was the world's first republic. Later, during the time of Alexander the Great in the 4th century BCE, the Greeks wrote about the Sabarcae and Sambastai states in what are now Pakistan and Afghanistan respectively, whose 'form of government was democratic and not regal' according to Greek scholars at the time. Another example was Gopala's rise to power by democratic election in Bengal, which was documented by the Tibetan historian, Taranatha.

SUCCESSES AND ILLS OF INDIA'S ELECTORAL PROCESS

Following centuries of feudal and colonial rule, the beginning of democracy in recent times in India is marked by Independence in 1947 and the constitution of the country as a republic in 1950. The Constitution serves as the framework of what has proven to be a robust and thriving democracy. India's general elections, when people elect those who represent them in Parliament, have always been well contested, noisy—often chaotic—celebrations of democracy, conducted in a free, fair

---

[2] From 'History of Democracy', *Wikipedia*, https://www.cs.mcgill.ca/~rwest/wikispeedia/wpcd/wp/h/History_of_democracy.htm, accessed on 17 March 2021.

and efficient manner. In this, the Election Commission of India (ECI) has played a key role, as have the mechanics of fraud-free voting (like the electronic voting machine [EVM]). These, therefore, deserve a more detailed exposition.

The ECI has been the bulwark of a smoothly functioning democracy. However, for many years, it was considered a toothless body, depending more on the moral force of its pronouncements than on action. One chief election commissioner, T.N. Seshan, changed this when he assumed office in December 1990. He not only found that the ECI, in fact, had considerable power, but began to actually use it. Through forceful statements, quotable quotes and an aggressive stance, he brought the ECI front and centre in the eyes of the people. Subsequent members of the ECI have carried forward this legacy, though possibly with lesser force or demonstrable neutrality than Seshan. In fact, at times, the ECI is believed to be pliant, especially in relation to the wishes of the party in power. Yet, overall, the electoral process enjoys general credibility and there is no serious question about the legitimacy of results. In such a vast country, with a massive electorate, this is indeed an achievement.

Apart from its role in election-organizing, the ECI under Seshan had also become a powerful watchdog, monitoring the total electoral process including the campaigning. Any infringement of the code of conduct laid down by the ECI immediately drew action against the erring candidate or party. On this, there are accusations of late about the ECI being soft on the ruling party, especially with regard to provocative or 'hate speech'.

Over the years, the ECI—mandated to organize and oversee the elections—has made the electoral process more secure and voter friendly. In the early days, there used to be accusations of impersonations of voters, double voting, even 'capture' of polling booths and 'stuffing' of ballot boxes. Such cases have practically disappeared after the ECI introduced EVMs in every state assembly election after 2001, and for the Lok Sabha from 2004. Also, voter ID cards and Aadhaar have made impersonation difficult, almost impossible.

The EVMs are tamper-proof (and efficient ways of recording and quickly counting votes). Yet, given questions about possible rigging of EVMs—proven to be unfounded so far—the ECI has also introduced a voter verifiable paper audit trail (VVPAT) system. All this has greatly enhanced the transparency and credibility of the electoral process.

In order to promote higher voter turnout, ECI undertakes voter awareness and education programmes, often using innovative and popular means (organizing music events, for example). It has also created greater transparency by getting candidates to declare their assets, educational qualifications and any pending criminal cases. The ECI has been suggesting further reforms, especially with regard to barring convicted criminals from contesting elections.

An ongoing concern is the role of money power in elections, with political parties or individual candidates seeking to buy votes. Money, or other allures like alcohol or gifts, are known to be used as methods of influencing voters. In every election, there are reports of ECI action to seize unaccounted cash intended as bribes to voters. In addition, there is a growing incidence of 'paid news' as a means of influencing voters, and of some media outlets putting out biased news reports so as to ingratiate themselves with the party likely to win the election.

With regard to money power, a major issue relates to unaccounted donations to parties or candidates by companies and individuals. This serves as a method to buy influence or, sometimes, is a coercive 'donation' demanded by the party. Ideas of how to curb this have been around for a while, as has recognition of the undesirability of this. A recent reform has been the creation of electoral bonds. Companies can buy these bonds and give them to a party of their choice. Thus, the amount is known but not the recipient. This has been severely criticized, in part because of the view that the government can access the name of the recipient (since the transaction has to be done through a state-owned bank), but the voters and other parties cannot. Thus, there is no transparency, and it seems that the ECI did not favour the issue of electoral bonds.

Reforms to tackle these issues of non-transparency and to reduce money and criminal power in elections have been widely discussed for many years, but successive governments have been reluctant to enact the necessary legislation. These concerns do dilute the strength and vigour of our democracy. Some civil society organizations have tried to counter this. An example is the Association for Democratic Reforms (ADR), which has been doing outstanding work in bringing about more transparency by researching candidates' backgrounds, analysing data about elected candidates and putting all this in the public domain. Such initiatives, along with much more intensive reporting by media, have ensured greater public awareness.

These pitfalls notwithstanding, India's success in the task of smoothly and efficiently conducting polls involving such a massive electorate is much admired around the world. Many countries have sought advice and help in emulating our tech-based system. The credibility enjoyed by the process and the role of the ECI too has won wide acclaim. This is an additional dimension of India's soft power. One, therefore, hopes that the independence and objectivity of the ECI—on which there have recently been some questions—is retained. This is critical for nurturing the strength and force of India's democracy in the years to come.

PITFALLS OF DEMOCRACY

The numerous steps taken by ECI have certainly resulted in a credible electoral process. The post-election scenario, though, is murky and has got worse with time. Here, apart from political games and fickle loyalties, money power is in full cry. 'Buying' legislators in state assemblies has become an almost routine matter. As a result, in many cases, it is not the number of votes, but the number of notes that determine which party will form the government. Many a legislator, elected as a member of one party, defects within days or weeks to another party. Enticed by power or money, such defections make a mockery of party manifestoes and ideology. An anti-defection law passed decades ago has loopholes that make possible such a switch of parties, especially when a substantial block of legislators can be lured. Money—or the means to make it through being a minister or equivalent—makes for frictionless movement from one party to another. Where there are multiple parties in the fray, with no single dominant party, the possibility of such note-based democracy increases. It is, then, not the voters who decide which party will form the government but the cash balances of various parties. Central to this is the flexible morality of legislators, which means that they have little compunction in changing parties, without any concern about the voters who elected them on the basis of the contestant being member of a particular party. A 'right to recall', through which voters can choose to recall a legislator (that is, to cancel his/her election as a legislator), has been debated, but is not in place yet. In some cases, pre-election alliances between parties are replaced by a completely different post-election combination. In these political manoeuvres, it is clearly the voter who is short-changed.

Some consider all this is part of the hustle-bustle and dynamism of democracy; others view it as being the antithesis of democracy. A free and fair electoral process is obviously an essential element, but true democracy extends well beyond this. Electoral procedures are but one part of a full democracy: what happens after an election is equally important. In this, unlike the voting process, India does not present a pretty picture, especially at the state level. Defections, shifting alliances, money inducements or coercive measures to vote one way or another on legislation: these have become almost commonplace across practically the whole political spectrum.

One result of such politics is the mistrust and disdain for politicians, in general, amongst the mass of people. In diverse and highly opinionated India, the one thing most Indians will agree on is that the majority of politicians are self-serving and corrupt. The idea that people enter politics to serve the people has long been buried. In fact, it is increasingly regarded as a business where politicians trade in money, power and favours. For example, it is alleged that a seat in the Rajya Sabha (to which members are elected through voting by members of state legislatures, with voting based on a party whip or diktat) can be bought. Former Congress member of Parliament (MP) from Haryana, Birender Singh,[3] is reported to have said that he knew a person who had earmarked ₹100 crore to become

---

[3] Singh had switched over to the BJP from the Congress ahead of the 2014 Lok Sabha elections.

a Rajya Sabha MP but managed to achieve his objective with ₹80 crore. Singh was quoted as saying, 'Not one, but I can tell you about 20 such people'.[4] While this pertains to 2013, it is more than likely that it continues at least in some cases. A rare individual may pay only for the privilege, status or visibility of being a MP; most would look for a return on their 'investment', either in direct monetary terms or through the power it confers. Little wonder that there were also reports of cash for questions (being asked in Parliament) and promotion of corporate vested interests. The former was exposed through a sting operation by two journalists, in 2005, which resulted in framing of graft and criminal conspiracy charges against 11 former MPs in 2017. Interestingly, these MPs straddled the political spectrum, including those from the the Bharatiya Janata Party (BJP) and Congress.[5]

Parliament (and each state legislature) has law making as its major role, but it is also intended to serve as a check and balance to the executive and the government. Clearly these roles are greatly eroded if MPs can be influenced by vested interests, through money or other inducements. Many of these ills are generic to democracy itself and to human nature; they are, therefore, not unique to India.

Another threat to true democracy is the worldwide trend of majoritarianism, led by a strong leader. In many democracies, one party has won an overwhelming number

---

[4] "Rs 100 Crore Can Buy You a Rajya Sabha Seat : Congress MP", *The Times of India*, 30 July 2013, https://timesofindia.indiatimes.com/india/rs-100-crore-can-buy-you-a-rajya-sabha-seat-congress-mp/articleshow/21472374.cms, accessed on 17 March 2021.

[5] "2005 Cash-for-Question Scam: 11 Former MPs to Be Put on Trial, *The Economic Times*, 10 August 2017, https://economictimes.indiatimes.com/news/politics-and-nation/2005-cash-for-question-scam-11-former-mps-to-be-put-on-trial/articleshow/60003803.cms, accessed on 26 February 2021.

of seats in Parliament, making it dominant. This has led to steam rolling of new laws or approvals, based purely on a massive majority. Democracy should mean that rights of minorities—religious, regional, gender, caste, opinion or anything else—need to be respected. However, there is a trend for strong leaders to consolidate and build their vote banks by demonizing one minority or the other. In India, this has been seen in the continuing efforts to consolidate the majority through a religious (Hindu) appeal based on a socio-cultural agenda (Hindutva) which 'others' minority religions (especially Islam). Such majoritarian politics may be a reaction to its obverse: minority (again, mainly religious, but also caste-based) vote banks, based on 'minority appeasement', a term used in India almost exclusively with regard to the Muslim population. Whether true or not, this labelling has been an important factor in enabling one party to consolidate a substantial part of the Hindus and garner their votes. This, in conjunction with allegations of corruption and scams that mired the United Progressive Alliance (UPA) government in a perceived 'policy paralysis' (especially from 2012), ensured a win for the BJP in the national election in 2014. The BJP scored an even bigger victory, in 2019, based again on a religious appeal, supplemented by a strong nationalistic posture.

Ultra-nationalism, jingoism and xenophobia seem to be the common elements amongst all the strong leaders in various countries, most of whom have used these to come to power with big electoral wins. Such ultra-nationalism is almost always based on—and draws strength from—the creation of an 'other'. Thus, an important element of identity is a shared dislike—more often hatred—of the other. Hate, not harmony, is the binding force, and arousing this from time to time is a necessary nourishment for sustaining a majoritarian approach.

Some of this is a common trait amongst many such leaders; in India, implicitly equating the domestic 'other' (the Muslim minority) with the demonized external enemy (present-day Pakistan or Muslim conquerors of the past) helps to not only bind together the Hindu majority, but adds the element of nationalism in the mix.

Majoritarianism in India has an additional dimension, not prevalent in all democracies. This is the first-past-the-post electoral system, in which the candidate who gets the maximum votes is declared the winner. This means that in a multi-party system, if there are many strong candidates in the fray in a constituency, the one who gets elected may well have got only 25–30 per cent of the votes. The remaining votes may have got divided amongst numerous other candidates in a manner whereby none of them has got more than that. Given the typical voter turnout of around 66 per cent[6] (2014: 66.4 per cent; 2019: 67.4 per cent including postal ballots), the winning candidate has the explicit support of only a small proportion of the total eligible voters: in this case, 16 to 20 per cent. Translated across the country, a party with a strong and dedicated support base of around 25 per cent of the population can sweep the polls, as long as most constituencies see multi-party contests amongst three to four strong candidates. For, if the party can mobilize its devoted support base to vote (even 20 per cent, if not all 25 per cent), it translates to 30 per cent of the polled votes in a 66 per cent total turnout constituency. With about a third of the votes, it can win quite easily in a multi-cornered contest between strong parties.

On the other hand, in the two-contestant scenario, where

---

[6]'Full Statistical Report', *Election Commission of India*, https://eci.gov.in/statistical-report/statistical-reports/, accessed on 17 March 2021.

all the parties ally to fight the dominant one or there are only two strong candidates, a 33 per cent vote will put the party on the losing side. This is brought out starkly with a concrete example. In the Delhi Assembly elections, the BJP polled 34 per cent of the votes in 2013 and won 31 seats (of 70); in 2020, its vote share went up to 38.5 per cent, but it won only eight seats! This was the result of the 2020 elections being basically a two-party contest (between the Aam Aadmi Party [AAP] and BJP, with the Congress being only a nominal contestant). Interestingly, just a few months earlier, in the 2019 Parliamentary election, the BJP had polled 57 per cent of the votes in Delhi (and won all seven seats).

The seemingly sweeping victory of the BJP in 2019, when it won an absolute majority (303 of the 543 seats in the Lok Sabha), was based on a vote share of only 37.4 per cent. With a turnout of 67 per cent, it means that the party had the explicit support of just about one quarter of eligible voters.

This highlights the pitfalls of the first-past-the-post system and explains (though it hardly justifies) the temptations of vote-bank politics in a fractured polity. A party with a core of dedicated and active supporters who actually vote, can win a disproportionate percentage of seats if contests are multi-party and amongst strong contenders. On the other hand, the run-off system followed in some countries (with the top two contestants in a multi-candidate election having to contest a 'final' election) ensures that the candidate finally elected has the support of a majority (more than 50 per cent) of the voters. This requires the candidate—and his/her manifesto—to have an appeal across various sections of a fragmented society. In a country like India, with historical and newly created divides, such a system may ensure that winners have a more inclusive outlook and promote cooperation and harmony amongst different groups. Such a radical reform of the electoral process may be well worth debating.

In the present system, the question that arises is whether a party whose voting support is just about 25 per cent of the total eligible voters can claim to speak for the majority of citizens only because it does have a majority in Parliament. The larger question, though, is whether—and how—democracy upholds the rights of various minorities and promotes their well-being, even if the party in power is elected by securing a majority of the total turnout.

It also raises the broader issue of whether the assumption of democracy being equal to freedom is correct. Many would argue that freedom is an inherent part of democracy. Yet, in India, as in some other countries, we see democracies pass laws—through a proper and due process—which substantially abridge freedom. We see executive actions and court rulings that, in effect, steal individual freedom. May be it is time to rethink the presumption that democracy and freedom are conjoined twins.[7] If they are not, is there an alternative system that assures freedom, human rights and dignity, equality and justice?

Another basic issue is whether democracy means that governance and laws only reflect and respect the views of the majority. If so, how will radical social reform take place? In the context of India, how would laws against sati, dowry or child marriage ever have come about? For, at the time they were enacted, it is most unlikely that they had the support of a majority of the people. The question, then, is whether leaders should follow or lead 'public opinion'? In a country like India,

---

[7] See 'Swaraja in Shackles?', Kiran Karnik, in *Tilak in Our Times*, ed. Dr Raghunath A. Mashelkar, Dileep Padgaonkar, Lokmanya Tilak Vichar Manch in collaboration with Pune International Centre, July 2016.

with a social structure rooted in the past, this is not merely a rhetorical or philosophical question, but one of contemporary relevance. In the past, we had great leaders and social reformers who led and shaped public opinion, sometimes going against 'popular' viewpoints. Unfortunately, in recent times, there have been few leaders who have ventured to lead public opinion in a progressive direction. One recent example of such failure is from Kerala. Traditionally, the much-revered Sabarimala temple in that state bans entry of 'menstruating age' women (those between 10 and 50 years). No political party or leader had seriously challenged this or called for reform. However, gender activists took this issue to court and the Supreme Court ruled in 2018 that this bar be lifted.[8] While the Left Front government bravely sought to implement this, other parties (expectedly, BJP but also the 'secular' Congress) opposed the move as an assault on 'religious tradition'. An amazing 620 km long human chain (stretching from the northern tip of Kerala to Thiruvananthapuram in the south) was organized on 1 January 2019 by about five million women in favour of lifting the ban.[9] Despite this, the government's position began to see a nuanced change. This is one more example of leaders succumbing to regressive public opinion rather than leading progressive change.

---

[8]'Women of All Ages Can Enter Sabarimala Temple, Rules Supreme Court', *The Economic Times*, 29 September 2018, https://economictimes.indiatimes.com/news/politics-and-nation/supreme-court-allows-women-to-enter-sabarimala-temple/articleshow/65989807.cms?from=mdr; accessed on 26 February 2021.
[9]'SabarimalaTemple: Indian Women form '620 km Human Chain' for Equality *BBC News*, 1 January 2019, https://www.bbc.com/news/world-asia-india-46728521; accessed on 26 February 2021.

'INNOCENT UNTIL PROVEN GUILTY': THE ROLE OF THE CRIMINAL JUSTICE SYSTEM

The judiciary is, both figuratively and literally, the final court of appeal for aggrieved citizens and groups. Its fairness, responsiveness and independence—in reality and in popular perception—is, therefore, of critical importance. In India, the independence and fairness of the judiciary, and especially of the Supreme Court, has rarely been doubted. Of late, though, there is definitely a perception of it being sometimes biased in favour of the government. Further, the interminable delays in the whole judicial process often thwart the ideals of justice. A massive backlog of pending cases and frequent adjournments of hearings results not just in endless delays, but also high cost. This makes a common man wary of the whole system. As of July 2020, over 29 million cases were pending in district and taluka courts, of which over three million were more than ten years old.[10] The cases pending in high courts were 4.35 million (June 2019)[11] and even in the Supreme Court, as many as 60,444 matters were pending (July 2020).[12]

The concept of courts as protectors of the rights of an individual citizen against large organizations or the

---

[10]"Data | 77 Cases Filed in the 1950s Still Pending in Courts across India", *The Hindu*, 29 July 2020, https://www.thehindu.com/data/data-77-cases-filed-in-the-1950s-still-pending-in-courts-across-india/article32219415.ece, accessed on 17 March 2021.

[11]"Out of 43 Lakh Cases Pending in High Courts, Over 8 Lakh a Decade Old", *The Economic Times*, 27 June 2019, https://economictimes.indiatimes.com/news/politics-and-nation/out-of-43-lakh-cases-pending-in-high-courts-over-8-lakh-a-decade-old/articleshow/69974916.cms#:~:text=Law%20Minister%20Ravi%20Shankar%20Prasad,pending%20in%20the%20Supreme%20Court, accessed on 17 March 2021

[12]"Statistics", *Supreme Court of India*, https://main.sci.gov.in/statistics, accessed on 17 March 2021.

government is an important element of democracy. This is even more essential if majoritarian tendencies increase and minorities are given short shrift. Will the courts step up to this challenge? From time to time, they have proven their ability and willingness to do so. Yet, there are times when they seem to falter and an individual citizen is left to wonder about what other recourse is there.

In some cases, including high-profile ones like the detention of top leaders (including former chief ministers) in Kashmir or matters related to police action in the campuses of Jawaharlal Nehru University (JNU) and Jamia Millia in Delhi in 2019–20, the courts have been slow and seemingly reluctant to ensure quick action. The same seems to be true with regard to the riots in northeast Delhi in early 2020. In fact, the Delhi High Court was pulled up by the Supreme Court saying that the delay (in hearing the pleas for arrest and prosecution of leaders who instigated the communal rampage in Delhi) was 'unjustified'. It requested Delhi High Court chief justice to decide the petitions 'as expeditiously as possible'.[13] Ironically, the Supreme Court itself has been more than lethargic in certain instances, especially in 'political' cases. On the other hand, in a recent case (November 2020), it showed extraordinary speed in granting bail to a vitriolic, pro-government TV anchor. As one report states: 'His release came a day after a huge controversy over the immediate listing of his plea for bail when the court was on a Diwali recess.'[14] To

---

[13]"Supreme Court Asks High Court to List Delhi Riots Cases on March 6", *The Hindu*, 4 March 2020, https://www.thehindu.com/news/national/supreme-court-asks-high-court-to-list-delhi-riots-cases-on-march-6/article30982103.ece, accessed on 26 February 2021.
[14]"Supreme Court Grants Interim Bail to Arnab Goswami in 2018 Abetment to Suicide Case", *The Economic Times*, 12 November 2020, https://www.

a common person, recent court proceedings certainly indicate a bias towards the government and its supporters.

As part of their 'nationalist' agenda, BJP-led governments—both at the central and state levels—have been trigger-happy in filing sedition cases. Some other (non-BJP) state governments too have been filing such cases for criticism or lampooning of their leaders. Using a colonial-era law, intended to curb the Indian independence movement, governments have registered sedition cases for various acts, almost all related to sloganeering, demonstrations and even a school play. Earlier judgments of the Supreme Court with regard to acts that would (and would not) invite charges of sedition are ignored by the police and lower levels of judiciary. Similarly, provisions of bail for the accused in various cases are often not followed. As a result, many persons, especially the poor and disadvantaged, suffer punishment by being in jail for extended periods even before the case is decided by a court. The massive number of undertrials languishing in jails is indicative of this, and makes mockery of the dictum 'innocent till proven guilty'. Of the 466,084 prisoners in various jails in India, almost 70 per cent were undertrials as of 2018.[15] This, despite Supreme Court judgments generally favouring bail. One wonders whether the Supreme Court is powerless with regard to non-implementation of its own decisions and judgments. If so, who will protect the constitutional rights of citizens when the executive rides roughshod over them?

---

firstpost.com/india/supreme-court-grants-interim-bail-to-arnab-goswami-in-2018-abetment-to-suicide-case-9003911.html, accessed on 26 February 2021.
[15]"Prison Statistics India–2018, Executive Summary', *National Crime Records Bureau*, https://ncrb.gov.in/sites/default/files/Executive-Summary-2018.pdf, accessed on 17 March 2021.

The situation regarding freedom and bail is worsened because of the delays in the judicial system. This results in extended periods in jail for undertrials. Thus, in effect, it is not the judiciary that decides whether a person is guilty but the police. Once a person is charged and arrested, the police may put him/her in jail with a low probability of being let out on bail. Even if the court finally pronounces the verdict of 'not guilty', s/he would already have spent months, often years, in jail (as numerous examples show). This is often justified by many on the grounds that getting a conviction is difficult, and that being set free on bail would allow known criminals to continue their 'profession'. This view is also shared by senior police officers, which is ironical, for it is slipshod investigation by the police that leads to a low percentage of convictions in court.

Long delays in the judicial system, compounded by poor police investigation leading to low rates of conviction, have another, far more serious consequence. This is the widespread acceptance (even support) for so-called 'encounters'—a euphemism for cold-blooded killing by the police of suspected criminals. There are many reports about such killings by the police of anyone they label as a Naxalite or terrorist, ostensibly in 'encounters'. Many of these are undoubtedly fake encounters, as has been clearly established by independent investigations. Such killings, which include those who are 'merely' criminals—a big step 'forward' from incarceration in jail without a trial or bail—are becoming more common. One reason could be the support, as noted above, for such vigilante justice (incidentally, romanticized and eulogized in popular movies too).

In July 2020, a well-known criminal in Uttar Pradesh (UP), reputed to have many political connections, killed some policemen. After an intensive hunt, he was arrested (in Madhya Pradesh) and being brought back to UP by a police party. On the way, he was killed while allegedly trying to escape.[16] While hardly anyone believed the story of his attempted escape, there was little outcry at what seems like a brazen murder; in fact, people feted the policemen concerned. Not surprisingly, the demolishing of the criminal's house a few days earlier did not even merit notice. By all accounts, the criminal was worthy of the most severe punishment. Yet, police playing the role of accuser, judge and executioner is not really the sign of a true democracy. It also raises the question of the role of the courts and the judiciary.

In a similar incident in 2019, persons accused of the rape and murder of a young woman in Hyderabad were arrested. In a few days, all four were shot dead by the police, ostensibly because one of them tried to snatch a police officer's gun when they were taken to the crime scene to reconstruct it.[17] There are enough indications to assume that they were, in fact, killed in cold blood by the police. Again, the police won wide praise and acclaim for the killings.

Uttar Pradesh has seen a spate of 'encounter deaths' in the last few years. The police claimed that these were during encounters and in self-defence. However, many in the country and outside doubt this. United Nations (UN) experts on human

---

[16]This was widely covered in media. For example, 'Vikas Dubey: India Police Murder Suspect Shot Dead after Arrest', *BBC News*, 10 July 2020, https://www.bbc.com/news/world-asia-india-53359221, accessed on 17 March 2021.

[17]This too was widely covered in media. For example, 'Hyderabad Encounter: All Four Accused in Telangana Doctor's Rape-Murder Killed', *The Times of India*, 6 December 2019, https://timesofindia.indiatimes.com/india/hyderabad-encounter-all-four-accused-in-hyderabad-vet-rape-murder-case-killed-in-encounter/articleshow/72392991.cms, accessed on 17 March 2021.

rights say that evidence indicates the killings took place in police custody, with the bodies having 'injuries indicative of torture'. They also highlighted their concern over statements issued by high ranking state government and police officials seeming to incite, justify or sanction killings.[18] This reinforces the widely held view that such so-called encounter killings have the implicit approval of the top leadership in the state, who favour the police taking the law into their own hands and delivering 'justice', rather than counting on—or waiting for—the judiciary to pronounce judgment.

It is an unfortunate fact that there is widespread support amongst the general public for such killings, as there is for use of so-called third-degree methods (torture, in direct terms) by the police. While India is a signatory to the UN 'Convention against Torture and Other Cruel, Inhuman or Degrading Treatment or Punishment' (UNCAT), it has not yet ratified the Convention (even Pakistan and China have done so).[19] In October 2017, the Law Commission presented Report No. 273, in which it recommended that India ratify the UNCAT. Earlier, the Prevention of Torture Bill, 2010 was introduced in April 2010, by the Ministry of Home Affairs, and was passed by the Lok Sabha in May 2010. It was then referred to Select Committee of the Rajya Sabha which submitted its report on 6 December 2010 but the Bill lapsed due to inaction and the subsequent change in governments in 2014. In September

---

[18] 'India: UN Experts Alarmed by Alleged Police Killings in Uttar Pradesh', *United Nations Human Rights Office of the High Commissioner*, 11 January 2019, https://www.ohchr.org/EN/NewsEvents/Pages/DisplayNews.aspx?NewsID=24066&LangID=E, accessed on 26 February 2021.

[19] 'United Nations Treaty Collection', *Convention against Torture and Other Cruel, Inhuman or Degrading Treatment or Punishment*, https://treaties.un.org/pages/ViewDetails.aspx?src=IND&mtdsg_no=IV-9&chapter=4&lang=en

2020, the Ministry of Home Affairs informed the Lok Sabha that it had no plans to bring legislation on custodial violence. One wonders what to make of all this.

Third-degree methods and 'encounters' continue to be seen as shortcuts to deliver justice: practical alternatives to overcome the indefinite delays in the judicial system. That they seem to subvert the very idea of justice does not seem to matter, nor the fact that this will make the courts redundant. A large part of the blame for the sorry state of affairs must rest with the judicial system. It is the known delays and overall time-scale for a final judgment that spurs people to accept— even applaud—the instant justice meted out by the police. While understandable in the context of years (even a decade-plus) for the judicial system to pronounce a judgment, such an approach is hardly conducive to promoting democracy and freedom, with the rights of an individual being suppressed (even extinguished) by the State machinery.

The growing partisanship of the police is yet another disturbing development. Apart from giving in to political pressures, there are indications of biases based on caste, religion and ideology. The belief that such biases exist was strengthened through recorded videos of events in JNU and Jamia, the merciless beating of demonstrators from one community and the wanton destruction of CCTV cameras to prevent recordings. With all this happening in the national capital, with its intense media attention, it is obvious (and known) that the situation is worse elsewhere. Such partisanship by the police bodes ill for democracy, for which the rule of law is foundational, and requires an independent, sensitive and unbiased police force as a necessary element. Unfortunately, the police have generally been found wanting on this count. Further, the politicization seems to have extended to other law-enforcement agencies like the Enforcement Directorate (ED), National Investigation Agency (NIA) and Income Tax Department. These agencies are now accused of being routinely used to conduct investigations and raids on opposition politicians or dissenters, seemingly at the beck and call of the political leadership.

A professional police force, with the capability and willingness to undertake rigorous and thorough investigation, complemented by an efficient and fair judiciary, could possibly begin to change the dismal scenario. In many instances, it is the politicization of the police and the pressure to show quick results that is a root cause. An upright police officer inevitably faces transfers and harassment, while a pliant one gets plum postings and promotions. The Supreme Court has asked for police reforms, based on multiple reports about what is necessary. These reforms could minimize political interference and provide fixed tenures of service in a particular posting. No state has yet fully implemented the court's directives. Once again, the question arises: are the courts powerless?

In supporting 'encounter' killings by the police, the general public also implies that it is acceptable to take the law into one's own hands. Little wonder, then, that the last few years have seen a big spurt in cases of vigilante 'justice.' It is now commonplace to read media reports about mobs dispensing instant justice. In most cases, the targets have been people belonging to the minority communities (mainly Muslims) or Dalits; sometimes, they have been youngsters subjected to 'moral policing.' If this continues to spread, it holds the possibility of degenerating into general lawlessness and the emergence of local warlords (a step further from the conventional 'Dada' who rules the roost in many areas). At some point, people may be overwhelmed by this, and there will be a yearning for a 'strong' law-and-order government: the perfect soil for an authoritarian/totalitarian government. Have we reached this point in some parts of the country?

Already, we have a number of draconian laws like the ones on sedition or those meant to control terrorism. There are long delays in getting a closure to cases. In addition, there is the high cost of litigation, a general reluctance of courts to grant bail, torture and encounter killings by the police and perceived political influence on both the police and judiciary. Taken together, these constrain democracy, limit freedom and deny justice. Of course, many of the issues mentioned may not occur frequently and a despondent view would, therefore, not be fully justified. However, in a true democracy, unfairly limiting the freedom of just a few or denying justice to even a handful, is not acceptable.

While the law on sedition dates back to British times (though in the UK itself the law has been repealed), its extensive and indiscriminate use (post Independence) is a recent phenomenon, attributable mainly, though hardly solely, to the BJP-led government. In this context, it is necessary to mention that almost all the other draconian laws, which seriously curb freedom and have no place in a civilized and free society, are the legacy of decades of Congress-led government. Similarly, the use of various 'investigative' agencies (like the ED, Central Bureau of Investigation [CBI] or the NIA; recently, even the Narcotics Control Board [NCB]) to harass and intern individuals, NGOs, or companies is also a tactic begun by Congress governments. Of course, BJP-led government have, in the last few years, amplified and taken this to a new level. The real victim is freedom.

Amongst the constraining, if not draconian, laws is the Foreign Contribution (Regulation) Act (FCRA). This has been used to increasingly bully independent civil society organizations, especially those involved with protecting human rights. The September 2020 amendment creates barriers for NGOs to even partner with each other, if they are receiving foreign funds. This affects the basic working model of NGOs. This is unfortunate because NGOs are a vital pillar of a democratic society, and governments—Centre or state—irrespective of their political orientation, need to engage with, and not stifle, NGOs. Again, while the BJP seems to be inherently against NGOs, the 'credit' for initiating harassment through the FCRA must go to the Congress. Interestingly, the constraints on foreign-funded NGOs with regard to policy advocacy are not applicable to foreign-funded corporates or to political parties. Needless to say, there is a consensus amongst parties on this!

DANGEROUSLY DIVIDED

As noted earlier, democracy is beginning to translate into majoritarianism, the rule of the majority, without a care about various minorities. In fact, electoral arithmetic can mean consciously ignoring or even attacking minorities so as to consolidate and win the vote of the majority. In India, this has been the implicit (and, at times, the explicit) strategy of many of the BJP's election campaigners. Some have used religion (Hindu versus Muslim), along with 'dog whistle'[20] tactics to implicitly condemn Muslims—also the Congress and the Left—as being supporters of terrorism or even anti-national. This combination of religion and nationalistic posturing

---

[20]'Amulya Gopalkrishnan; Dog-Whistling, the BJP's Art-Form of Choice', *The Times of India*, 13 October 2016, https://timesofindia.indiatimes.com/blogs/to-name-and-address/dog-whistling-the-bjps-art-form-of-choice/, accessed on 26 February 2021.

(the use of the Pulwama killings and the action by India in Balakot was a major campaign plank) was supplemented by a black or white 'with me or against me' stance, and proved a big winner in the 2019 elections. Many blame the Congress, viewing them as the initiator of communal politics by creating a sense of insecurity amongst Muslims and positioning itself as their patron or protector. Given this, it is easy for the BJP to allege 'Muslim appeasement' by the Congress and to promote the idea that the Congress is a party that favours Muslims. Building on selective historical facts and perceptions, the BJP has very successfully woven a narrative of Hindu victimhood, branding itself as a strong, assertive party that would right the perceived discrimination and ensure Hindu domination. Clearly, this line has resonated in the national elections in 2014 and 2019, backed by Modi's powerful oratory, nationalistic fervour and extraordinary ground-level organization effort. Opposing political parties were also characterized as being incompetent or corrupt. In addition, the Congress was attacked for '70 years of misrule' and especially for dynastic rule. Some of these allegations stuck, being based—at least in part—on fact, and certainly on widespread perception.

The election campaigns implied a connection between the Congress party (and some other parties), Muslims and Pakistan. For example, Amit Shah, then president of the BJP, said that 'If BJP loses Bihar … firecrackers would be burst in Pakistan.'[21] The BJP would, of course, boldly put Pakistan (and, presumably, Congress and Muslims) in their place.

Though electorally unimportant, 'liberals' (labelled as

---

[21]'If BJP Loses, Crackers Will Go Off in Pakistan: Amit Shah', *The Economic Times*, 29 October 2015, https://economictimes.indiatimes.com/news/politics-and-nation/if-bjp-loses-crackers-will-go-off-in-pakistan-amit-shah/articleshow/49586000.cms?from=mdr, accessed on 26 February 2021.

'Lutyens' elites' or 'Khan Market gang,' after locations in Delhi) were attacked by similarly equating them with leftists, communists, Naxalites and, therefore, anti-national. The students and professors from institutions like JNU were all clubbed together with fringe groups (*tukde-tukde gang*, the words signifying a breaking up of India, and allegedly used by some students as a slogan in the JNU campus) as being anti-national, and had sedition cases slapped against them.

Reprehensible as this may be, such characterization of various political parties and groups seemed to be acceptable to a large proportion of voters. While the Congress did well in elections in some states (including Gujarat, Rajasthan, Madhya Pradesh and Chhattisgarh), it was later decimated—even in these states—in the Parliamentary elections in 2019.

The success of a vitriolic, hate-based campaign in 2019 was depressing to more than a few thinking people (not all of whom are lackeys of the Congress party, as the BJP often portrays). It seemed that this would now be the template for all parties in future elections, hoping to create their own vote bases by inciting hatred against some defined 'other'.

It was in this scenario that various groups began protesting against the Citizenship (Amendment) Act (CAA) in late 2019. The CAA had been approved by Parliament, despite the widespread feeling that it was discriminatory. It aimed at granting citizenship to refugees from some neighbouring countries, but specifically excluded Muslims, on the argument that these countries were Muslim countries, and so there could not have been persecution of Muslims there. Many saw the CAA as being contrary to the Constitutional principle of secularism. Further, the CAA was seen as a prelude to National Register of Citizens (NRC). The home minister has often spoken of the two in the same breath and more than hinted about their connection. Though he has sometimes said that there is no link, he has asked people to understand the 'chronology' where the CAA would be followed by the NRC.[22] This has caused great concern because of the experience in Assam, where a very large number of people were excluded from citizenship on the basis that they did not have the requisite papers to prove their Indian citizenship (and so, must be illegal migrants from Bangladesh). These worries added fuel to the protests against the CAA.

Protests multiplied after the police chased and beat up students in Jamia Millia Islamia University in Delhi. Soon, video clips of apparent police brutality and destruction of property (including the university library) went viral, triggering wide media coverage and public outrage. This ignited more protests in Jamia and elsewhere. One such anti-CAA protest was organized by women, who began a 24x7 sit-in at Shaheen Bagh in Delhi. This drew women of all ages, mainly from the Muslim community living in the area. Given its uniqueness, media attention was immediate, amplifying its visibility and impact and attracting many others who shared the anti-CAA perspective. Someone smart and politically astute initiated the reading of the Constitution's preamble (which mentions the secular nature of the Indian republic) as part of the protest, along with holding up the national flag and singing the national anthem. This sought to recapture the 'nationalistic' space from the BJP. In days, Shaheen Bagh became an iconic site (like Tahrir Square in Cairo and Taksim Square in Istanbul) and a metaphor for anti-CAA protests. Its model of women-led

---

[22]'Amit Shah Says No NPR–NRC link, His Govt Linked It 9 Times in House', *The Indian Express*, 25 December 2019, https://indianexpress.com/article/india/npr-nrc-link-amit-shah-central-government-parliament-6183572/, accessed on 26 February 2021.

and women-dominated protests was replicated in many cities across the country. Reading the preamble of the Constitution and singing the national anthem became an integral part of protests everywhere. Most observers acknowledged that these demonstrations were spontaneous and organic, not organized by any political party. In any case, the fact is that political parties were wary of being associated with a mainly-Muslim protest, given what they perceived as the nationwide domination of a majoritarian view.

Elections for the Delhi Assembly came up in early 2020, amidst these ongoing protests. The BJP ran a campaign that was even more hate-filled than the one for the national elections held only a few months earlier. The ultra-nationalist tone was topped by much rhetoric against the protests; much of it indirectly (and, at times, directly) anti-Muslim, clearly an attempt to polarize voters. The incumbent, AAP, however, did not take the bait: instead of responding to the BJP campaign line, it focused on the down-to-earth issues of governance and those of immediate concern to the local voter—especially water, power, health, pollution, education and safety. I summarize it as SHE—safety (especially of women), health and education—with the acronym also indicating the gender focus. Apart from highlighting its programmes of free water and electricity, AAP showcased its work on education and health: vastly improved government schools and 'mohalla clinics' in each locality. In the national elections in 2019, the BJP had swept Delhi, winning all seven Lok Sabha seats, with the AAP winning none. The expectation was that it would again win hands down, with a similar campaign, aided further by a possible backlash (amongst the Hindus) against the Muslim dominated anti-CAA protests in Shaheen Bagh and elsewhere in Delhi. Top BJP leaders predicted winning 45 of the 70 Assembly seats.

Finally, when the results came in, the BJP had received a severe drubbing, winning only 8 of the 70 seats. It is unclear as to whether its defeat was due to a reaction against its excessively acerbic rhetoric, or the fact that local issues mattered more in a state election (and the AAP was generally perceived as having performed well in its five-year stint). More unlikely, but not impossible, is the conclusion that the mood of the electorate had changed.

One impact of these developments (the reactions to incidents in JNU and Jamia, the Shaheen Bagh protest, and the BJP's electoral defeat in the Delhi state election) is the willingness to speak out. While, as on some other issues, government leaders are in denial, the fact is that there has been much caution—to put it mildly—in voicing views that are critical of government policies, actions or speeches of leaders. An atmosphere of fear-based self-censorship (not seen since the Emergency in 1975–7) has now given way to more articulation of views that oppose many actions and words of those in power. The wariness (amongst non-politicians) of speaking out in public—often, also in drawing rooms—has decreased, and dissent and argument are, once again, being heard. Of course, armies of trollers continue to react venomously to any views against the policies and actions of the government, or of certain leaders. Also, there are worries about one or the other regulatory agency (even the police) acting against dissenters. In many instances, this has actually happened. Yet, the willingness to voice criticism has visibly increased.

Unfortunately, despite proudly claiming a heritage of tolerance, India has increasingly become a highly intolerant society, where one or other of the many identity-groups takes great umbrage and offence at any perceived slight. Contrary opinions are shouted down and even innocuous comments are interpreted as causing deep hurt. Most Indians have, indeed, become so aggressive and touchy that characterization as jaguars and porcupines—ever ready to attack, and bristling at the slightest touch—may not be inappropriate.[23] This is the very antithesis of democracy, an essential element of which is the right to dissent, have contrary opinions, even offend. One often wishes that there was a law safeguarding the 'right to offend'! In this, France seems to have captured well this characteristic of democracy: speaking in the context of seemingly offensive (religious) cartoons, President Macron has said, 'To be French is to defend the right to laugh, jest, mock and caricature...'.[24]

THE DEFINING DECADE

We have dealt at length with the recent political scenario because it forms the basis of making a prognosis for the decade. The trend curve only shows a steady worsening, and its projection to 2030 is frightening. Imagine a scenario of vigilantes and lynch mobs, organized and egged on by hate-mongering leaders, taking the law into their own hands, with the police acting as mere bystanders or, worse, joining them. Shops and houses are selectively vandalized and destroyed;

---

[23] As described in 'Do We Really Want a Superpower India Populated by Angry Indians?', Kiran Karnik, *The Economic Times*, 7 August 2012, https://economictimes.indiatimes.com/opinion/et-commentary/do-we-really-want-a-superpower-india-populated-by-angry-indians/articleshow/15382725.cms, accessed on 17 March 2021.

[24] 'To Be French Is to Defend the Right to Mock, Macron Tells New Citizens', Reuters, 4 September 2020, https://in.reuters.com/article/us-france-politics-macron/to-be-french-is-to-defend-the-right-to-mock-macron-tells-new-citizens-idUSKBN25V1O1, accessed on 17 March 2021.

cars and motorbikes are set afire; individuals are beaten and some killed. If this sounds an extreme and exaggerated scenario, keep in mind that all this actually happened in Delhi in 2020. If the trend continues, it will not considerably stretch the imagination to foresee how much worse things may be in 2030. Violent mobs controlled by local warlords, creating chaos and destruction: this is generally thought to be something from the distant past or the situation in some exceptional country, for a brief period. Is this India's future? Or will the majority assiduously 'weed out' all perceived 'others', consigning them, at best, to terrible ghettos far removed from the mainstream?

India 2030 could well be a theocratic State (even constitutionally; as Indira Gandhi demonstrated, major changes in the Constitution are possible with a brute majority in Parliament and a strong leader), in which religious minorities are second-class citizens with limited rights. The secular imperative of separation between State and religion has been ignored sometimes in the past, but never as completely as in the last few years. The foundation-stone-laying ceremony for the Ram temple in Ayodhya was, for all practical purposes, a state event. Interestingly, except the Left parties (which are now marginalized, except in Kerala), no political party spoke up against this; if anything, they were falling over each other in praise of the event. Given this, a theocratic State is possibly not far away.

In such a scenario, ideological dissenters would be silenced through fear of violence, and of a law enforcement machinery that can intern them on any wild charges. Courts would tend to favour the State; even if they are finally declared innocent, the legal process could take years. For example, in a 'transistor bomb' incident (a series of bomb blasts across north India in which 69 people died and another 127 were injured), as many as 30 accused persons were declared not guilty in 2020 in a case that dates to 1985: a time lag of 35 years![25]

The government would be equated with the State, so all criticism of the government would be deemed anti-national and any dissenter could be charged under the sedition law. Troublemakers would be kept in check or in jail. Dissidents, particularly from the minorities, would be in detention centres which may be renamed—as in Xinjiang, China—'re-education centres'.[26] In such a climate, differing views would be silenced. Laws and codes on how not to dress, unacceptable behavior and on food that cannot be eaten will be enforced by the police and by vigilantes serving as moral police. There would, of course, be 'peace' and, most likely, the economy would be doing well.

It is possible to further flesh out this scenario, and elaborate on what life in such a dystopia would be like. It is, of course, possible that a large proportion of the citizens—maybe even a majority—would be happy with the situation and may look at it as an utopia rather than a dystopia.

Around the world, there are countries that have one or the other characteristic of such a dystopia, or—depending upon one's point of view—utopia. China, for example, has a strong government, an all-powerful leader, brooks no dissent, runs detention ('re-education') facilities and has a police/

---

[25] 'Delhi Court Acquits 30 in Transistor Bomb Blasts Case', *The Hindu*, 9 March 2020, https://www.thehindu.com/news/national/other-states/delhi-court-acquits-30-in-transistor-bomb-blasts-case/article31026088.ece, accessed on 18 March 2021.
[26] "Xinjiang: China Defends "Education" Camps', *BBC News*, 17 September 2020; https://www.bbc.com/news/world-asia-china-54195325, accessed on 26 February 2021.

justice system that is effectively at the command of political masters; it also has high economic growth and internal 'peace'. Pakistan is a country in which terror groups often run amok, and, as a theocratic State, religion is given pride of place. Israel—considered by some in the BJP as the right model for India—is a theocracy, a 'muscular' and strong State that pre-emptively and ruthlessly attacks its enemies. Its citizenship model for incoming Jewish migrants is not unlike what India has emulated for Hindus. Countries like Sudan and Libya have gone through times when a strong leader has, due to external intervention, given way to chaos. Local warlords emerged, who controlled specific areas, and there was little by way of law and order.

Is India likely to head in the direction of one or the other of these countries? Some look at history and see parallels between today's India and Germany of the mid-1930s. Possibly, this is an exaggerated view of desperate opponents of the present government. At the same time, an objective assessment can hardly fail to note the striking similarities: a government that is perceived as being corrupt and ineffective, leading to yearning for—and an ushering in of—a strong government; election of a party that promises to be nationalistic and to put a religious minority as also ideological opponents in their place (Jews and communists, in the case of Germany in the 1930s); a powerful leader who can sway masses; ultra-nationalism and a militaristic stance vis-à-vis neighbours.

Is such a trajectory inevitable? Are there alternative scenarios that are equally likely? As an optimist, one would certainly believe so. After all, India's own history indicates how it quickly transited from the Emergency to again emerge as a vibrant democracy, how it quelled communal hatred after Partition in 1947 and how it overcame the Khalistan issue in the 1980s. Each of these has left a residue, as have other events like the razing of the Babri mosque in December 1992 and the Gujarat riots of 2002, but the country has been able to contain and minimize their impact.

Providing a basis for optimism are Shaheen Bagh (and its clones elsewhere) and, more recently, beginning towards the end of 2020, the farmers' agitation, with their peaceful, grassroots-originated protest (there is yet controversy whether the unseemly events and violence on Republic Day 2021 were an aberration or caused by a few saboteurs). Another cause for optimism has been student protests around the country. For the last two decades or more, many felt that the idealism of youth had been supplanted by materialism-driven greed. The ferment of ideology, it seemed, had been abandoned in favour of discussions on campus (job) placements and salary levels. From 2019, it seems that campuses around the country are once more alive with discussion, dissent, the passion of ideology and the fire of idealism. Also, women, long on the sidelines of most movements, are now centre stage, with Muslim women—long disadvantaged by gender, religious practices and as a minority—being in the lead. They are playing an active role in the farmers' protest too. Whatever one's political leaning, these need to be recognized as powerful portents of a resurgent democracy. The strong movements involving grassroots mobilization—of both rural and urban people—as also their grit and determination provide hope that dystopian scenarios like the one painted earlier are unlikely.

The contrary voting trends between state and national elections do convey a message: voters want a strong, nationalistic and corruption-free government at the Centre, led by a forceful and popular leader, but at the local (state) level—which is about their day-to-day life—they want social harmony and focus on the needs of mundane, daily living ('*bijli, sadak, paani*' [electricity, roads, water]). Jobs, education and health too are key factors, along with safety and transportation in urban areas.

Political parties are known to quickly pick up signals sent out by the electorate. Therefore, it is certain that each party will begin to modify its strategy to meet voter expectations. It is then fair to assume that the decade will see a trend towards the creation of greater social harmony, with less divisive tactics. The need for jobs will shift the focus towards economics, reducing the emphasis on politics (seen especially after 2019). As the youth become more active, there will be need to pay attention to the future rather than the past. The constant harking back to 'a glorious past', continuous reminders of destruction and crimes by the Mughal rulers (that is, Muslims) and '70 years of misrule' (by the Congress) will reduce, if not cease. In its place, there would be a future orientation, a positive vision of where the country could be and what needs to be done to get it there. Social harmony in a cohesive society, with full freedom and a vibrant democracy, are pre-requisites for the country to realize its full potential. In a positive scenario, all political parties will recognize this, and those that do not will be promptly punished at the polls.

Given this, the decade of the 2020s is likely to see a transition, a movement away from the hate-filled, divisive, communal and intolerant political scenario seen in the latter half of the last decade. It will also witness governments that are less corrupt, more transparent and accountable than those of the past. New political formations may emerge. Forward-looking and younger people will be leaders, and will promote flowering of creativity, innovation and entrepreneurship. Economic growth will be more sustainable, equitable and inclusive than in the last few decades. Decentralization will be a key philosophy and not just states, but municipalities and panchayats will be the major stakeholders, enabling grassroots participation in decision-making.

Is this too fanciful: a scenario as unlikely as the dystopian one outlined earlier? One hopes the probabilities are not the same, and that one is not only more desirable than the other, but also more likely. Take your pick on which one.

Either way, this is truly the decisive decade, and will determine the velocity—both direction and speed—of India's progress.

2

SECURITY

Maintaining Social Harmony and Peaceful Borders

Security is at the core of the very concept of a nation-state. Defined as it is by geography, the integrity of a country requires the protection of its boundaries. Thus, the State must have the means of deterring or preventing—and, if necessary, repelling—any incursion across its border. This has long been the crux of the sovereign duties of a State, giving security the pride of place amongst its various functions.

THE THREE THREATS

In earlier years, the primary threat was a direct attack, across the land or sea frontiers, by an adversary. War would ensue, and the more powerful State would emerge victorious. Those States that could, often took on a proactive aggressor role, seeking to pre-emptively subdue potential enemies or to expand their territorial limits through conquest. Thus, European colonial powers fought each other, either across their own borders or in their colonial territories.

For over four decades—till the reunification of Germany—

after the Second World War (1939–45), borders in Europe were relatively stable, and the cross-border incursions were mainly in developing countries. Tribal and regional loyalties led to conflicts that were much exacerbated by the way the boundaries of countries had been arbitrarily drawn by the former colonial powers. This led to territorial disputes, which were sometimes settled by the force of arms. Fuelling this were two other factors. The first was the US–Soviet Union (the Union of Soviet Socialist Republics, as it then was) Cold War. The ideological battle between the two superpowers took on a 'hot' form in the so-called Third World: in Asia, Africa and Latin America. In any dispute, while one superpower backed a particular country, the other allied with its enemy. Sometimes, the foes were factions within a country, engaged in a civil war (as happened in Vietnam and Angola in the last century, and in Syria, more recently). This vicarious battle between the two superpowers, played out far from their shores, was exacerbated by the second factor: the lucrative business of selling weapons. In effect, this provided an incentive to arms lobbies in both countries (and some of their developed country allies) to stoke conflicts around the world.

With the disintegration of the Soviet Union in 1991, some of these conflicts—though not all—abated, but a residue of mistrust and enmity remained. Thus, secure borders and the need to maintain a deterrent—even aggressive—posture meant that external security continued to be a priority. One example is the India–China relationship. After discussions on disputed border claims (a legacy of British colonialism) in the 1950s, amidst apparent bonhomie (a popular slogan was '*Hindi-Chini bhai-bhai*' [Indians and Chinese are brothers]), action moved from the conference table to the battlefront in 1962. Within a few weeks, things quietened down. Following this, there have been only occasional and limited skirmishes on the border (up to mid-2020), and many instances of close cooperation between the two countries on some global issues like climate change. Trade between the two has soared, to the extent that China is India's second-largest trading partner. Yet, both countries maintain large security forces on the border, now further enhanced after the clashes in Ladakh. China has galloped far ahead of India in both economic and military terms, and is now fast becoming the second pole in a bipolar world (reminiscent of the 1950–90 period). The ascent of China and its implications for India, as also events from mid-2020, are discussed later.

Meanwhile, many countries face a second security challenge, in the form of cross-border terrorism. Unlike a direct, frontal attack by the armed forces of a country, this takes the form of insidious forays across the border (and, sometimes, deep within the country) by small groups of trained and well-armed people (apparently civilians, or pretending to be so, rather than regular military personnel). The Arab–Israeli conflict in West Asia has seen this for many decades now, on both sides of the divide. India too has been a major sufferer, for three decades or more, with Pakistan being the source and supporter of such terrorists.

Many in the world saw such terrorist attacks as local— limited to a few countries only. However, after the terror strikes in the US in 2001 (generally known as '9/11', signifying September 11, the date of the attacks), this was acknowledged as a global problem, especially after there were terrorist attacks in other countries too. Following 2001, US actions in many countries, including Afghanistan, Iraq, Libya and Syria, had the effect of giving a further boost to terrorist groups. After Al-Qaeda, which claimed responsibility for the 2001 attack, was contained by the US, a new and more extreme group—the so-called Islamic State of Iraq and Syria (ISIS), also known by its Arabic acronym 'Daesh'—became the most organized and powerful terrorist organization. Its brand of fundamentalist Islam, combined with its anti-American stance, won it many adherents. In its heyday from 2014 to 2017, it overran and controlled large swathes of territory in Iraq and Syria, and declared an Islamic Caliphate in June 2014. It had operations in many countries and these were serious threats to the governments. Concerted moves by many countries—with the US and Russia working together in many instances—were able to first stem the tide and then roll back the Islamic State's advance. In a few years, it has been practically defeated, though it continues to hold on in a few pockets.

Importantly, the rise of the ISIS indicates that there are, globally, large numbers of disaffected people who are willing to not only buy into their propaganda, but to join them and take up arms. The ISIS was able to recruit citizens of many countries, both developed and developing, including a small number from India. Many attribute this to discrimination and lack of integration of minorities (particularly migrants in Europe). It is also indicative of one's dominant identity; if it is religion, then almost inevitably some proportion of people will fall prey to an extreme and fundamentalist form as has been seen in some horrific instances—for example, in France and New Zealand in recent times. This is especially true of monotheistic religions, the writings of which can be interpreted to not only separate the 'other', but to even demonize them. Blaming them for one's woes—or those of co-religionists—becomes easy, and acting against them is only a step away.

All this is, of course, backed by powerful propaganda, based often on a core of fact. This is disseminated through a variety of means, including social media. Soon, the echo-chamber and confirmation-bias nature of media provides both credibility and justification. For example, an actual image—which may well be a few years old—of a (white) policeman beating up an (Islamic) migrant in one of the European countries would cause outrage. Widely circulated and going viral on social media, many who are already predisposed to assume police racism and violence against Islamic people will take this as further proof, and feel justified in attacking any white policeman.

Terrorism may have its roots in the diversity, quirks and animalistic nature of the human mind. However, the number of those who, for one reason or another, are inherently prone to follow a violent path against fellow humans would be small. The growth of terrorism, therefore, depends on the number of people who feel disaffected, discriminated and unfairly treated. They begin to see some truth and justification in terrorist propaganda, and it is this that provides a fertile ground to terrorists for sympathy first, then sanctuary, and finally recruitment.

The third challenge to security is primarily internal. Serious dissensions within a country, which evolve to take the form of an armed challenge, are not new. Civil wars have long been prevalent around the world. The slide from dissension and dissent to armed insurrection takes place most commonly when the space for differing viewpoints is constricted, and a change of leadership through peaceful means is perceived as not being possible. Therefore, it is mainly totalitarian States that have witnessed civil wars. However, smaller or limited armed insurrections are not uncommon in democracies too. Such exemplars of democracy like the UK have also gone through this in recent times (in Northern Ireland, through the Irish Republican Army). In our neighbourhood, Sri Lanka, a robust democracy, experienced a long and often-brutal civil war, which began in 1983 and continued for two decades.

India has had to cope with a direct military challenge practically from its birth as an independent country in 1947. Wars and major skirmishes with Pakistan had been a regular feature, including the attempted invasion of Kashmir in 1947, and wider wars in 1965 and 1971. Since then, barring the Kargil incursion in 1999, that country has seemed to change track: while there has been a lot of cross-border firing, its strategy after 1999 appears to concentrate on initiating and supporting terrorist attacks. The exception is the attempted aerial attack in 2019, after India's bombing in Balakot in retaliation to a terrorist attack. Therefore, even as India has to stay prepared to handle any direct military attack or to take pre-emptive military action, its attention must increasingly shift to the terrorist threat.

Countering this is far more complicated than facing a military threat. Such asymmetric means of warfare always gives the attacker an advantage. Unlike a cross-border military thrust, a terrorist attack can take place at any time and any location, with no indication of a build up. Just one person can cause mayhem—for example, through a suicide attack in a busy place like a shopping mall or a railway station or airport. The formulation of a strategy to counter such attacks is not easy. Strong measures aimed at deterrence and prevention are probably the best bet, but may mean cross-border action (against terrorist training camps, as was done in Balakot); retaliation too would need the same. Any such strategy would have to take note of likely escalation and draw clear red lines. It would require the use of India's soft power (and economic muscle) to avert diplomatic pressure from other countries. This must also be pro-actively used to deter terrorist attacks and seek to move Pakistan away from its strategy of using terrorism. Financial and economic pressure is one strong method of doing this, especially given the somewhat precarious state of Pakistan's economy. The threat of blacklisting of the country by the international Financial Action Task Force (FATF) seemed to have an immediate impact, and more such actions may have some effect. Amongst the various actions that can be taken to counter terrorism, putting a squeeze on their funding is one of the effective methods; after all, recruitment, logistics and weapons require money.

Terrorism requires local support for logistics, safe houses and other assistance. Without such support, terrorist action—beyond small incursions across the border—is just not possible. Conversely, a sympathetic local population—even pockets of support—can greatly facilitate terrorist strikes. Therefore, one important way of curbing terrorism is to ensure that such local help is not forthcoming.

Unlike terrorism, which is now acknowledged as a global problem, internal insurgencies are specific to each country. India has faced this through the last seven decades, right from Independence in 1947. Some have simmered almost continuously (in Nagaland, for example); others have seen a shorter, sharp upsurge and then died out (the Khalistan movement is an instance). Militancy in Kashmir has its genesis in a cross-border invasion (from Pakistan) in 1947–48. Since then, the degree of internal militancy has, on and off, added to cross-border terrorist action. The Khalistan insurgency too was partly based on external support (Pakistan and foreign Khalistanis from countries like Canada played a major role). Of course, wherever there is an internal insurgency, foreign enemies are eager to provide support to it. This is as true for Nagaland as for Kashmir.

Internal militancy in the very heart of India ('Left-wing extremism' [LWE]) and its point of origin (Naxalbari in West Bengal in the 1960s, though some may date it further back to Telangana in the immediate aftermath of Independence), and a whole range of militant/separatist movements in the Northeast, are all driven mainly by an agenda and leaders who are very much local (Indian). However, in almost all cases, external vested interests have provided support—arms, funds, training and sanctuary, etc.—to these movements. Prime Minister Manmohan Singh considered LWE as India's 'biggest' challenge. Whether the biggest or not, the internal security threat is certainly a major one in India, especially when any of these link up with terrorist groups operating from (and often supported by) a country hostile to India.

In Kashmir, it is deep-rooted and endemic, with occasional periods of relative peace. The same has been true in parts of the Northeast. In central India, LWE has been a challenge for many decades.

As a result, Indian security forces have been deployed in many of these areas for long periods of time. This has its own consequences, with respect and trust being casualties, along with people. Considered essential by some and a license for breach of human rights by others, draconian laws like the Armed Forces Special Powers Act (AFSPA) have been invoked in some of the troubled areas—sometimes for years and years. Many security experts see such laws as being a necessity—even if an unfortunate one—to counter the threat of terrorism and militancy through immediate and extreme action. However, such laws have further embittered and alienated many in these areas, besides being criticized by civil liberties organizations everywhere. Every aberration which is covered up by invoking the AFSPA causes great resentment against the armed forces. This becomes fertile soil for militants to build a base of sympathetic locals: an essential necessity for terrorism, as noted earlier.

From time to time, various governments at the Centre had tried to negotiate settlements with groups that are disaffected and want some form of autonomy or freedom (not necessarily secession). Some of these have fructified into agreements which have ushered in peace; unfortunately, many have failed and militancy has continued. Governments have swung between negotiations or conciliation, and tough or determined action (by deploying more security forces or more firepower). Khalistan and some parts of the Northeast present examples of success; Kashmir and LWE areas represent long-standing failure.

Even as Pakistan and China, especially the former, continue to provide active support to some of the militant and terrorist groups, both countries also pose a more direct military challenge. Given the close relationship between the two, India has to prepare for the contingency of a two-front war. In addition to the rapid build-up of its army and air force, China has also considerably augmented its navy, and its warships now regularly patrol the Indian Ocean. This poses a new challenge to India, especially as China uses its economic and political clout to seek access to ports in our immediate neighbourhood, including in Myanmar, Sri Lanka and Pakistan (and, more recently, in Iran). Its Belt and Road Initiative (BRI), promising Chinese investments in infrastructure, gives it access to Bangladesh and Nepal too; in effect, it has built possible logistic or military relationships with all the countries in India's neighbourhood, except Bhutan.

Though India's military expenditure as a percentage of government expenditure was 8.8 per cent in 2019 as compared with China's 5.4 per cent, the fact that China's economy is about five times as large means it completely outspends India: China spent an estimated $261 billion, dwarfing India's $71 billion.[27] A result of this is that militarily, China is now in a different category and streets ahead of India in terms of size and capability of its armed forces. Even a cursory look at the comparative figures tells the story. China has 74 submarines and 1,232 combat aircraft, compared to India's figures of 16 and 538.[28] This large disparity extends to all other major weapons systems, as also to nuclear bombs. Qualitatively, too, much of China's military might is known to be more advanced than India's. Yet, India needs to maintain at least a minimal deterrence capability—a task that has become increasingly difficult.

This challenge can only be met by changing the context away from direct India–China military confrontation. One option is to ally with another country that would enable the balance to be more even. Our strategic partnership with the US sometimes seems to veer towards this aim. An alliance with Russia, the one other country whose military might could help us to checkmate China, could have been a possibility. However, this no longer seems to be an option, in the light of growing China–Russia ties, on the one hand, and a definite cooling off in our traditionally strong relationship with Russia (especially compared with the ties during the days of the Soviet Union). Also possible are multilateral alliances like the Quad

---

[27] 'SIPRI Military Expenditure Database', *Stockholm International Peace Research Institute*
[28] "To Take on Chinese "Wolf Warriors", India Must Fix Military Asymmetry', *The Times of India*, 28 June 2020, https://timesofindia.indiatimes.com/blogs/academic-interest/to-take-on-chinese-wolf-warriors-india-must-fix-military-asymmetry/, accessed on 18 March 2021.

(Australia, Japan, India and the US) or working with other like-minded countries (France, Vietnam and South Korea).

There is one other way to change the context away from a direct one-to-one military engagement. This is to engage China in dialogue, increase interdependency through trade, and utilize India's growing soft power in a world where this is becoming even more important. Meanwhile, the border dispute and the territorial counter-claims have to be kept on the backburner. This has been the de facto position on both sides for almost six decades and has worked successfully, barring a few, relatively minor, border skirmishes. However, in mid-2020, this changed. China has adopted an aggressive stance, altering the status quo in a limited way along the Line of Actual Control (LAC) in eastern Ladakh. It has apparently made a foray into the demilitarized no-man's land, between the Chinese claim of where the LAC lay and the Indian one. An active Indian reaction to this led to a clash in Galwan, resulting in the death of 20 Indian soldiers and an unspecified number of Chinese. Surprisingly and strangely, neither side used firearms, and the deaths were due to cruder methods, including clubs and sticks embedded with nails and stones! Barbaric though this is, it indicates that both sides respected the long-standing protocols between the two countries, which were intended to maintain peace along the LAC. Subsequent to this, both countries have amassed considerable military strength near the border, and the dangers of escalating clashes are very much present. Meanwhile, talks to defuse the situation are on between army commanders of the two sides and diplomatic efforts to do so have now been raised to the ministerial level.

There are two immediate outcomes of this. First, China's strong support of Pakistan through arms, diplomacy and financing, which has been of ongoing concern, now necessitates our contingency planning for a two-front war. This appears a real possibility, given Pakistan's attitude and its inclination to fish in troubled waters. Second, an active LAC and preparations for a two-front war imply big increases in our defence spending, with substantial impact on both investments on the social front (education, health) and on economic growth. Fortunately, there is so far little evidence of any substantial or increased support by China to any of India's internal insurgencies.

Pakistan continues to be an implacable foe. Unlike China, it has not been amenable to putting contentious issues on the back-burner and building positive relationships in other areas. Its very existence seems to be predicated on an antagonistic relationship with India. Many there—most of all, its all-powerful military and intelligence establishment—have a vested interest in continuing a hostile position with regard to India. From time to time, there have been glimmers of hope, and sustained peace seems to be just around the corner. Each time the light at the end of the tunnel has proved deceptive. Of late, domestic politics in India seems to be drawing us too into a posture of complete hostility, with no major political party willing to espouse the cause of peace with Pakistan. This means that apart from the military need to be prepared for any contingency vis-à-vis Pakistan, there is also a certain political compulsion—and mileage—to be belligerent, and even to possibly take pro-active or pre-emptive action.

The hawkish military posture against Pakistan has, though, hardly been reflected in government's fund allocations: the share of defence in India's GDP has, in fact, remained almost static—2.41 per cent in 2015 and 2.40 per cent in 2019.[29] As

---

[29]'Military Expenditure (% of GDP)', *The World Bank*.

much as three-fifths (about 58 per cent) of India's defence expenditure goes into salaries and pensions,[30] leaving but a little for acquisition of new equipment or for replacement of obsolete hardware. As a result, the modernization plans of the three services are way behind the conservative timeline, and there is little funding for new areas like cyber and space. R&D is stymied by funds and other constraints, while indigenous production is woefully slow. Therefore, India imports most of its arms, making it the world's second-largest importer. Despite some efforts and many announcements, domestic production is limited to older-generation planes, ships, submarines and tanks: these too are mostly the result of technology transfer from foreign suppliers, and have a high proportion of imported components. New generation equipment—be it any of these platforms or precision-targeted smart bombs, unmanned aerial vehicles, air defence missiles or attack helicopters—are all imported. This means dependency, vulnerability and high costs. Besides, rapid scaling up at a time of need will be difficult. Meanwhile, import dependency has imposed another huge penalty: given the unbelievable delay—a decade is not exceptional—in the convoluted procurement process for key equipment like aircraft, India's armed forces have to make do with obsolete equipment. Further, by the time orders are placed, based on specifications finalized years ago, and new equipment arrives, it is often already obsolete. Thus, if and when India actually gets its intended hundred-plus Rafale fighter planes (a requirement dating back about 15 years), a new generation of aircraft will already be fully operational.

---

[30]"To Take on Chinese "Wolf Warriors", India Must Fix Military Asymmetry', *The Times of India*, 28 June 2020, https://timesofindia.indiatimes.com/blogs/academic-interest/to-take-on-chinese-wolf-warriors-india-must-fix-military-asymmetry/, accessed on 18 March 2021.

The impact is a triple whammy: facing the enemy with outdated equipment, inadequate spares means fewer numbers, and end-of-life equipment failures, which put the crew at risk.

FUTURE WARS

As we continue to invest in traditional armaments, the contours of any possible future war are rapidly changing. New technology is revolutionizing warfare, not just in support functions like command, control and communications, or intelligence and surveillance, but in core functionalities. Thus, the infantryman of the future will have his sight, hearing, body armour, physical capability and armament greatly enhanced by technology. In fact, the infantryman may no longer be 'man' (or woman), but a robot. With today's capabilities, this is no longer sci-fi or cinematic imagination; it will be tomorrow's reality. Planes and ships may be fully automated and unmanned. Cyber-attacks may cause more damage than bombs. Wars may well be more like video games, but with consequences, damages and deaths in the real world. This, we need to understand, is closer than it may seem.

Before this becomes a reality, frontal attack wars between nations may become a rarity. Proxy wars—through terrorism, instigation or support to internal insurgencies, economic and cyber-attacks—will increasingly be the norm for attacking an enemy country. A lot of this is in action already (as India knows from its own experience), and will only increase—in both scale and sophistication—as capabilities in these areas spread.

Clearly, external threats, terrorism and internal insurrections are amongst the vital issues facing countries around the world today. However, security is now a much broader concept. Its dimensions range from food security to ecological sustainability, and cover aspects such as personal safety, healthcare and economic, social and data security. This broad concept of security is certainly a substantial departure from the traditional one, limited to countering an overt military attack by an enemy country. Even in that sphere, security is not limited to concerns of an armed incursion, but also about an enemy country unleashing biological warfare, cyber-attacks, psychological warfare and economic or financial disruption. Given this broader definition of security, the task of protecting the State requires a multi-pronged response involving a variety of stakeholders.

The devastation that biological warfare can cause is massive, and can well bring a country to its knees. COVID-19 has provided a glimpse of what could happen. Modern biotechnology, unfortunately, provides the capability of designing and creating similar viruses. Issues related to this are discussed in the chapter on health.

Many of these forms of non-frontal attacks can be mounted by non-State groups too. Some, like cyber-attacks, do not need vast financial or human resources, and are also not easily traceable. Thus, a country can face a serious threat even from a small group of people who can stay anonymous. Such groups can, therefore, wreak considerable havoc with little danger of retaliation. The difficulty in tracing the precise point of origin and the inherent plausible deniability enables an enemy State too to mount such attacks.

In the 2020s, it is likely that these types of attacks will increase, rather than direct military action. In fact, despite rhetoric from both sides, India and Pakistan are unlikely to go to war against each other, or even have a major skirmish. While one might hope for peace, even friendship, the immediate outlook—over the next three or four years—is one of continued pinpricks from Pakistan. Cross-border firing is likely to continue on and off, with each blaming the other for initiating it. Terrorism, sponsored by one or the other arm of the State, is likely to persist. The occasional retaliation by India will be restrained enough to prevent an escalating spiral. In any case, other countries—including both China and the US—are certain to step in and prevent any large-scale military action by either side.

LEAPS INTO A BETTER FUTURE

In the medium and longer term—beyond 2025—a most likely Indo-Pak scenario is an uneasy but cooperative peace, similar to the India–China relationship till early 2020. This will be predicated on mutual interest in trade and cultural exchanges (both driven by the private sector), people-to-people interaction and tourism. As the dominant economy in the region, India will have to be magnanimous in relation to imports and tariffs. This could well be a positive spiral and the stronger it gets, the more difficult it will be to disrupt it through any occasional terrorist attack by some fringe group. In this, India will have to be strong and firm but restrained, with a clear understanding that the main purpose of any such attack will be to disrupt the Indo-Pak relationship.

Is this an excessively optimistic view? Probably not. Already, there seems to be a growing weariness in Pakistan—and an understanding of the futility—regarding their quest to wrest Kashmir. Just as India has realized that talking of getting Aksai Chin back from China can only be rhetorical, Pakistan too has begun to understand that the borders of Kashmir will remain what they are. Clarity on this—understated as it may be—is the key to a better, even positive, relationship. Maybe, somewhere in the mid-20s, India will have the self-assuredness and confidence to propose an agreement between India, China and Pakistan to freeze the borders of Kashmir and Ladakh in keeping with the reality on the ground. Simultaneously, this will include an agreement with China that formally recognizes the present positions as the formal border along the rest of the India–China boundary. In our interest, we may also insist on a similar China–Bhutan agreement as a prior condition.

Any such tripartite deal would be a political hot potato in all three countries, but especially in India and Pakistan. All political parties will have to be taken on board, and a national consensus reached. In India, this would require careful preparatory steps, including lowering the temperature and moderating the political rhetoric against Pakistan and China. Cross-border firing incidents must be prevented and, if at all they happen, be immediately quelled. Media, especially India's noisy, hyperventilating and hate-spewing TV channels, will have to be managed. An overall positive climate will have to be carefully built regarding any such deal.

An agreement to formally make a permanent change in India's borders may be inevitable. However, if such a bold move is not considered politically palatable and is seen as too radical, then an intermediate option could be considered: an agreement to freeze borders and 'temporarily' recognize these for the next 25 years. The matter can be reopened and negotiated for a final permanent settlement by 2050. This may not pose too difficult a problem between India and China (despite China's sometimes very vocal and aggressive claims on Arunachal Pradesh), but—as in all matters—the India–Pakistan issues will be contentious. Yet, if the leaders can agree, selling this to their domestic constituencies may not be an insurmountable problem.

Such a deal will only be recognition of long-standing ground realities, which have been accepted de facto. Yet, any government in India that can pull this off would deserve great kudos. It can transform India, enable us to shift funds from defence to development and provide a considerable economic fillip to trade, especially if easy transit across borders (particularly with Pakistan) follows. It will also free India from its obsession with Pakistan, re-energize South Asian Association for Regional Cooperation (SAARC) and wider regional cooperation and enable us play a far bigger role on the world stage.

Importantly, it will greatly reduce—if not altogether eliminate—terrorist attacks, as also much of the militancy and separatism, in Kashmir. Obviously, no-support-to-terrorists clauses will have to be part of any deal on borders. Amongst the advantages of a trilateral agreement is the likelihood that not only will China pressurize Pakistan to sign up for a border freeze, but also for no-terrorism (or support for it) clauses.

Further, given that communal tensions between Hindus and Muslims are sometimes linked to Pakistan, a conviviality—or, at least, a non-antagonism—with that country may well make for greater social harmony in India. A spin-off would be more inclusive—and possibly faster—economic growth.

Many in India may look askance at involving China in India–Pakistan issues, which we have always maintained must be sorted out bilaterally. Of course, the reality is that China and the US are very much involved, especially when matters escalate. Yet, if there is hesitation, the solution would be to negotiate separate treaties with China and Pakistan.

Clearly, this is a very ambitious agenda and requires great optimism to even imagine that it will find support in any of the three countries, leave alone all of them. Yet, in a rapidly evolving global scenario, it is quite possible that all three see this as being in their own enlightened self-interest. It will require statesmanship of the highest order, but all the countries do have leaders capable of this. We have seen rapprochements galore amongst enemies throughout history; there is no reason to imagine that this great civilizational area is incapable of similar leaps into a better future for each.

The alternative of adopting an aggressive or muscular policy may sell well domestically in India, and even win elections, but is hardly a wise option for India. Such an approach will inevitably lead to confrontations, for which we will pay a heavy price. Even if we do not end up with a bloody nose (as was the result of Nehru's aggressive 'forward' policy on the India–China border, 60 years ago) and many military deaths, it will drain our resources. Big increases in military spending will be required, diverting funds from social and economic needs. Lower economic growth and poor social indicators in critical areas like health and education will be amongst the fall-outs. A lot of India's diplomatic capital will be consumed and India will remain locked into a limited sphere with little strategic autonomy. These are hardly outcomes that the country would want. The suggested option of bold and radical thinking, if it succeeds will, on the other hand, propel the country into a different orbit.

Internal insurgencies are another key factor. These are unlikely to altogether fade away in the 2020s. Though an agreement on Kashmir, as suggested above, may effectively end—or drastically reduce—militancy there, tribal and ethnic-related issues in the northeast, and the problems in the mainly-tribal LWE areas are likely to continue. Optimistically, stronger integration of people from the Northeast, and rapid economic development in central India will substantially reduce militancy. Both depend a great deal—but not only—on economic growth and more jobs for the people concerned. More accountable, better and a service-oriented rather than feudal style of governance is essential. Local participation and decentralization in decision-making is also a must, especially vis-à-vis corporates and organizations involved in forest, mining and industrial activities in central/eastern India.

Reduced militancy in these areas might appear an optimistic expectation, especially given the growing clout of the corporate world and the government's focus on economic development (sometimes at the cost of the local population and the environment). However, there is a strong counterweight of growing public awareness and media attention that may force both, corporates and the government, to be more mindful about the interests and concerns of the local population. Doubtless, this can be ignored for a while, and there will be those who support 'strong' and hawkish action to quell any disaffection. Yet, as the government becomes more sensitive and the world moves to greater emphasis on social indicators of progress, there is hope for a dialogue—rather than force—to settle issues. Optimism with regard to internal insurgencies may, therefore, not be unwarranted.

OTHER CHALLENGES

Finally, a brief look at 'black swan'[31] events that may affect India's security. One is the possible resurgence of a global organization like the ISIS, which may want to target India.

---

[31] The term 'black swan' here refers to low-probability events, and is drawn from *The Black Swan: The Impact of the Highly Improbable*, Nassim Nicholas Taleb, Penguin, 2008.

Given the assumption of an agreement of some sort with Pakistan, that country may not be the launch pad or support base for terrorist attacks. However, a Taliban-ruled Afghanistan could well nurture training camps and provide the arms for terrorists who could foment trouble in India. Another possibility—remote though it may seem—is for a reversal of Bangladesh's present trajectory, and that country serving as a terrorist base. Given its large and porous land, riverine and sea border with India, this would certainly be a dangerous development. Pre-emptive action may be both necessary and tempting, but could lead to on-going problems through the decade. The best defence against any such scenario would be complete social harmony within India.

For decades during colonial times, the 'great game' was played out in Afghanistan between the Russian and British empires. Is there a possible modern day equivalent that may happen between a resurgent Russia and a growing India? This would be an extreme black swan event. Given realities on the ground, a China–Russia or a China–India rivalry is more likely. Of course, an unstated, low-key India–Pakistan rivalry has been on in Afghanistan for quite some time now and may continue—so this is hardly a black swan.

Two low-probability, though sometimes predicted, events are a break-up of Pakistan and its descent into an ungovernable chaos, like the present situation in Afghanistan. Though some may welcome this as a fitting punishment for an enemy, it would spell disaster for India. A nuclear weapons State, with well-armed military forces, breaking up into a chaotic mess, with no clear central leadership, would be a nightmare for India. Even a less extreme disintegration or merely chaos may well trigger an influx of millions of refugees into India. Again, a disaster India would not want.

As India becomes powerful—economically and militarily—will the US want to hold it in check? Unlikely though this may seem, the US does have a strong strategic establishment that looks far into the future. Certainly, one of the scenarios in the decades ahead would see India emerging as a major global power in the second half of the century. Unless China hits a major roadblock, as likely as not, it will be India and China which will dominate the world in the latter part of the 21st century. For some time now, the US has recognized China as a challenge to its power and has tried to contain it, sometimes using India as the counterweight. In the years ahead, it is entirely possible that India moves to the 'frenemy' category and then to being considered a rival. Though many consider the Indo-US nuclear deal—Manmohan Singh's great victory—as signifying the start of a strategic partnership, one can also view it from a different perspective. It acknowledged India's nuclear weapon State status and promised to end India's exclusion (self-chosen, a fact that most tend to overlook) from various nuclear cartels, but at the cost of constraining India's nuclear programme and even abridging its sovereignty (via inspections and curbs on nuclear exports). Much touted access to new technologies never happened, and the sale of nuclear power plants to India, at exorbitant and unaffordable cost, has long been stymied for various reasons. Clearly, if one wanted to slow down India's nuclear program, the Indo-US nuclear deal—sold to the Indian public as a game changer—was a clever way doing so. Very few took this point of view at the time the deal was signed.[32] Might we see such subtle

---

[32] As one observer noted in: 'Indo-US Ties: Eco-cultural Adhesive', Kiran Karnik, 2 November 2010, https://economictimes.indiatimes.com/opinion/et-commentary/indo-us-ties-eco-cultural-adhesive/articleshow/6856386.cms, accessed on 18 March 2021.

plays from the US, or even overt obstacles to India's progress? Unlikely, yes; impossible, no.

Other black swan events are some form of military challenge from one of the two large and potentially powerful countries in our neighbourhood: Iran and Indonesia. Our present relationship with both is positive, and there are no contentious issues with either. In fact, there is a shared cultural and civilizational history. Additionally, both may prefer to work with India, as China expands into areas of interest to them: Southeast Asia in the case of Indonesia, and Central Asia in Iran's case. Any confrontation between India and either of these countries is, therefore, largely unlikely.

SECURITY SCENARIO: 2030

The overall security scenario by 2030 that we would consider most likely, then, would be as follows. First, there will be no direct military confrontation with any of our neighbours. Skirmishes too are unlikely, and even the presently frequent cross-border firing between India and Pakistan will practically come to an end. The clashes with China in Ladakh will see a diplomatic settlement. An agreement with Pakistan and China, as proposed earlier, will enable considerable cuts in defence budget, even as we move towards a smaller, leaner, but potent and new-age security force.

As a result, forces along the borders with both countries can be thinned out, and there will even be scope to reduce the overall force strength. The defence budget will see much larger allocations for cybersecurity (defensive and offensive); intelligence and reconnaissance, especially from space; unmanned aerial vehicles; technology-enabled infantryman and robots; missiles, defensive and offensive and highly automated ships and submarines. While all this will be expensive, there will be considerable savings by reducing human power and conventional armaments.

Second, terrorist attacks will reduce considerably. However, the dangers of fewer but bigger and more damaging attacks will loom large, as will the scope of the attacks, encompassing areas like cyber and bio weapons. Increasing sophistication, the use of high-technology and diverse—even unidentifiable points—of origin will make pre-emptive action and deterrence difficult. A lowering of attention would, therefore, not be possible. Intelligence and other agencies will need to be on their toes and augment their presence in potential points of origin abroad. However, the easiest, cost-effective and probably strongest safeguard will be a harmonious society which provides no sanctuary or support to terrorists, and no 'causes' for them to rally around. Yet, terrorism is likely to be India's biggest security concern in 2030.

Internal insurgencies, in this somewhat optimistic scenario, will practically die out by 2030. This is, of course, contingent on the 2020s focusing on building a more equitable society (both, economically and socially) and the creation of enough opportunities of livelihoods for all. A strong and universal social security net will underpin this, with assured rights to employment, food and shelter, and possibly a minimum income for all. These are expensive and difficult propositions, but not beyond the country's affordability. They will provide an impetus to economic development and faster growth, making these investments rather than expenditures. More importantly, they will ensure a happier country. The consequent reduction in internal insurgencies will, in a positive feedback cycle, enable people-focused development in these areas.

Will there be new hotspots of serious disaffection elsewhere in the country? In a country as large and diverse as India, this is certainly likely: there will always be some issue or the other on which a part of the country, or a group of people, will be seriously unhappy. It could be perceived neglect or inequitable treatment with regard to economic, social, regional or cultural issues. Hypothetically, one can think of many such issues, which may antagonize some group of people. However, it is difficult to conceive of one that may result in any form of armed insurgency of the type presently seen Kashmir, the northeast, or in LWE areas. It is, therefore, reasonable to predict that by 2030, serious internal insurgencies will become history.

Thus, the three dimensions of an armed challenge to security—direct military confrontation, terrorism, and internal insurgencies—seem to be waning, and our prediction is that by 2030, these will not pose a serious problem for India. This may seem like wishful thinking, yet, we feel this optimistic scenario is entirely possible, even likely.

However, in this scenario, too, the country must prepare for more subtle attacks, from both, other nations and also non-State groups. These may take the form of cyber, financial, psychological or biological warfare. These forms of asymmetric warfare generally give the attacker an advantage. Since attribution is difficult and often unprovable, deterrence too has to be subtle and unattributable. This would require high and continuous investments in technology and talent, and a very effective global intelligence system. Such 'unarmed' attacks may pose the biggest challenge to India's security by 2030.

Broader dimensions of security were mentioned earlier. Some are global (climate change and trade, for example) while others are domestic (personal safety, food security). Thanks to COVID, awareness about global pandemics and the dangers they pose are now top of mind. Health security is no longer just a national issue, but—like climate change—has become one of global concern. In this context, India would do well to avoid the vanity of thinking of itself as a near-superpower, and so preferring a unilateral or bilateral approach to global issues (as, for example, the US has been doing). It must continue its past policy of preferring multilateralism and strengthening global institutions like the UN, World Health Organization (WHO), World Trade Organization (WTO) and others. Of course, as is now widely recognized, these organizations need restructuring so that they better reflect the new realities of global power and influence. Global problems—be they related to space, the oceans, climate, cyberspace, trade or health—require international compacts and global agencies. India must play a role to ensure the reform and strengthening of global institutions. Its increasing clout would be best used to enhance its role as a rule-maker within a multilateral framework, rather than falling into the trap of unilateralism. This will enable it to face the challenges of global issues which threaten its own security.

Amongst such global issues, one of direct concern to India is climate change. It must play a forceful role in this area, even if it means taking on the US (the one country that has been most reluctant to accept global consensus on climate and environmental action; hopefully, President Joe Biden will change this). The effects of climate change are already visible in India. Extreme weather events have been increasing. For example, 'extremely heavy rainfall' events have increased by 100 per cent in three years: from 261 in 2017 to 554 in 2019. Also, the number of cyclones in the Arabian Sea and Bay of Bengal went up from three in 2017 to eight in 2019.[33] Given

---

[33]Data given by Minster of Earth Sciences in Rajya Sabha, as quoted in

this country's vulnerability to climate change, it must be at the forefront of pushing global action.

India's ambitious renewable energy programme is an example to others, but it needs to do far more to reduce pollution due to use of coal, especially for power. The answer here may lie not in abandoning coal (which it cannot afford to do), but to vigorously push R&D in areas like coal gasification, emission control, and carbon sequestration. In this context, the temptation (and increasing actions) to ease environmental regulations so as to promote investment and score on Ease of Doing Business rankings must be avoided. Such relaxations can endanger our long-term future for some limited immediate gains. Already, pollution in many areas (including the national capital region) have reached extreme levels, with serious health effects. According to one report, two-thirds of the world's most polluted cities are in India (21 of the top 30, and 6 of the top 10), with Ghaziabad (a Delhi suburb) being the worst in the world, and Delhi itself at number 5.[34]

Energy security is a major issue for India. The dependence on imported crude oil and gas will continue, and energy security will require a number of actions. First, a big increase in production of renewable energy (solar, wind and hydro); as a corollary, domestic production of solar cells. Second,

---

"'Extremely Heavy Rainfall' Events Up 100% in 3 Years", *The Times of India*, 17 September 2020, https://timesofindia.indiatimes.com/india/extremely-heavy-rainfall-events-up-100-in-3-years/articleshow/78158286.cms, last accessed 18 March 2021.

[34]From the 2019 World Air Quality Report, quoted in 'Two-Thirds of Most Polluted Cities Are in India: Global Report', The Indian Express, 26 February 2020, Indian Express, https://indianexpress.com/article/explained/two-thirds-of-most-polluted-cities-are-in-india-global-report-6286708/#:~:text=India%20accounts%20for%20two%2Dthirds,IQAir%20and%20Greenpeace%20on%20Tuesday, accessed on 18 March 2021.

vigorous prospecting for on-land and undersea oil and gas reserves. Third, more productive coal mines and technologies for cleaner (less polluting) coal-based thermal power (by coal gasification, for example). Fourth, vigorous development of next-generation nuclear power, especially fast-breeders and thorium plants. Fifth, R&D to quickly operationalize electric vehicles. Finally, R&D on hydrogen, nuclear fusion and other new, 'clean' power sources. In addition, knowing that continuing oil and gas imports are inevitable, ensuring energy security will require eco-diplomatic efforts to diversify sources and also tie-up long-term supply arrangements.

Food security is highly unlikely to be an issue for India in the 2020s. Even the dependence on imports for (cooking) oil and pulses will decrease considerably, as India's domestic productivity and production goes up. Meanwhile, agricultural exports continue to be substantial.

Personal security and safety could be a matter of concern, especially if the present trend-line of crime continues. In particular, crimes against women have shown a big increase, despite much lip-service about steps to prevent them. Many factors drive crime, and high inequality is definitely one amongst them. A more equal society—which we have predicted will be the evolutionary direction in the 20s—will dampen crime. Yet, if society continues to focus strongly on materialistic aspects and adopts a 'greed is good' outlook, crime—including a lot of white-collar types—will flourish.

To summarize, the main challenges to India's security—and, therefore, the ones that will shape its posture and outlook—in 2030 will be terrorism (especially from untraceable sources, and including cyber-attacks), energy security and personal security/safety (which includes health and livelihood security). The external challenge needs to be neutralized through clever diplomacy and a statesman-like long-term strategic perspective; if not, the biggest and most daunting challenge would be the possibility of a joint China–Pakistan attack.

If India can face up to and overcome these challenges, it can take on a greater role in its extended neighbourhood—from the Horn of Africa to the Malacca Straits. Peaceful borders, internal harmony, a booming economy and greater soft power will together position India to begin playing a big global role from the 2030s. In this scenario, it will without any doubt, be one of the two or three major global powers by 2050.

3

HEALTH

Adding Years to Life and Life to Years

India is widely acknowledged and respected for its achievements in many fields—in space, nuclear technology, information and communications technology, agriculture and diplomatic acumen. Over the last quarter-century, its overall economic performance too has been seen as exemplary. Yet, there is one area in which it ranks poorly: social indicators related to human development. On most of these, it performs worse than its peers at comparable levels of development. Even in its own neighbourhood, Bangladesh and Sri Lanka do much better on many counts, despite lower per capita incomes. India's overall rank of 131 (amongst 189 countries) for 2019 in UNDP's Human Development Index compares poorly with Sri Lanka (72) and China (85).[35]

Health, in particular, has been India's big failing. In key indicators like infant, child and maternal mortality, it has done very badly. In children, three indicators are generally used to indicate overall health and nutrition. These are stunting (height for age), wasting (weight for height) and

---

[35]'Human Development Report 2020', *United Nations Development Programme*, http://hdr.undp.org/sites/default/files/hdr_2020_overview_english.pdf, accessed on 18 march 2021.

underweight (weight for age). India's figures for these tell a sad story, but what makes it worse is a comparison with some of India's neighbours whose per capita income is, in fact, lower than that of India. Stunting, wasting and underweight amongst children under 5 years in India (as indicated in the Comprehensive National Nutrition Survey, 2016–18) was 34.7 per cent, 17.3 per cent and 33.4 per cent, respectively. The figures for Bangladesh are 30.8 per cent, 8.4 per cent and 21.9 per cent, better than India on all three indicators. Sri Lanka too has better figures than India: 17.3 per cent, 15.1 per cent and 20.5 per cent. We have a lot to learn from the success of these countries, especially Bangladesh (given its size and where it began from, after its independence in 1971). India can learn even more from within the country: the best-performing state outperforms both our neighbours. The figures and best states for the three indicators are: 15.5 per cent (Jammu & Kashmir), 5.8 per cent (Mizoram) and 11.3 per cent (again, Mizoram).[36] India's poor performance affects not only the physical health of children, but also their cognitive development. Certainly, this is serious enough to cause deep concern and ensure more attention and resources.

Another indicator of significance is Maternal Mortality Ratio (MMR), representing the number of women who die from pregnancy-related causes while pregnant or within 42 days of pregnancy termination per 100,000 live births. India's

---

[36]'Comprehensive National Nutrition Survey, 2016–18', *National Health Mission*, https://nhm.gov.in/WriteReadData/l892s/1405796031571201348.pdf, accessed on 18 March 2021; 'Sri Lanka: Demographic and Health Survey 2016', *HIV and AIDS Data Hub*, https://www.aidsdatahub.org/resource/sri-lanka-demographic-and-health-survey-2016, accessed on 18 March 2021 and 'Bangladesh: Demographic and Health Survey 2017–18', The *Demographic and Health Surveys Program*, https://dhsprogram.com/pubs/pdf/PR104/PR104.pdf, accessed on 18 March 2021.

MMR was 145 in 2017, again comparing poorly with Sri Lanka's 36 and Vietnam's 43 (and just seven in Germany).[37] Sample Registration System (SRS) 2016–18 has a lower figure for India, but even that is as high as 113.[38] This reflects poor nutrition and bad health, as also the sorry state of India's healthcare system.

Of course, much progress has been made. An overall indicator like life expectancy at birth is evidence: this has gone up from 49.7 in 1970–75 to 69.4 years in 2014–18. While this may seem quite impressive, it is worth noting that China reached this level in 1990, and is now at 76.7 years. Even Bangladesh and Nepal—behind us in 1980—are now ahead at 72.1 and 70.5, respectively.[39]

As a result, the next generation is growing up amidst a dismal health scenario, and the primary homemaker is not properly taken care of. The neglect of public health is at the root of the problem. Despite much lip service over decades, the public expenditure on health continues to languish at less than 2 per cent of the GDP; in fact, in 2019–20, it was 1.29 per cent.[40] Even including private spending, the total healthcare expenditure in 2017 was 3.5 per cent; as a comparison, China

---

[37]'Maternal Mortality Ratio', *The World Bank*, https://data.worldbank.org/indicator/SH.STA.MMRT.NE?locations=LK, accessed on 18 March 2021.

[38]'Special Bulletin on Maternal Mortality in India 2016–18', *Census of India*, July 2020, https://censusindia.gov.in/vital_statistics/SRS_Bulletins/MMR%20Bulletin%202016-18.pdf, accessed on 18 March 2021.

[39]'State, Area and Gender Key to Life Expectancy, Shows Data', *The Times of India*, 28 September 2020, https://timesofindia.indiatimes.com/india/state-area-and-gender-key-to-life-expectancy-shows-data/articleshow/78354844.cms, accessed on 18 March 2021.

[40]'India's Economy Needs Big Dose of Health Spending', *LiveMint*, 8 April 2020, https://www.livemint.com/news/india/india-s-economy-needs-big-dose-of-health-spending-11586365603651.html, accessed on 18 March 2021.

spent 5.15 per cent, and the UK 9.63 per cent. The US spends an amazing 17 per cent of GDP on health.[41] While expenditure is only an input index, and outcomes depend on other factors, it is nevertheless of vital importance.

Over the years, a health system structure has been built up: beginning with accredited social health assistants (ASHAs), primary health centres (PHCs), community health centres, district hospitals and specialized referral hospitals. On paper, this looks like a good system that should meet all needs, from minor ailments to major medical problems. In reality, the system is broken. Far too many PHCs have no doctors, sometimes no paramedical staff. Where there is a doctor, s/he often lives in a different location and is often absent. Medical stocks at the local level are frequently not available. As a result of this, and frequent bad experiences, trust in the system is low, and most people prefer to go to a private doctor, if they can afford to do so. This is part of the downward spiral, as seen in education too, where private schools—which charge fees—are preferred to free education in government schools. Data bears this out: private expenditure is 63.2 percent of the total expenditure on healthcare,[42] despite the free services offered by the government system. This spells disaster, especially for

---

[41] "Current Health Expenditure (% of GDP)", *The World Bank*, https://data.worldbank.org/indicator/SH.XPD.CHEX.GD.ZS, accessed on 18 March 2021.
Estimates of current health expenditures include healthcare goods and services consumed during each year. This indicator does not include capital health expenditures such as buildings, machinery, IT and stocks of vaccines for emergency or outbreaks.

[42] "National Health Accounts Estimates for India, 2016–17", *National Health Systems Resource Centre*, October 2019, http://nhsrcindia.org/sites/default/files/FINAL%20National%20Health%20Accounts%202016-17%20Nov%202019-for%20Web.pdf, accessed on 18 March 2021.

the poor: a single episode of serious illness can drive a family into poverty (taking millions each year to below-poverty-line level), as many studies have established. Death or debt seems the only choice for many.

To provide a safety net that will safeguard against large expenditures on medical exigencies, the government launched Ayushman Bharat Yojna in 2018. This ambitious initiative—aimed at covering 500 million people[43]—ensures, through an insurance scheme, free treatment for the poor in hospitals for a wide range of medical problems. However, the majority of health issues do not require hospitalization and, as is well-known, the overall health scenario depends on the efficacy of basic healthcare. Preventive work in public health requires strengthening of the system at the PHC level. While this is included in the government plan (through local wellness centres), there is too little focus and too few resources devoted to it.

The chronic, long-standing inadequacies in basic healthcare are highlighted when there is any major headline grabbing news (like dozens of children dying of encephalitis, or women dying in family planning camps). Sadly, these are soon forgotten. Investigation results in reports, which, with the recommendations, are generally fated to remain in cupboards. Public reaction, after the initial media-fuelled burst of indignation, is short-lived. Many of those directly affected see it as fate or destiny; those who do not, feel helpless. Most others, who are influential and matter, see this as an unfortunate problem of the poor and rural, not as a systemic problem that demands immediate action. Political parties and

---

[43]'Getting Coverage Right for 500 Million Indians', *Pradhan Mantri Jan Arogya Yojana*, 13 November 2019, https://pmjay.gov.in/node/1247, accessed on 18 March 2021.

their election manifestoes generally ignore health, even as they touch on a range of other issues. One exception is the AAP, which, in the 2020 Delhi assembly elections, made this a major issue, highlighting their creation of 'mohalla' (locality) clinics by its government. Earlier, it had initiated a campaign against dengue, focusing on basic public health and involving the people in tackling issues like cleanliness (no stagnant water). In 2020, it is running a campaign highlighting pollution, asking drivers to switch off their engines at traffic (stop) signals. The key elements of awareness, community involvement and behaviour change have been brought home most forcefully through the COVID pandemic. Even as scientists search desperately for both a cure and vaccine, it has been established that the best preventives are three simple, low-cost measures: physical distancing, frequent handwashing and a face mask. If rigorously adopted, these can hugely slow the spread of the disease. Sadly, in many developing countries, these are not easy to practise. In urban India, with its high population–density slums and cramped and crowded homes, physical distancing is just not possible. With half a dozen (or more) living together in a small room, houses cheek-by-jowl in narrow lanes and common toilet and water facilities, what kind of physical distancing can one expect? Further, where money for food is scarce, how much can be spared for enhanced purchase of soap for frequent handwashing? And is there water for it? These are challenges with no easy answers.

The epidemic has highlighted the dismal state of India's health system, including the inadequate numbers of doctors, nurses and hospital beds. This was particularly evident in epidemic hotspots like Mumbai and Delhi. Initially, vital needs like personal protective equipment (PPE) for frontline staff and ventilators for the seriously ill were scarce and had to be imported on a war footing. Testing kits—to diagnose patients by detecting the presence of the virus—too had to be procured from abroad. To the government's credit, they quickly established and ramped up local production of these, in collaboration with industry. Efforts within the country to work for a cure or vaccine are also being supported. Yet, the long neglect of public health—especially in certain states, and in most rural areas—is starkly visible, and could have disastrous consequences.

COVID has brought attention to the poor state of healthcare, thanks to media coverage. However, media has, by and large, focused on the disease and not so much on the system. Stories about hospitals have mainly been human interest stories, and there has been little discussion on the chronic under-investment in health and the general neglect of this area.

Even now, there are few signs of any major effort for basic improvements in the health system. As part of the economic revival package, the finance minister announced (in June 2020) a whole host of reforms and funds provision, incentives and investments, but there was hardly a mention of health. In recent years, governments at the Centre and in states have been able to provide or ensure funds for such showpiece (and very political) projects like a massive statue in Gujarat, a grand one offshore in Maharashtra and plans for the 'biggest and tallest' one in UP. The one in Gujarat, along with associated infrastructure around it, was completed in record time. The home minister promised that the extraordinary statue in UP would be completed in a few months. Yet, no government—at the Centre or in the states—seems able to find the funds and will power to transform the health infrastructure or to create showpiece public hospitals.

When such projects are announced, they take long years to be completed and, when operational, are always short of funds for proper maintenance and upkeep. The dirty, crumbling facilities in most public hospitals tell their own tale. Yet, in many cases, they have the most dedicated and knowledgeable doctors. In this pandemic, they have heroically worked for endless hours, at considerable personal risk and often staying away from their families, so as not to endanger them. Certainly, they deserve better facilities?

COVID has received widespread attention, yet, the spread and devastation caused by it is far less than a disease like tuberculosis (TB). Testing, diagnosing and providing remedial medication are all grossly inadequate for TB. With limited focus and resources dedicated to it, TB continues to be rampant and is the cause for an estimated 450,000 deaths a year in the country, despite the availability of a cure. Not perceived as a disease of the well off, it gets little attention or funding. Fortunately, another affliction—polio—has been successfully countered and practically eradicated, thanks to a sustained effort in ensuring awareness and providing vaccinations.

However, the simple underlying problems of illness—lack of clean drinking water, poor sanitation and malnutrition—continue to take a large toll, especially amongst children. Government schemes exist for each of these, but must deliver on the ground. The Swachh Bharat programme, for example, has concentrated on constructing toilets. However, they will not be used unless availability of water, means to clean them and their maintenance is ensured. In addition, there is a challenge in changing traditional beliefs and behaviour with regard to use of toilets.

These and other instances indicate the futility of investing merely in infrastructure. This is, of course, easy and visible;

it is also expensive and involves contracts with third parties for construction, furniture, equipment, etc., which, as is well-known, is often an 'incentive'. While infrastructure is essential, without an overall or system view, it is often wasted. PHCs without doctors, toilets with no water connection, hospitals without specialists, non-functioning equipment: these are incapable of delivering results. None of this is new or unknown, but government's siloed ways of working, improper metrics and perverse incentives contribute to the problem. For example, if the metric is number of toilets built, the action is a flurry of construction—sometimes of questionable quality—to meet the target. If, instead, the metric were number of regular users, one would get a different thrust.

BEHAVIOURAL SCIENCE AS A MEDICAL TOOL

Health, it is well known, is crucially dependent on behaviour: be it handwashing, regular exercise, taking medicines as prescribed, or using a toilet instead of defecating in the open. This has to begin with awareness and information, and often has to overcome traditional beliefs or customs. Communication is key to ensuring this and triggering desired changes in behaviour. Unfortunately, the importance and attention given to this is minimal, with health being perceived as only a medical issue. Large-scale communication campaigns have been launched, starting from the early days of the family planning programme (most older people yet remember the '*Hum do, hamare do*' [We two, our two] campaign). However, these are rarely thought-through efforts that understand the psyche of the intended 'target audience', or use the multidisciplinary methods of behaviour change communication as they have evolved in recent years.

In India, this approach for effective communication was used as far back as the 1970s. It was extensively utilized by Indian Space Research Organisation (ISRO) in the Kheda communication project, initially a part of the Satellite Instructional Television Experiment (SITE). India's first TV station dedicated to serving rural areas was set up in the Kheda district of Gujarat. It broadcast programmes focused on relevance to the viewers in Kheda, in Gujarati and often in the local dialect, Charotari. These were the product of teams comprising social scientists, content experts, and creative and technical professionals. Thus, the teams brought together people who studied and understood the audience (sociologists, anthropologists, psychologists) with experts who knew the subject (health, agriculture, social change). Creative professionals (writers, directors) and those who handled the production equipment converted this subject-and-people knowledge into interesting TV content. Ideas and pilot programmes were often pretested with the audience through focus group discussions and interviews, before operational production. Even prior to this, social scientists identified the obstacles, issues and possible 'entry points' for communication, through interaction with the audience. A 'brief' was prepared for each programme. This was converted into a script by the writers, and given creative video form by the producer-director and the production team. An audience profile, needs-assessment and testing of a pilot were steps before regular programme production, followed by feedback and evaluation. Thus, behaviour change needs were identified and specifically addressed through the communication.

Teamwork of this nature is not easy: its interdisciplinary character means the team members do not speak even the same 'language'. Each one fights any perceived dilution of their viewpoint, and yet the final product obviously has to make trade-offs (for example, between pedantic presentation of all the facts versus creative liberties to sustain interest). Yet, such teams are essential for effective communication—be it health, or other issues.

Behaviour change communication is sometimes embedded into a genre called education-entertainment, similar to the example of the ISRO TV programmes for Kheda in the 1970s, recounted above. Soon after, based on the success of a series on Mexican TV called *Ven Conmigo*, Doordarshan embarked on serials such as the immensely popular *Hum Log* (dealing mainly with family planning, and also gender and social issues). A contemporary example is the series *Main Kuch Bhi Kar Sakti Hoon*[44] (produced by Population Foundation of India and broadcast by Doordarshan), which uses the positive deviance approach to behaviour change communication to address issues of gender equality, family planning and health.

Behaviour change is of particular relevance and importance to health-related issues, re-emphasizing the fact that a holistic view of health issues would be far more beneficial and effective than a narrow medical one. Take children's health. A major cause of high mortality is poor nutrition, which also results in being underweight, as well as stunting and wasting, besides affecting cognitive development. It is known that an important reason for child malnutrition is frequent diarrhoea, caused by poor quality drinking water. The 'medical' solution is to recommend that drinking water be boiled, ideally for 20 minutes. A communication campaign on this would be a standard follow-up action. Effective communication may

---

[44]For more on *Main Kuch Bhi Kar Sakti Hoon*, see the website: www.mkbksh. org.

succeed in getting the message across. However, for poor households, which depend on firewood, twigs and picked up animal-dung, fuel even for cooking is scarce. Using some of it for boiling water (and for 20 minutes) is unthinkable.

With economic growth and schemes for subsidized cooking fuel (including gas), this particular problem is less widespread now than it used to be. Even so, it has not quite gone away, and the need to tackle the root causes remains. Take the other (medical) solution to child (and general) health: better sanitation. Open defecation having been identified as a problem, the immediate response was a scheme to build toilets. Welcome as this is by itself, non-medical research would have pointed to the fact that where toilets had been built, many were used for storage or as goat-sheds or were just crumbling. Lack of downstream or cleaning arrangements, of water and maintenance, were inhibitors to usage, but equally important were widely prevailing beliefs—and tradition—which favoured defecation in the open. It would, therefore, have been more appropriate to begin with campaigns and communication aimed at overcoming these beliefs, thereby creating a demand for toilet facilities. However, the supply-side push is always easier, more convenient, and hence preferred by government agencies, though it is generally ineffective without a demand pull.

Many health issues are caught up in a whole web of traditions, superstitions or beliefs and social pressures. These cannot be tackled without changes in attitudes and behaviour, through processes that are necessarily slow. Consider an issue like preference for the male child. This leads to many unwanted pregnancies, low spacing between children, domestic violence and neglect of girl children: all with serious gender consequences, including on the health of women. Occasionally, there are horrendous reports about murder of infant girls, and in many cases technology is being misused for prenatal sex determination followed by abortion (if the test indicates a girl child). Changing this historical preference for male progeny may take years, even a decade or more, of sustained work. Progress—leave alone results—may not be visible for years, unlike construction of a building. Yet, tackling this issue is of vital significance.

All this indicates the importance of behavioural science in the overall healthcare system. An interesting example of its use comes from a very different field. A large number of people in India are injured or die while crossing railway tracks. The problem is particularly acute in Mumbai, where the number crossing the tracks and the frequency of the local trains are both high, resulting in 10 deaths each day (apparently, the largest cause of unnatural deaths in the city). Behavioural science provided a crucial insight: humans systematically underestimate the speed of large moving objects. This led to a simple solution. Yellow lines painted across the track provided trespassers a visual and non-conscious reference of the speed of an approaching train. According to the company that led this effort (Fractal Analytics), tests of this solution by Indian Railways brought down accidental deaths by 75 per cent.[45] Clearly, there is need and scope to use behavioural science in various fields, including health, where behaviour change is vital.

---

[45]'Supercharging the Public Sector—Why AI Won't Be Enough?', *National Conference on e-Governance*, 9 August 2019, https://nceg.gov.in/sites/default/files/AI%20for%20Governance%20-Sandeep%20Dutta.pdf, accessed on 18 March 2021.

PUBLIC HEALTH: A COMPONENT OF NATIONAL SECURITY?

Considerable controversy has surrounded the origin of the COVID virus. Most scientific evidence now points to this as a zoonotic disease (originating from animals), which began in the 'wet markets' of Wuhan in China, where a whole range of products (including bats, a possible source) are sold for human consumption. However, speculation—and allegations—of it being a 'lab created' virus has continued. It seems that extreme theories of the virus being part of work on biological warfare, which escaped from a laboratory in Wuhan, may be more imagination than truth.

However, the fact that some scientists consider this to be a possibility is indicative of what could happen—even if, this time, it did not. It is no secret that some countries are actually working on biological weapons. Irrespective, the very fact that genetic engineering and science enables the creation of such viruses is truly scary. Sci-fi scenarios of engineering a virus to selectively attack certain populations may no longer be fiction. Like cyber-attacks, these viruses too will be untraceable as regards point of origin. Thus, a covert attack can be undertaken with full 'plausible deniability'. While the kind of investments required may limit the creation of such biological agents to nations, it is not impossible for a sufficiently well-funded non-State actor to create such viruses. Also, it could be stolen from a government facility. These possibilities, and the devastation that they can unleash, should give pause to all nations.

A Biological Weapons Convention has been negotiated, and was signed in 1972. As many as 183 countries have signed and ratified this, but a few countries have not.[46] Worse, as there

---

[46]"The Biological Weapons Convention (BWC) At A Glance", *Arms Control*

is no clause for verification of compliance, it is entirely possible that more than one country is violating this. For example, according to reports, Boris Yeltsin (former president of Russia) confirmed that in earlier years, the Soviet Union did have a clandestine biological weapons programme, which he ordered to be terminated in 1992.[47] Meanwhile, there are rumours from time to time of similar clandestine programmes in one country or another. One can only hope that the worldwide devastation caused by COVID will persuade all countries to sign, ratify and respect the Convention.

Till this is done, and having experienced how a pandemic can not only cause untold human suffering but also put a whole country's economy in reverse gear, health will become a key security concern for all countries. Each one will take steps to protect its own interests. India, too, needs to consider health security as an integral part of overall national security.

In this context, COVID has thrown up an interesting dilemma facing each nation and the global community. On the one hand, there is the rapid global spread of the pandemic pointing to the close trade and tourism linkages between countries: in less than a year from the first cases in China, the virus had infected over 60 million people in 190 countries, and resulted in more than 1.4 million deaths.[48] The development of a vaccine and the testing of possible cures requires cooperation of researchers across national

---

Association, https://www.armscontrol.org/factsheets/bwc, accessed on 18 March 2021.
[47] From https://www.britannica.com/event/Biological-Weapons-Conventions, accessed on 18 March 2021.
[48] 'Coronavirus pandemic: Tracking the global outbreak', BBC News, 27 November 2020. Covid-19 pandemic: Tracking the global coronavirus outbreak—BBC News

boundaries if these are to be done in the shortest possible time. Also, cross-national exchange of data and experiences in handling the outbreak would immensely benefit all countries. These factors emphasize the need for global coordination and cooperation.

On the other hand, contrary to these positive reasons and benefits of global cooperation, there is nationalistic pressure within each country to safeguard its own narrow interests. Thus, if—for example—the US view is that it is ahead in vaccine development, it may be tempted to not join a cooperative international effort. Instead, developing its own vaccine will give it huge commercial and strategic advantage. The companies which produce the vaccine will make a lot of money, and the country can export the vaccine selectively, providing it to allies and friends, while withholding it from enemies. There are already many indications of such 'vaccine nationalism'. This will be a further step to protectionism that such a pandemic engenders. To protect their citizens, countries had closed their borders (many, like India, barred any incoming passenger flights or vehicles). Even as these are slowly reopened, the protectionist sentiment is unlikely to go away. Meanwhile, the disruption in global supply chains—partly due to lack of production because of lockdowns in various countries and partly because of difficulties in logistics—has ignited action to move manufacturing back 'home', rather than contract it to companies in other countries. Therefore, as a result of COVID, one is likely to see de-globalization gather momentum.

COVID has brought us face to face with a deep question: do we value all lives equally? This is no longer an issue in the realm of philosophy, but has become an immediate moral issue which will dictate our actions when faced with the poser:

to whom do you give the next hospital bed? The Lombardy region of Italy, when faced with this issue in the context of an acute shortage of hospital beds to take care of pandemic-affected patients, decided that priority would be given to the young. They had longer to live, and so could contribute more to the economy, and their chances of survival were greater. Though it may seem callous to leave the old to die, it was a necessary decision to a practical problem involving hard choices. Others could have used the logic of determining whose need is greater, and come up with a contrary answer (obviously, in general, the elderly would be in greater need of hospital care). In a pure capitalist society, the allotment of hospital beds could be on the basis of pricing, which would have ended up as practically an auction. In this case, the rich would get medical care, and the poor would be left to die.

With the rapid rise in cases, Mumbai began to face the issue of shortage of hospital beds. Delhi, too, at one point seemed to have almost no available ICU beds. It is not yet known what criteria the authorities will follow in such cases. Doubtless, hospitals elsewhere are faced with similar dilemmas in regard to hospital beds, ventilators, ICU facilities, medicines and doctors. A similar dilemma will arise when vaccines become available: who will get it first and what will be the order of priority? These issues are both practical and philosophical, and there are no easy answers.

Earlier, the possible consequences of the epidemic were posed as a broader issue: lives versus livelihoods. The lockdown, it was posited, would affect livelihoods (due to a near halt in economic activity), but save lives (by slowing transmission of the virus). This seemed to be a moral dilemma and policymakers decided that lives being more important, a complete and very severe lockdown was essential. It took some weeks to modify this. The primary reason for the change was horrendous pictures of jobless and penniless migrant-labour families (carrying their meagre belongings and children) trudging along roads to walk hundreds of kilometres to their home villages. This prompted the new mantra of lives *and* livelihoods. While a complete lockdown may be an appropriate strategy for more prosperous countries and those with a good social security safety net, in a poor country like India—with a few hundred million people below or just above the poverty line—lives depend upon livelihoods on a day-to-day basis. Any major disruption in livelihoods (as was triggered by the lockdown) means no income, no food and, soon enough, death due to starvation or other causes. In a country where 450,000 people die each year due to TB—a disease with a known cure—mainly because of lack of healthcare or of availability and affordability of medicines, greater poverty can only mean a huge spike in deaths. In this, as in COVID, it is the elderly who are vulnerable, but here it is also young, malnourished children. There is, as yet, no count of the number of deaths resulting from lack of access to health facilities due to the lockdown. One can only be sure that it is very large, given the weeks-long closure of practically all healthcare, except for COVID cases.

These issues thrown up by COVID—health security, protectionism and nationalism, globalization, moral choices and more—will continue to be with us, and debated, even after COVID becomes only a memory. We do need an ongoing dialogue on them, even as we strengthen health facilities and prepare for another, yet unknown, viral epidemic.

If COVID acts as a wake-up call, both to the governments and the people, about the crucial importance of healthcare, it would at least have been of some long-term benefit. Will it succeed in getting health into the priorities of governments and put it upfront in the minds of voters? Will powerful and influential people realize that their own health depends upon the health of all others, epidemics spare no one, and that large investments in public health are essential? Could this result in a free, public universal healthcare system?

HEALTH IS HAPPINESS

Optimistically, one can see a scenario unfold in the 2020s in which, thanks to the lessons of COVID, the country dramatically increases its attention to and investments in healthcare; government increases its health budget to at least 3 per cent of GDP; state governments vastly increase their health spend and a countrywide free healthcare system is introduced. Such a scenario would see a quantum leap in the number of medical colleges and in the yearly throughput of well-trained doctors and nurses. It would see rural facilities for basic healthcare being as good as those in urban areas. While the prime focus may be preventive health, high-quality hospitals will be spread across the country, with tertiary or specialty hospitals available within a few hours' drive from most locations in the country. Large states will have more than one super-specialty hospital, while smaller states may have only one. India will become a hub for medical education, as also for healthcare. While private hospitals will be welcomed, the aim will be for the public hospitals to set the benchmark (analogous to what the Indian Institutes of Technology [IITs] and Indian Institutes of Management [IIMs] have done, in their respective field, and All India Institute of Medical Sciences [AIIMS] Delhi in healthcare).

As a hub for education and healthcare, India will attract

many foreign students, and medical tourism will become a large export industry. The country is already known for its efficient and large-scale production of generic and off-patent pharmaceuticals. It is famous for its role in saving the world from a major HIV-AIDS epidemic through the production of large quantities of anti-HIV medicines, sold for a fraction of the price being charged by other foreign manufacturers (this is discussed further in the chapter on technology).

With further investments in developing and producing new drugs and enhancing its healthcare infrastructure, India could position itself as a hub for comprehensive medical care. A well-thought-out plan, backed by facilitative policies, can develop this concept through this decade so that, by 2030, India indeed emerges as a global hub for high-tech medical care.

A further extension of this, which would be a unique factor, is to add yoga to the package, making it truly comprehensive: from mental (and possibly spiritual) well-being to good physical health. With or without this, healthcare promises to be the sunrise industry of the 2020s, with a large segment of it melding into the information technology (IT) industry. While it could be one of India's major 'exports', there is need to ensure that the business and commercial considerations do not distort domestic healthcare through high ('dollar denominated') costs. The best safeguard against this is to have a strong public health system and universal, free healthcare.

On the other hand, an alternative pessimistic scenario would see health once again go to the back-burner as the threat of COVID recedes a year or so from now (thanks to a cure, vaccine, herd immunity or a combination of these). Lip-service will, of course, continue. Meanwhile, the government will abdicate its role, creating even more dependence (and individual health expenditures) on private health facilities. Medical tourism will continue, and increase, resulting in escalating charges in private hospitals. There will be some concern about a future and unknown virus, but the COVID experience will foster a sense of complacency of being able to manage it. A part of 'managing' the pandemic was based on a control-and-command, law-and-order approach, with the home ministry—rather than experts or the health ministry—calling the shots. Given possible negative trends in governance, this will be the template for the future. While this has implications for governance and democracy, it clearly has a serious impact on the health sector too.

Further, the pessimistic forecast would see the COVID pandemic lingering for long, creating misery on a scale not seen in generations. This will not only be in terms of illness and mortality due to COVID, but also the amplified effect of other diseases, not treated because of the complete focus on COVID. The collateral economic impact will push at least 100 million—maybe even 200-plus million—into deep poverty. This may well trigger a reaction that has fortunately been almost unseen in India: riots to raid shops, and possibly even homes. It will invite intervention by the police—and, over time, by the military—and set off a vicious cycle of increasing violence and chaos. Healthcare and the economy will dive downwards. Stability may return, but only after all development is effectively set back by a decade or more.

The point of sketching this horror scenario is—as for all dystopias—to think, in advance, of ways of avoiding it. At the same time, action has to be taken to bring to reality the optimistic projection.

One hopes that the trauma of COVID—from the health dimension to the economic one to, especially, the human dimension—would galvanize the collective energy of all Indians. The massive human tragedy that forced millions to lose their livelihoods should lead to introspection about the skewed development which results from a model that creates—and amplifies—vast regional and individual economic disparity. The images of thousands of poor trying to walk back to homes that are hundreds of kilometres away should stay seared in all minds, as a reminder of what must never recur.

One lesson from COVID is the importance of agility and flexibility in decision-making based on specific situations in small geographical areas. This requires decentralization and the devolution of authority. A corollary is community involvement, especially in tracing, tracking and isolating cases. Both are particularly important from the viewpoint of tackling health issues, but also have wider ramifications. Community involvement requires a strong bond of mutual trust between government and the people. This bears emphasis at a time when some sections of the population are feeling alienated or discriminated against. A re-building of trust is a necessity and the prime agenda for the 2020s, if the country is to move ahead and achieve ambitious goals by 2030. If this can be done, and actions taken to ensure the realization of the 'optimistic scenario' outlined earlier, India 2030 should, from all points of view, be a healthy country.

Health is obviously important for our well-being and hence the strong plea here for far greater attention to it, as also for a large increase in investments in public health so as to ensure free, universal, high-quality healthcare. There are those who argue that while this is desirable, India cannot yet afford it and we must await economic growth. Recent research provides a direct counter-point: it shows that while happiness does vary with gross domestic product (GDP), the effect of health and life expectancy is larger. A one-year increase in longevity has the same effect on national happiness as a 4.3 per cent increase in GDP.[49] Even if the figure is overstated by a large factor, the very fact of a relationship is significant.

So, through this decade, ensuring the health of all Indians must be very high on the agenda. For, a healthy country is a happy country.

---

[49]From 'Reading between the Lines', *The Economist*, 19 October 2019, https://www.economist.com/science-and-technology/2019/10/19/how-to-reveal-a-countrys-sense-over-the-years-of-its-own-well-being, accessed on 18 March 2021. The article refers to research done in Britain which uses a very interesting methodology of analysing millions of books and articles published in four countries since 1820 to develop an objective measure of happiness

4

EDUCATION

Building a Knowledge Society

To say that human capital is now more important than financial capital is a well-worn cliché. Nevertheless it is a fact.

Over time, the world has seen an evolution in the primary factors of production. Human capabilities have always mattered. In ancient times, it was physical prowess: the ability to protect oneself against animal or man, to ensure that one's possessions were not appropriated by another. While this continued to be a factor, in later times it was the number of cattle owned or the size of the farmland cultivated that were as or more important. For a while, the number of people in one's army was crucial, but, very soon, it was the weapons that determined outcomes of battles. With superior weapons, even a small army could decimate a bigger force.

In this, finance was very important: whether for recruiting and paying soldiers or for buying weapons. However, money became the truly dominant factor only in comparatively recent times, with large investments required for land and equipment for factories. With the growth of financial markets, capital became a means of generating even more wealth. Thus, capital emerged as the dominant element in the three conventional factors of production—land, labour and capital.

In more recent times, there is now recognition of one more factor of production beyond the standard three: technology. Not only does technology lead to greater productivity and superior products, it often creates altogether new ones. As a result, in many sectors of the economy—as also in day-to-day life—technology has become the driving factor. Of course, technology has always been a part of the production process—be it in agriculture or in industry. The difference is that the impact of technology is now far greater. Also, the speed of change and the frequency of disruptions have increased. The rapidity with which new technology spreads and penetrates, and its higher value-add further amplify its impact.

Technology itself is the outcome of efforts undertaken by researchers, and is a concrete manifestation of the intellectual capital generated by high quality human resources. It is, therefore, the human and intellectual capital of a community or country which, increasingly, determines its success. Power too now flows from collective brainpower, rather than from the barrel of a gun. Today, the most valuable asset of the company or a country is its intellectual property.

India has recognized the importance of human capital, and every government has indicated its commitment to education as a means of upgrading the country's human resource. Of late, vocational training and skill development too have seen a lot of emphasis. Despite all this, the outcomes have been rather poor. One indicator—particularly important in a globally competitive environment—is the annual ranking in the Human Development Index. India is currently (2019) ranked 131 out of 189 countries, compared to 119 out of 169 in 2010.[50]

Education is obviously a crucial element in developing the country's human resources. Over the years, the extent of literacy has seen a steady increase, from 64.8 per cent in 2001 to 77.7 per cent in 2017–18.[51] However, the rate of progress has been slow, compared even with countries at the same level of per capita income or our culturally similar neighbours. As a result, while we had achieved around 74 per cent adult literacy in 2018, this was only the same as Bangladesh, and far lower than Sri Lanka's 92 per cent.[52] Particularly hurtful is the fact that even as recent years have seen boastful pride in India being 'the fastest growing free market economy' or, in the last few years, 'the fastest-growing big economy', it is also the country with the world's largest illiterate population. This, despite decades of lip service about the importance of education and various programmes to promote adult literacy.

As in much else about India, the overall statistics are an average of some successes and many failures. Literacy in

---

[50]'Human Development Report 2020', *United Nations Development Programme*, http://hdr.undp.org/en/2020-report, accessed on 18 March 2021 and 'Human Development Report 2010', *United Nations Development Programme*, http://hdr.undp.org/sites/default/files/reports/270/hdr_2010_en_complete_reprint.pdf, accessed on 18 March 2021.

[51]For 2001 data: 'Status of Literacy', *Census of India*, https://censusindia.gov.in/2011-prov-results/data_files/mp/07Literacy.pdf, accessed on 18 March 2021. For 2017–18 data see 'Indicators Relating to Literacy, Status of Education and Vocational/Technical Rraining', in 'Household Social Consumption on Education in India', Ministry of Statistics and Programme Implementation, http://www.mospi.gov.in/sites/default/files/NSS75252E/KI_Education_75th_Final.pdf, accessed on 18 March 2021.

[52]'Literacy Rate, Adult Total', *The World Bank*, https://data.worldbank.org/indicator/SE.ADT.LITR.ZS, accessed on 18 March 2021. Adult literacy rate is the percentage of people aged 15 and above who can both read and write with understanding a short simple statement about their everyday life.

Kerala was 96.2 per cent in 2017–18, but only 66.4 per cent in Andhra Pradesh (considered a progressive state) and just around 70 per cent in Rajasthan and Bihar. Importantly, the gap between male and female literacy rates in 2017–18 was just 2.2 per cent in Kerala, but was as much as 23.2 per cent in Rajasthan, 19.2 per cent in Bihar and 18.4 per cent in UP.[53]

School education has been expanding and the Right of Children to Free and Compulsory Education Act, 2009 (popularly known as the right to education [RTE] Act), gave a considerable impetus. As a result, enrolment at the primary school stage has reached an impressive 113 per cent (2017) of the relevant age group.[54]

As noted earlier, figures are often misleading. Even as one notes the impressive enrolment ratio, it is necessary to point to the dismal quality. Surveys show that the educational outcomes are extremely disappointing. For example, in rural areas, around half of Class 5 students cannot read a Class 2 text; as many as 72.2 per cent of Class 5 students are unable to do a simple arithmetic operation (dividing a 3-digit number by 1 digit).[55]

In general, the quality of education in schools is extremely

---

[53] See 'Literacy Rate (in per cent) among Persons of Age 7 Years and above for Different States', in 'Household Social Consumption on Education in India', *Ministry of Statistics and Programme Implementation*, http://www.mospi.gov.in/sites/default/files/NSS75252E/KI_Education_75th_Final.pdf, accessed on 18 March 2021.

[54] 'School Enrolment, Primary (Gross)', *The World Bank*, https://data.worldbank.org/indicator/SE.PRM.ENRR, accessed on 18 March 2021. Gross enrolment ratio is the ratio of total enrolment, regardless of age, to the population of the age group that officially corresponds to the level of education shown.

[55] 'Annual Status of Education Report (Rural) 2018', AESR Center, January 2019, http://img.asercentre.org/docs/ASER%202018/Release%20Material/aserreport2018.pdf, accessed on 18 March 2021.

poor. Many argue that this was worsened by the no-fail policy laid down earlier in the RTE law, as a result of which children are automatically promoted to the next class each year, irrespective of their academic performance, till Class 8. This viewpoint finally prevailed, though many consider it regressive, and it is now left to the states whether to continue the automatic promotion.

The present method of testing in the school-leaving (or Board) examination has led to 'marks inflation', creating an illusion about students being very bright. In earlier days, at the time my generation graduated from school, 'first class' (marks of 60 per cent or more) was considered creditable, and a matter of pride for both the student and the parents. Now, anything below 90 per cent in the Class 12 examination is a cause for mourning in many homes. Apart from inflated marks—made worse by school boards in different states vying to show better results—the limited number of high quality colleges and standalone institutions has resulted in intense competition for admission. Some have their own admission test, but many admit students based on the Class 12 marks. In University of Delhi, for example, the cut-off for entry into the better known colleges is well over 95 per cent. Despite this, the quality of school education for a vast majority of students is yet subpar.

A related issue is the lack of skill education at the school level. The limited efforts at introducing vocational training in the curriculum have not been successful. Even when such courses have been introduced, the poor facilities and generally obsolete curriculum mean that the students are not work-ready. This results in poor employment prospects, despite demand for trained resources in industry. This, and the fact that vocational courses in schools are generally looked down upon and seen as being for those who are (academic) failures, makes such courses unattractive. Little wonder, then, that efforts to integrate vocational courses into the school curriculum have not met with much success.

Industrial training institutes (ITIs) were set up many decades ago, as a means of providing training in specific skills for school students who did not want—for financial reasons or lack of academic capability—to go to university. The intent was to provide industry with well-trained human resources and to equip youngsters with skills that would result in immediate employment. While this worked to an extent, the poor quality of training in many ITIs impacted the employment prospects of the students. Over time, this became more serious as the curriculum lagged the needs of the technologically evolving industry.

Partnership of ITIs and industry has been tried and now a few of the ITIs are actually run by individual companies. This is, however, a very limited effort and while industry continues to bemoan the shortage of appropriately skilled workers, youngsters continue to face unemployment. This paradoxical situation highlights the mismatch in both relevance and quality between what the ITIs produce and the needs of industry. Meanwhile, India continues to have a very low percentage of workers who have been through a formal skilling course.

For long, India has supplied skilled human-power to countries in the Gulf region. Masons, plumbers, electricians and carpenters from here have built the impressive buildings and infrastructure in the region, though most of them have no certified qualification in their trade. The informal apprenticeship model, through which they have acquired their skills, worked in a static world. However, as the pace of technological change accelerates, there is need for a strong foundation of basic knowledge on which training in the use of new materials, equipment, devices and technology is imparted and then updated from time to time. If such a system can be evolved, with an assurance of quality through well-recognized certification, and if it can be scaled, India can be the major source for global supply of skilled human resources.

A parallel exists in the field of IT: India is the source for more than half the globally outsourced IT services, and part of this is through the export of people; in addition, a very large number of Indian IT professionals are employed by foreign companies in countries around the globe. In this case too, while the quality of their education spans a wide spectrum (from world-class to mediocre), a sufficiently large number of them have skills adequate for their jobs. Contributing in a big way to this relative abundance are those who learned their skills at one of the private training institutes. These places were geared to meet the requirements of industry and quickly modified their training content to meet evolving technological needs.

Given its demographic profile, and the fact that it has a massive working-age population, which will to grow to 1,025 million by 2031 (more on this in Chapter 6), jobs are one of India's biggest concerns.[56] This population bulge in the 18–65 years age group is both an opportunity and a challenge. Experience elsewhere shows that this population age-distribution can boost economic growth. However, this would depend on the proper utilization of the working-age group in a productive manner, for which a prime necessity is education and skills. Even with this, there may not be enough jobs

---

[56]Calculated from 'Population Projections for India and States 2011–2036', *National Health Mission*, November 2019, https://nhm.gov.in/New_Updates_2018/Report_Population_Projection_2019.pdf, accessed on 18 March 2021.

domestically. Fortunately for India, the developed economies (including China) face a problem of ageing populations, with degrowth in the working-age population. They are, therefore, likely to face a shortage of workers, opening up a big opportunity for India, provided that we can generate a sufficient number of appropriately skilled workers. Education and skilling are, therefore, vital pivots that will determine not only the job opportunities for youth, but also the speed of the country's economic growth.

UNDERSTANDING THE STRUCTURAL FLAWS

Of key importance here is quality and relevance of learning. As far as quantity is concerned, India seems to have achieved what it should in terms of enrolment at the school level—at least at the primary stage, as noted earlier. Dropouts at secondary and higher secondary levels are still a problem, but the absolute number who finish school education is yet large enough for ambitious economic growth. Livelihood and development opportunities for school dropouts are yet a serious problem, but this is a human and social challenge rather than an economic issue at the macro level.

Similarly, the growth in the number of those taking up tertiary (university) education is adequate for immediate economic needs. Further, the gross enrolment ratio at this level is targeted to go up from 26.3 per cent in 2018 to 50 per cent in 2035.[57]

The big challenge—whether at the school level or in

---

[57] Figures mentioned include vocational education and are from 'National Education Policy 2020', *Ministry of Human Resource Development*, Government of India, https://www.mhrd.gov.in/sites/upload_files/mhrd/files/NEP_Final_English_0.pdf, accessed on 18 March 2021.

the ITIs or universities—continues to be the relevance of what is taught and the learning that takes place. It is widely acknowledged that only a quarter of university graduates are directly employable. The others have serious lacunae either in their own discipline (subject) or in soft skills (like communication, teamwork, sensitivity to gender/intercultural issues) or both; some are yet 'trainable'—involving time and money for the employer—while others are a write-off. Clearly, at all levels of education, and also in training institutes, there is need to continuously review what is taught, and how much is learned.

The rapid expansion of education, especially higher education, has necessitated a large number of teachers. Given the existence of other opportunities—often more lucrative—attracting qualified persons to the teaching profession is a big challenge. This begins at the very foundation: few bright students want to do a doctorate, particularly when job opportunities after their first professional degree (BE/BTech, MBA, etc.) are attractive. This limits the pool for selection of university teachers. Of concern here is that pressures to expand doctoral programmes have led to a lowering of quality. The result is that a great many PhDs are of poor quality. Inevitably, they are bad teachers too, and are unable to ensure quality learning for the vast numbers that they will teach in the course of their teaching career.

The present structure of higher education and the regulations have been factors that contribute to poor quality. State universities account for the bulk of students in higher education. Inadequate funding over the years has resulted in poor infrastructure. In many universities, buildings and classrooms are so badly maintained that they seem to be crumbling. Laboratories have old and generally obsolete equipment, and this too is often not properly functional. State-of-the-art laboratories—so necessary for science and engineering—are rare, giving students no exposure to current equipment and facilities that may be widespread in industry. Researchers can hardly do cutting-edge work with obsolete equipment. Funds for libraries are very limited, constraining access to the latest publications, whether in print or online. With so little to support their work, is it any surprise that few researchers from these universities make a mark globally, or that only a handful of Indian institutions figure even in the top 500 worldwide?

Adding to these obstacles to quality is political interference in appointments and recruitment. Widely known and frequently criticized, such interference has not stopped. It begins with the appointment of the vice chancellor (VC), who is then beholden to his/her political benefactors. This means that recruitment of professors and others too gets influenced, with merit being a small and subsidiary consideration. The structure in the university is such that the VC can, if s/he so chooses, be a virtual dictator, with powers to make unilateral decisions in many key matters. Universities have various bodies that could act as a check and balance, but the VC—especially if s/he has political backing—can ride roughshod over them.

The central universities and institutes that have a Parliamentary mandate (like the IITs, IIMs and AIIMSs) are generally better governed and traditionally had less political interference. However, in recent years, even this has begun to change and there is a widespread sense that appointments— whether of the VC or of faculty—are being influenced by political factors. At least one VC, who has completely antagonized a majority of both teachers and students in his university, continues to sit pretty—despite calls for his resignation—only because of political support.

The tendency to centralize, control and micro-manage has resulted in curbing the autonomy that at least some institutions enjoyed. Despite a forward looking Act for the IIMs (passed by Parliament in 2017), the detailed rules framed by the bureaucracy have imposed unnecessary constraints. What could potentially have been an exemplary move towards autonomy for universities has turned out to be disappointing. The Ministry for Human Resource Development (HRD) assumes that it has direct authority over these institutions and issues diktats from time to time. More than one minister for HRD has given instructions to institutions like the IITs and IIMs and unfairly berated their directors in large meetings. While the law, unfortunately, still vests a great deal of authority in the ministry and the minister, the routine use of such power completely erodes the concept of autonomy and independence of these institutions. Such an approach ensures that Indian universities will never be in the top global rankings.

Aspirations to excel are nullified by the bureaucratic tendency to standardize, which results in a 'lowest common denominator' approach. This has a direct and seriously adverse impact on quality and innovation. One example of moving towards standardization is the creation of a Coordination Forum, comprising not only the head of each IIM, but also bureaucrats. A similar council has existed for the IITs, but there was none for the IIMs. Now, instead of liberating the IITs from the standardization that such a body inevitably brings about, the IIMs are regressing towards it. Such a forum could, at best, have been a body for sharing experiences and discussing common, broader issues; unfortunately, it is seen as a decision-making body where the minister and ministry give instructions to all the institutions. In the former case, there was little need to have any of the ministry bureaucrats as members. The fact that they are members indicates the intent.

The penchant for standardization and simplistic solutions is seen in the push for a common ranking list for the IIMs Common Admission Test (along the lines of the IIT Joint Entrance Examination). Such an approach negates the genius and special character of each institute. This differentiation meant, for example, that for long years, IIM Calcutta was seen as the place for more quantitative-oriented management courses whereas IIM Ahmedabad was the mecca for qualitative-oriented ones. While the test for admission was common, the relative weightages given to different sections of the test varied between the two institutes, enabling each to draw up its own shortlist for interviews. Further, each institute had its own interviews to finally select students who were best suited for its course. This was good for students too: those with a stronger capability in a certain field could possibly get admission in one institute when they may not have got into the other. It also made for greater diversity in overall admissions. This is unlike the IITs, which seem to admit clones of standardized 'meritorious student'. Little wonder, then, that a place like Kota has developed as a factory for producing IIT-worthy students and that there is no such equivalent for the IIMs entrance test. The bureaucracy would, of course, want a single merit list for IIMs too, as part of standardization. I remember discussing this extensively with the higher levels of government over a decade ago, and trying to quell their enthusiasm and push for a common ranking. It is fortunate that the IIMs have not succumbed to this yet. Hopefully, the academic community can prevail over the powerful bureaucracy.

In University of Delhi, one of its best colleges—Lady Shri Ram College (LSR) for Women—had its own test for admissions under the quota for 'extra-curricular activities' (ECA; like performing arts). This ECA quota was an enabling provision permitted by the university for up to 5 per cent of the seats, allowing a compensation of up to 15 per cent in marks. This enabled students with exceptional talent in sports or cultural activities to have a better chance of admission, and ensured diversity in the student composition. Now, possibly because of misuse of such quotas by a few colleges, the test has been centralized and a common merit list is prepared. If misuse existed, it has now only moved up to a more central level, and involves a larger number of students. The autonomy that enabled an individual college like LSR to make its own decision, based on its own criteria and judgement, has been taken away. As is often the result of such standardization and centralization, the baby has been thrown out with the bathwater.

The obsession with uniformity and standardization ensures one thing: mediocrity. And, of course, centralized control. In a country like India, with its many and vast diversities, uniformity and centralization makes no sense. The few institutions that have guarded their autonomy and maintained their freedom have been able to prove the value of these by being the top institutions in their field. These include a few of the IIMs, some IITs, the Indian Institute of Science (IISc) and JNU.

The large number of private engineering colleges set up during and after the 1990s played an important role in creating the massive base of human resources that the IT industry tapped into. This made India the IT outsourcing hub of the world and Indian IT professionals a ubiquitous presence in countries around the world. Many of these colleges produced below-average and often unemployable graduates, yet, quantity trumped quality, and the smaller percentage of acceptable graduates were sufficient in number to meet India's and global demand. In recent years, as demand has somewhat slackened, quite a few of these private colleges have had to close down because they could not attract a sufficient number of students. Clearly, students are voting with their feet, seeking admission in those colleges that are perceived as offering better quality. In higher education, such competition is welcome, as long as it is on a fair basis, and students are able to make an informed choice (which means greater transparency about the institution).

An increasing number of states now have private universities and, in recent years, some of them have been able to establish a good reputation. Of course, Birla Institute of Technology and Science (BITS) Pilani has enjoyed special recognition for a few decades now. Amongst the newer institutions, Indian School of Business (ISB), Ashoka University and Symbiosis International (deemed university) are generally highly regarded. Ashoka, beginning with a focus on humanities and now going into the sciences, has been able to establish an enviable reputation in a very short period of time. A key ingredient of its success is its ability to attract top-notch faculty. The fact that it is not legally constrained with regard to its student fees has led to fees which—by Indian standards—are exorbitant. This, in turn, has facilitated payment of a high compensation to the faculty, making it easier to attract the best talent (even though, admittedly, money is not the only factor that determines their choice).

The government has made efforts to raise quality by upgrading the Regional Engineering Colleges to National Institutes of Technology. However, apart from some incremental funding, this has by and large been only a change in nomenclature. The setting up of a large number of new IITs and IIMs has, arguably, eroded their brand value due to the lower quality of most of these new institutes, mainly due to a paucity of good faculty. Now, employers and others are no longer satisfied that the candidate is from an IIT or IIM; they ask 'which IIT' (or IIM). Similarly, the setting up of Indian Institutes of Science Education and Research (IISERs)—modelled on the lines of the successful IISc and seeking to emulate it—has not been the game changer it was intended. While a few of them (like some of the new IITs and IIMs) are doing quite well, almost all suffer from a shortage of really high quality faculty.

The new scheme of identifying and recognizing 'institutes of eminence' promises greater autonomy and funding to them. It may be too early yet to reach definitive conclusions, but the initial start—including controversy around some selections—has not been too promising. A new National Education Policy (NEP 2020) has now been formalized, but this may well turn out to be merely one more well-intentioned but little-outcome effort. For, over the years, a number of committees have been set up and each has come out with an excellent set of recommendations—all to no avail because of hindrances of one kind or another and poor execution. Between vested interests and the bureaucracy (including the academic bureaucracy), no radical change in governance of higher education has been made. Attempts at improving quality and ensuring greater autonomy by creating new models—like public–private partnerships between the government and industry, for example—have come to naught because the overarching regulatory framework remained the same: the University Grants Commission (UGC) or the All India Council for Technical Education (AICTE). The stifling controls and the mindset of ensuring uniformity meant that there was little innovation in courses. Even a change from the conventional three-year degree programme in humanities and sciences to a four-year one—common in other countries—was shot down by the UGC and government. Now, NEP 2020 calls for the setting up of a Higher Education Commission of India (replacing UGC and AICTE), but the role envisaged (despite emphasis on its 'promotional' role) yet seems to be in 'control' mode.

The issue of permitting foreign universities to operate in India has long been controversial. Discussed for decades and sometimes on the verge of being approved by Parliament, this issue remained unresolved for years. The NEP 2020 now proposes a legislative framework facilitating the entry of the top 100 universities in the world, which will be given special dispensation regarding regulatory, governance, and content norms on par with other autonomous institutions of India.

Meanwhile, the paucity of quality educational institutions has resulted in thousands of students going abroad. Recent figures indicate that about 1.09 million Indians (as of July 2019)[58] are pursuing higher education abroad, spending around $2.8 billion (2017–18).[59] Places like Singapore and Dubai have been able to attract top-notch universities to set up 'offshore campuses', benefiting local students and also enticing foreign students. Apart from the US and the UK—traditional foreign destinations for Indian students—countries like Australia and Canada are now luring thousands of Indian

---

[58] 'Students Registration Portal', *Ministry of External Affairs*, https://www.mea.gov.in/Students-Registration-Portal.htm, accessed on 18 March 2021.

[59] Based on RBI data; sourced from 'More Indians Going Abroad for Studies, but Foreign Students Aren't Coming in', *LiveMint*, 17 August 2018, https://www.livemint.com/Education/qVtlWO1E9D923fiDD2o69I/More-Indians-going-abroad-for-studies-but-foreign-students.html, accessed on 18 March 2021.

students. They thrive on the large number of those who could not get admission to the very limited number of high-quality institutions in India, especially in certain fields. In medicine, for example, the very limited number of seats in Indian colleges has led to students going to non-traditional destinations such as China, Kyrgyzstan, Philippines, Ukraine, Russia, Poland, Germany and Belarus.

It is ironic that the situation is quite the opposite of what it should be: given its advantages, India could well be one of the biggest global educational hubs, attracting students from around the world. Its low living costs—lower not only than the US, the UK, Canada or Australia, but also less than those in Singapore or Dubai—and the benefits of scale due to a large domestic market, add to its educational attractiveness. Further, it has an image as a creator of human resources that have made it a tech power, a long history of Indian teachers (though mainly in schools) in countries in Africa, and its ancient heritage as a centre of learning and wisdom. Its art and culture makes it an attractive place for learning in a range of humanities and arts. Nalanda could, metaphorically, be reborn and foreign students could once more flock to India.

Instead, we have a regulatory framework that, through myriad regulations and constraints, inhibits the emergence of world-class institutions. The world has now understood the importance of cross-disciplinary linkages, where STEM (science, technology, engineering, mathematics) has already become STEAM (with the addition of arts), design thinking is the new buzzword in technology and psychology is an element of artificial intelligence (AI). In this world, Indian regulators draw rigid lines between technology and humanities, even between medicine and biology. At a time when diverse fields have to converge (electronics and neurology, or machine learning/AI and oncology, for example), we deal with these fields through different regulators and build walls between them. Even in NEP 2020, health and legal education has been kept out of the ambit of the Higher Education Commission of India (HECI).

The idea of converging all higher education under a single framework and a single promotional (not regulatory) body has been floated in the past, but given the structure of government (different ministries, all touchy about anyone else stepping on their turf), this is highly unlikely in the near future. Hopefully, changing times and emerging requirements will ultimately bring this about.

One driver of education is technology. Not education about technology, nor even technology in education—though both are important—but education through technology. Increasingly, technology is being used to deliver education. Broadband networks, computers and low costs have enabled learning to be delivered on multiple user devices, 24x7 and interactively. This includes even mobile handsets, making access easy, affordable and increasingly universal. Online learning (including Massive Open Online Courses [MOOCs]) is now available on almost any subject. There are both free and paid courses, the latter generally providing certification too. Top global universities are amongst those who have created online courses. For example, Coursera, a popular online education platform, offers a master's degrees in Computer Science (from the University of Illinois) and in Applied Data Science (from the University of Michigan) as paid courses.[60] The same platform offers another course from the University of Illinois—a Data Mining

---

[60]Master of Computer Science (MCS) | UIUC | Coursera; Master of Applied Data Science | Michigan | Coursera

specialization[61]—which can be audited without any payment. Many other universities, too, offer free courses, often with an option to obtain a certificate on payment. This includes global leaders like Harvard University.[62] Indian universities (including the IITs), too, are increasingly adopting this trend.

These online courses generally include built-in tests, enabling self-assessment, and pace or provide content that matches the student's level of comprehension. Some provide for a measure of online interactivity, so as to clear doubts or answer questions. The 'massive' element of MOOCs provides enough data for meaningful analytics—both quantitative and qualitative—enabling continuous improvement and changes in content and pedagogic methods so as to maximize learning. Though there are some similarities, MOOCs are a far cry—a radical improvement—from one-way delivery of content: via television or online.

India is a major consumer of global MOOCs. Local entrepreneurs have also tapped into the latent demand and created a huge market—for language learning, for example—especially through mobile phone apps. Most of the demand is for learning English, and a lot of it emanates from smaller towns. This is not surprising, since English is the stepping-stone for mobility: both, upward economic mobility for employment (many jobs prefer English speakers and pay a premium for this), and geographical mobility (village to urban centres—for jobs and, often, to escape social oppression). Recently, there has been a sudden upsurge in the demand for courses on coding. The marketplace reflects this best: a recent online coding-classes start-up, just about two-years old,

---

[61]Data Mining | Coursera
[62]CS50: Introduction to Computer Science | Harvard University

was acquired by a big ed-tech company for a whopping $300 million. This is not another Silicon Valley dream-story: both the start-up (WhiteHat Jr.) and the acquirer (Byju's) are Indian companies.[63]

The trend is now towards blended learning, comprising a combination of online and face-to-face. A number of institutions have adopted the approach of shifting some courses to online learning, with the (physical) class session becoming a tutorial for clarifications of doubts by the teacher and for discussion. This also means a new and different role for the teacher.

A major use of the online method in India is for supplementary learning and for coaching for entrance tests (for jobs, as also for educational institutions). These courses extend from school level to postgraduate. Many coaching institutions have adopted online courses in a big way. The best known is Byjus, which claims to have more than 70 million registered students. One indication of its standing and prospects is its ability to raise funds. It has now garnered over $1 billion from investors. Another is its market valuation; this is now an astounding $11 billion.[64]

---

[63]'Byju's Buys Online Coding Classes Startup for $300m', *The Times of India*, 6 August, 2020, https://timesofindia.indiatimes.com/business/india-business/byjus-buys-online-coding-classes-startup-for-300m/articleshow/77382275.cms?UTM_Source=Google_Newsstand&UTM_Campaign=RSS_Feed&UTM_Medium=Referral, accessed on 18 March 2021.

[64]'Byju's Onboards New Investors, Valuation now at $11.1 Bn', *LiveMint*, 22 September 2020, https://www.livemint.com/companies/start-ups/byju-s-onboards-new-investors-valuation-now-at-11-1-bn-11600798077568.html, accessed on 18 March 2021.

A NEW PARADIGM

It seems clear that with all the technological change, with the availability of online courses created by the world's top experts, the old approaches and methods need to metamorphose. Keeping up with the rapidly changing needs of industry, and the opportunities available due to new technologies and pedagogic methods, requires agility, innovation and speed. The present ossified and rigid structures, combined with overregulation, are an antithesis of these needs.

Education is a good in itself, and every individual must be given the opportunity to access the best possible learning so as to attain his/her full, inherent capability. Also, learning must no longer end when one leaves the portals of an educational institution. Emerging technologies and the changing world demand continuous upgradation of knowledge. Lifelong learning is, therefore, essential. Online courses now provide the means for doing this easily and cheaply, at a time, place and pace that suits each individual. While this is invaluable to working people to continuously update and upgrade their knowledge, it is also a boon to all others—including the growing number of elders, retired from jobs—who want to learn something new purely out of interest.

Now, online education is no longer merely supplementary or a means of knowledge upgradation for working professionals. Telescoping into months what was expected to possibly evolve over years, online education for formal learning is here. The COVID pandemic and the lockdown, as also the continuing need to maintain physical distancing, has made online a necessity; in fact, for over six months, it has been the only form of formal education. Schools and colleges around the country, shut by the lockdown and regulations, have had to quickly transform teaching to this mode, and even tests or examinations have been held online. This has meant serious challenges, not just for the teachers who have had to learn how best to use this new pedagogic method, but also for students. The latter have been faced with serious and varied challenges: availability of devices (computer or smartphone), Internet connectivity, a quiet place in the home to work from and much-reduced ability to interact with teachers and peers. These challenges are obviously greater for the disadvantaged and those in rural areas, leading to the danger of further increasing inequity in the educational system. A survey indicates that only 15 per cent in rural areas have Internet access; even in urban areas, it is only 42 per cent. As far as computers are concerned, access in urban areas is just 23 per cent. Access to computers in rural areas (at 4 per cent) is almost non-existent.[65] So, while online education opens up limitless possibilities, access and the inequity are serious problems, with no immediate or easy solutions.

Education, skills and knowledge are, of course, directly connected with the economic prospects of an individual and of the country. The correlation between the two has grown stronger as the world moves towards a knowledge economy. Little wonder, then, that countries seek to prioritize education and skills. One example of this is China, which has given tremendous importance to upgrading its higher education

---

[65] '23% of Urban Popn Has Access to Comps, Only 4% of Rural: Survey', *The Times of India*, 21 July 2020, https://timesofindia.indiatimes.com/india/23-of-urban-population-has-access-to-computers-only-4-of-rural-survey/articleshow/77075283.cms, accessed on 18 March 2021. Based on 'Household Social Consumption on Education in India', *Ministry of Statistics and Programme Implementation*, http://www.mospi.nic.in/sites/default/files/publication_reports/Report_585_75th_round_Education_final_1507_0.pdf, accessed on 18 March 2021.

system. As a result, many of its universities figure in the global rankings and some of them (Tsinghua, Beijing) are amongst the best regarded ones. Another example, at school level, is Vietnam. In 2015, it ranked number 8 in the global rankings in science in the well-regarded Programme for International Student Assessment (PISA) list, well above the Organisation for Economic Co-operation and Development (OECD) average and above countries like the UK, Germany, Australia, the US and many Scandinavian countries.[66] So, it is hardly surprising that its economy is doing well and it has increasingly become a destination of choice, particularly for companies looking for an alternative (or an addition) to their China operations. India seems to have come off only second best in this competition to attract job-creating and value-adding investments.

A major driver for the knowledge economy is research. While its foundation is education (beginning from school level), it requires not only strong research and doctoral programmes in universities, but also large monetary investments to promote and fund such research and to provide the necessary R&D infrastructure. While R&D too—like education—is a well-recognized priority for countries, not all countries have the human-resource base to do it yet. Those who do, and have invested in R&D, reap rich benefits. Apart from the US and many European nations, Japan, Israel, Korea and China are amongst those that exemplify this. These countries have built a strong human resource base by investing in education, and provide substantial support to R&D. Indicative of this is their R&D expenditure as a proportion of their GDP. As against

---

[66]'PISA 2015 Results', *OECD*, https://www.oecd-ilibrary.org/docserver/9789264266490-en.pdf?expires=1601186629&id=id&accname=guest&checksum= 6C32C73CE2DB1D5E3DFA4BABE4CCAD4A, accessed on 19 March 2020.

a figure of around 0.65 per cent for India, China invests 2.2 per cent, Korea 4.8 per cent and Israel 5 per cent (all 2018 figures).[67]

Apart from a much higher investment in R&D, many of these countries have focused programmes that concentrate on and build excellence in a few selected fields. Israel, for example, is a leader in cybersecurity; China has chosen to be a top player in AI. Amongst the other fields it has identified as priority are transportation, including electric cars and high-speed trains; electronics and telecommunications. It has already made a mark in all these, thanks to the priority accorded to creating educational institutions that produced a strong base of well-qualified experts, combined with high investment in R&D.

As technology becomes ubiquitous and more pervasive in day-to-day living, and its role in the economy grows, the importance of knowledge will increase manifold. The wealth of a nation may well be measured through indicators like the patents or intellectual property rights (IPRs) that it owns, or the number of doctorates and refereed publications that it produces. India needs to quickly pull up its socks in these areas, if it wants to be competitive and take a place amongst the global leaders.

This decade will see a transformation in the overall ecosystem of education. Even as technology becomes a major tool and means for learning—just as the textbook did, centuries ago—non-STEM subjects will assume greater importance. Since path-breaking innovations most frequently happen at the intersection of different disciplines, multidisciplinary courses

---

[67]'Research and Development Expenditure (% of GDP)', *The World Bank*, https://data.worldbank. org/indicator/GB.XPD.RSDV.GD.ZS, accessed on 19 March 2021.

or the flexibility to study any combination of courses must be an essential part of the university system. For example, insights from insect behaviour and abilities have helped in designing drones (unmanned aerial vehicles) that can avoid unforeseen obstacles. This requires knowledge of biology and a number of branches of engineering. While a team that brings together experts specializing in their own discipline is the answer, ideally there should also be a few people who understand both major aspects: engineering and biology. Examples of this type abound, and will be more the rule than the exception, pointing to the importance of providing full flexibility in combining varied subjects to earn a degree. This will also enable students to study subjects of their choice, not all of which may be within one broad area (science, for example). Thus, someone with an interest in physics but also in sociology should be able to study both, though one may be taught in a school of sciences and the other in a school of social sciences or humanities.

The years ahead are likely to see trends that are contradictory. On the one hand, there will be far deeper specialization, as disciplines get more complex. Be it medicine, engineering or humanities, there will be super-specialization, with experts who have ever greater knowledge of ever narrower areas. On the other hand, there will be those who prefer breadth and are familiar with a broad range of disciplines, but have lesser knowledge of each. There will be demand for such people too: those who can lead multidisciplinary teams, with enough knowledge to speak the language of each, without necessarily having deep expertise in any one.

The other contradictory trend is with regard to the preferred discipline. The excitement of rapid progress in technology and in biological sciences is likely to see continuing—even growing—demand for STEM courses. At the same time, there will be many who opt for arts and humanities. Here, too, the job market is likely to see demand for both. In the case of STEM, especially technology and engineering, it will represent a continuation of the present trend. At the same time, the need for professionals in arts and humanities—presently very muted—will see a considerable uptick as growing prosperity expands the market for experience and entertainment. This will include music and drama performances, art exhibitions, theatre, books and all kinds of content delivered via social media, streaming, television and film. In addition, technology and product companies will need experts who can design hardware, study and enhance consumer experience, understand human behaviour at individual or group levels, and carry out a range of other functions that require expertise in one or the other discipline of humanities or the arts.

The third trend where there is apparent divergence is the aspect of academic or intellectual knowledge as different from skills. The former would seem to be more important as the economy becomes more knowledge-based. In India, the preference for such courses is very marked, as noted earlier. This may well have to do with the country's 'brahmanical' tradition, in which thinkers are seen as 'superior' to doers. This may, therefore, reinforce the sense that both the job market and the compensation level for such graduates will be greater. Yet, there has always been high demand for skills, though the compensation has been lower. Now, with sophisticated technology, the skill requirement has increased considerably (and so have salaries).

It is true that obsolescence with regard to skills is high and, with robotics and automation, certain skills are no longer required (stenography, for example) and many more will face extinction (computer programming code-writers and testers, for example). Yet new needs are fast emerging and very high skills are required for maintaining, operating and repairing—even replacing—sophisticated new equipment. The demand for such high skills is bound to grow. This demand, though, will keep changing as technology advances and ever newer equipment and devices enter the market. Continuous updating and upgrading of skills will, therefore, be a necessity. Meanwhile, the requirement for skilled human resources in 'conventional' areas—carpenters, electricians, plumbers, masons, etc.—is unlikely to decrease. Even here, though, continuous updating will be required.

A fourth trend will be simultaneous automation and its opposite—greater humanization. Technology, cost, efficiency and reliability will drive automation, resulting in devices and software that replace humans in a variety of functions. Quite apart from industrial automation, we see human-replacing devices being used far more extensively even in the home (a trend that has been accelerated after the COVID-induced lockdown). One example is the cleaning robot, replacing the floor-sweeping function in households. These robots are likely to become ubiquitous in middle-class households, being less bulky, more efficient and cheaper than a vacuum cleaner, which was a rarity in countries like India. Similarly, new versions of washing machines and dishwashers will increasingly replace human labour (and househelp). At the same time, there is growing automation in the workplace too. Unskilled workers, employed in lifting and shifting materials, have been replaced by fork-lift trucks; robots have replaced humans in many assembly operations and skilled technicians have given way to digitally driven machines for tasks like metal-cutting. This growing level of automation in both workplace and home is likely to generate a backlash, with people longing for human interaction. An early indication of this is the number of people who recognize the ease and efficiency of an interactive voice response system (IVRS), but yet hanker for a human being at the other end. While Alexa may answer all your queries efficiently and correctly, it is not an adequate replacement for a person-to-person conversation.

Contemporary lifestyles (in India as much as in the West) leave little time for friends and socializing. Growing automation and high quality communication infrastructure reduce direct human contact even at work. Thus, a lot of teamwork now involves colleagues who are not geographically co-located, and interaction is through the intermediation of communication technology. The lack of direct human contact often leads to loneliness and a strong desire for human interaction. Thus, it is more than likely that the rise of automation will be tempered or balanced with the simultaneous growth in human-provided services. Future systems may, for example, provide an option between man and machine ('Dial 1 for a human; dial 2 for an automated response'). Many are trying to marry the two contrary needs by devising AI-based chatbots: automated robots that can chat with you in a manner that is almost indistinguishable from human. This may well be a solution—one that combines the advantages of a machine with the flexibility and warmth of a human. Yet, for other functions (for example, healthcare), and especially for the home-bound, the human touch (literally and metaphorically) may be preferred. Even in the case of education, a human teacher may be seen by many as the first choice—especially for young children—as against an automated teacher, even though the latter may be more efficient. Here too, a combination may work best, with automation at the back-end providing the appropriate content and data analytics, and a human teacher at the front-end ensuring the empathy, warmth and understanding necessary for students.

These and other trends are indicative of what direction education should take to meet the emerging needs of the future. Diversity and flexibility are clearly key elements that the education system must respond to in shaping its governance, structure, courses and syllabus.

REGULATION TO PROMOTION: AN ACTION PLAN

These requirements, combined with the rapid expansion of the system for higher education and skills training, call for immediate and radical changes. Moreover, as observed earlier, the quality of education—right from primary school to the doctoral level—has to be hugely improved. Without this, the growth of individuals to their full potential will be stymied, and the nation will not attain the sustainable social and economic development that is within its capability.

To meet the challenges and take advantage of the emerging opportunities, a number of initiatives are necessary. The start of a new decade is an appropriate time for a fresh beginning. The NEP 2020 does attempt to address these issues and outlines a number of very worthy steps. The problem, especially with regard to higher education, is that while it mentions the appropriate approach (decentralization, autonomy, innovation, etc.), the operational parts negate much of this. As a result, apart from challenges of execution, it does not reflect the radical and bold actions that are required to truly transform or revamp the education system. The vital steps that are necessary can be summarized as follows:

- Liberate the education system from the stranglehold of excessive and obsolete regulations. The NEP falls short on this count: replacing UGC and AICTE by a new regulator seems like old wine in a new bottle. What is needed is the scrapping of all regulatory and control agencies for higher education (not only UGC and AICTE, but their equivalents in all disciplines), and their replacement by a single, overarching promotional and facilitating body. This would cover all disciplines and branches, including engineering, technology, physical and social sciences, arts and humanities, law and medicine. Its role will be limited to a promotional one.

- Give universities and institutions full academic autonomy, including for the design of their own academic credits structure and requirements for degrees and certification, starting new courses, and giving credits for fieldwork or online courses. They must also have the freedom to decide their own admission criteria, recruitment policy and salary structures. Within affiliating universities, each college must also have similar freedom and flexibility. No centralization, no standardization and minimal 'regulatory' control: this will be the guiding philosophy. Innovation, experimentation and 'nudging' through incentives will be the watchwords.
- Mandate the Higher Education Promotion Commission (HEPC) to ensure complete transparency of the universities and ensure healthy competition. For institutions registered with it, the Commission will specify the information that must be displayed on university/institution websites and will evolve criteria for rating institutions on an annual basis. It will accredit courses and universities on the basis of clearly defined parameters. Institutions who do not want to subject themselves to such transparency are free to function, but will have to declare 'not registered with HEPC'.

- Recognizing the importance of inter-disciplinarity, existing 'specialized' institutions (in medicine, law, management, technology, architecture and design) will be encouraged to broaden their ambit and become true, full-fledged 'universities'. One way is to first build strong academic partnerships, and then move forward to a merger of diverse institutions in a given location (Université Paris-Saclay provides an example of this approach[68]). A more difficult possibility that could be explored is the merger of some research laboratories (for example, some Council for Scientific and Industrial Research [CSIR] facilities) with universities.
- Inclusion and diversity in admissions is most desirable. This could be done through a points-based system, derived from the excellent system devised by and successfully operational in JNU for many years. A reasonable proportion of foreign students too would be included for diversity. Similar inclusion and diversity is desirable amongst faculty. However, there should be no 'reservation' or quota in faculty recruitment. The HEPC will seek to ensure such inclusion/diversity through incentives (in ranking, funding or other innovative means), tweaked over time to ensure that the objective is met. Government institutions will necessarily follow this, but will receive the same incentives.
- There will be no cap on student fees in public (government) institutions too. However, no fee (or hostel fees) will be charged from any student in the 'reserved' category (in a points-based system, for anyone crossing a

---

[68] The merger brought together two universities, ten grandes écoles and seven national research institutions. These details are from *Building Research Universities in India*, Pankaj Jalote, Sage Publications, 2021.

specified limit) or from a minimum of 5 per cent of other students. Based on an annual cost accounting report, the HEPC will give a grant to the institution covering the cost-per-student for 100 per cent of these students. This will include the salaries—as specified by the HEPC—for staff and faculty (with numbers calculated on defined criteria, like teacher–student ratio and staff–faculty ratio), as also adequate funds for maintenance of all infrastructure. For other students, there will be numerous scholarships, and all those studying in HEPC-registered institutions will be eligible for student loans that cover all costs. Beyond the HEPC-specified compensation for staff and faculty (which will be the minimum to be paid), the institution is free to pay an additional amount to faculty/staff, based on its ability to raise other resources.

- The HEPC will give a fixed grant for research on a per-faculty-member basis to all public institutions. They will be expected to seek research grants, and the HEPC will then provide an additional matching grant. This will incentivize institutions to actively make proposals for research grants.
- There will be no cap on student fees or faculty compensation in private institutions. However, at least 20 per cent of the students (the percentage can be redefined with experience) will be charged no fee (or hostel charges). Institutions which follow the specified points-based system for deprivation (4 above) will be reimbursed a per-student fee at the rate calculated for public institutions (5 above).
- The HEPC will define criteria for 'recognition' for getting research or other grants from government. Only such institutions will be eligible to grant degrees. States will be encouraged to adopt the same model criteria.

- Special projects and grants will be given to explore and optimize the use of technology in education, especially to increase reach and inclusivity or improve quality. Pedagogic research on appropriate content, use of technologies like augmented/virtual reality, AI and data analytics will be encouraged through funding support.
- Support will also be given to regular studies on job market needs, emerging areas and student interests. These will be disseminated widely to the academic community as also to students. Close collaboration with industry will be an essential element of these studies.
- Special and generous funding will be provided to institutions that prove their ability to excel.
- Industries will be given incentives (for example, tax benefits) for investing in education and collaborating with academia. It will also be encouraged to continuously upgrade the capabilities and knowledge of its own employees.
- The overall philosophy will be for the government—through the HEPC—to extend a helping hand; define (very broad) boundaries; collaborate with universities; help to indicate future needs and possibilities; encourage innovation in courses, pedagogy, use of technology, and in research; facilitate links between industry, academia and R&D organizations and provide funding. Institutions will be encouraged to compete but also collaborate. The HEPC will safeguard the interests of students and the autonomy of the institutions.

Much more needs to be done, but the steps detailed above will be a good start. A similar clear and well-defined approach is required for skills training, which has seen slow progress despite good intent.

Tremendous effort is required to raise the quality of education for children, beginning at the pre-school stage. It is now clear that children from better-off families (with higher parental education) already have an edge at the Class I level itself. The gap between them and the disadvantaged grows further with time. One corrective could be a strengthened Anganwadi programme. Presently focused on nutrition and health, a pre-school education component could be added, helping to raise the ability of children at the time they enter regular school. The NEP 2020 has adopted such an approach. However, there are concerns that need to be addressed, particularly with regard to the specialized training required to teach children in the pre-school age group.

There are many other complexities in education at the school level. The NEP 2020 has addressed many of these. Issues like the medium of instruction and language policy are controversial, sometimes political. Increasingly, textbook content too is getting politicized. The other elephant in the room is the extent of privatization of school education. Over the years, due to apathy, neglect, and a host of other factors, the quality of education in almost all government schools is abysmal. In many states, there are teacher shortages; these are made worse by their absenteeism and lack of motivation or incentives. As a result, privatization has proceeded apace. Figures indicate that almost half the school students are now in private schools. Yet, there are examples of successes of government schools (Kendriya Vidyalayas, in their heyday; Delhi government schools, in recent years). These need to be emulated. Unlike higher education, school education needs to be primarily government-funded and government-run. The NEP, by not taking a clear stance on this, is seen by many as supporting privatization in an oblique manner.

The many and complex issues concerning school education are not further addressed here, as they may well take a separate chapter, if not book. School education, as has been emphasized elsewhere too, is the very foundation of human capital. Yet, in terms of the impact on India 2030, we have taken the view that higher education will be a more important influencer, and hence the focus on it.

Revamping of the full education system, from preschool to doctoral level, is badly needed. The year 1991 marked a watershed in the economic sphere, with the ushering in of major structural reforms. A similar overhaul of education is now needed, beginning with the structure. While there have been periodic actions to formulate and adopt new education policies, little progress can be made without real structural changes. If this is done, it can usher in a new era of education in India, one that combines reach and inclusion with quality and excellence, teaching with research and experiential field-based learning with theory. The NEP 2020 speaks of some of this, but is inadequate.

With the demographic profile which it has, India can be *the* global source for high-value talent, as also for vocational skills. Further, just as China has become the 'factory of the world', India could well be the 'university of the world'—a hub which attracts the brightest youngsters from all countries to its universities.

At a time when education, knowledge and skills will be the true wealth of nations, India is well positioned to be amongst the wealthiest. This decade will be the crucial one for making the necessary reforms and ensuring excellence in the education system. If this is done, by 2030, India should be well on its way to being a knowledge powerhouse.

5

ECONOMY

Eradicating Poverty, Reducing Inequality

'Let the whole world hear it loud and clear. India is now wide awake. We shall prevail. We shall overcome.'

This ringing declaration of intent and resolve—reminiscent of Nehru's famous 'tryst with destiny' speech on India's independence in 1947—was proclaimed by Manmohan Singh, then India's finance minister, in 1991. It marked the announcement of major structural reforms, aimed at transforming the economy, and moving radically away from a closed and quasi-socialist one to an open and near-capitalist one.

Amongst the slew of noteworthy reforms were a slashing of import duties, encouragement to foreign direct investment (FDI), devaluation of the rupee and loosening of restrictions on foreign exchange. Industrial licensing was abolished for almost all products, limiting the industries reserved for the public sector to defence equipment, atomic energy generation and railways. This opened up airline, telecom, TV broadcast and insurance sectors for private players.

The most important change, though, was in the mindset. The siege mentality embedded deeply in the country's psyche—possibly due to historical experience with the East India Company—looked askance at foreign capital. This, as also foreign goods, was to be kept out as far as possible, and (as in a siege) high walls offered the best protection—in this case, high-tariff barriers. The new mindset required openness: minimal barriers and a welcome to foreign companies and investors. Permissions, licenses and an obstacle-track maze of bureaucratic clearances: all were almost done away with, and replaced by automatic approval for investments in a host of sectors. This included foreign investments, up to a defined percentage (including 100 per cent in certain sectors). The private sector was looked upon as a partner in the country's development, rather than a greedy, avaricious and untrustworthy entity. All this required a near 180-degree change in the approach of the bureaucracy and the thinking of government.

This change in 1991 has widely been seen as revolutionary; some have even called it the 'second independence'—ushering in economic freedom, like 1947's political freedom. The change from socialism, though, really began earlier. After three decades of an economy that adopted (or sought to adopt) the socialist pattern of development, the early 1980s saw Indira Gandhi (back as prime minister, after the drubbing she received in the 1977 elections) move tentatively—even surreptitiously—towards a more open/capitalistic economy. After her death, Rajiv Gandhi, who became the prime minister, took more steps down the same path. Thus, for about a decade, through the 1980s, the country certainly moved 'rightward' in economic terms. However, the steps were incremental and the change, slow.

Rajiv Gandhi had fuelled growth on the back of borrowed foreign capital, without the reforms necessary to make India competitive in a fast-globalizing world. Soon, the chickens came home to roost and an unprecedented foreign exchange crisis faced the country even as it was going through a period of political instability after the 1989 election. Gold from India's reserves had to be sent abroad to make sure that the country did not default on its debt-repayment obligations. This trauma prepared the ground for the general acceptance that major changes in economic policy were essential.

In 1991, a coalition headed by the Congress was back in power, with Narasimha Rao as prime minister. He appointed Manmohan Singh—an economist with a long record in government officialdom—as finance minister. The Narasimha Rao–Manmohan Singh team (the former deserves more credit than is generally given) bit the bullet, making full use of the crisis to usher in big-bang reforms ('why waste a crisis' may well have been the thought!). These began to pay off, and the two decades that followed saw India emerge as a shining star on the global economic firmament—a close second to China, and often seen as an even better prospect in the long run.

Another brief period of political instability in the late 1990s followed the 1996 election. However, there was no drastic reversal or change in economic policies, as some had feared. The new coalition (the National Democratic Alliance [NDA]), anchored by the BJP and led by the charismatic Atal Bihari Vajpayee, came to power in 1999. The next five years saw further reforms, including bold steps in privatizing some public sector enterprises. India became a favourite of foreign economic commentators and forecasters. Multinational companies (MNCs) rushed to set up operations in India. To the world at large, it was certainly 'India shining'. However, this campaign line of the NDA did not carry credence with the voters and, against all odds, the NDA was defeated in 2004 by the Congress-led UPA. In a surprise move, the Congress chose to make Manmohan Singh the prime minister. The next five years saw unprecedented growth and—despite the dependence of the UPA on the outside support of four Left parties—a continued opening up of the economy. Even the global economic crisis of 2007–08 was weathered by sound policies, establishing the resilience of the Indian economy and the strength of its key institutions.

Though voted back to power in 2009, the new UPA government—still led by Manmohan Singh—seemed to have lost its way. It was soon mired in charges of corruption and allegations of various scams. A report of the Comptroller and Auditor General (CAG) give substance and credibility to allegations of massive scams, and an anti-corruption movement led by Anna Hazare suddenly galvanized huge support. His fast in the midst of Delhi drew nearly 24x7 media coverage. The urban middle class—normally passive, and probably the biggest beneficiaries of economic reforms and growth—rather than crediting the UPA or Manmohan Singh for their well-being, became active participants in the anti-government rallies. The allegations of scams and the anti-corruption protests led to 'policy paralysis' within government. This, and a retrospective tax introduced in the budget in 2012, affected not just business 'sentiment', but the economy itself.

Following the drubbing of the Congress and many of its allies, the BJP-led NDA came to power in 2014. The expectation was that under the leadership of a business-friendly leader like Narendra Modi, the government would not only take forward the economic policies of Vajpayee's NDA-I, but would usher in even bolder economic reforms. In fact, many expected another '1991'. However, possibly spooked by Congress leader Rahul Gandhi's jibe of a *'suit boot ki sarkar'* (literally, a government of the well-off), the government seemed to develop cold feet. Few major reforms were undertaken, and the buzz was that ministers were told to avoid interacting with business leaders. There was, though, a strong focus on improving the Ease of Doing Business (EoDB). India's ranking in the World Bank index went up from 142 in 2014 to 63 in 2019. The target set by the prime minister—of being in the top 50—seems close to realization. However, this improvement in ranking came primarily from incremental changes, and not from any radical reforms. The two substantive reforms were in the bankruptcy process (through the enactment of the Insolvency and Bankruptcy Code (IBC) in 2016) and the introduction of an integrated Goods and Services Tax (GST) in 2017. The latter was an initiative of the UPA/Congress government and was stalled for many years mainly by the BJP, with Modi (then chief minister of Gujarat) being the major opponent. Ironically, it was first proposed by the BJP-led Vajpayee government, nearly two decades ago.

On 8 November 2016, the government announced the demonetization of high-value currency notes (of ₹1,000 and ₹500), catching the country by surprise. Probably the biggest economic policy decision of the government in its five-year stint (2014–19), this was—literally—a disruptive 'reform', creating unprecedented difficulties for everyone. The demonetization of the high-value notes meant sucking out 86 per cent of money from the economy. For some days, the amount of withdrawals permitted from bank accounts and from ATMs was restricted. Businesses and contractors had difficulties in making the usual cash payments for daily wage labour, and many did not get paid for days. As a result, a lot of daily wage workers, especially in the construction industry, went back to their villages. Getting them back, as things settled down, took a while and this caused delays in all construction projects. The middle class was hit hard by the limitation in how much they could withdraw from their own bank account, and by the long wait in endless queues at ATMs. Further, housewives who had assiduously squirrelled away money for a rainy day by saving small amounts from household expenses over years, and had stored this in high-denomination notes, suddenly found that the money had no value. They would have to take the notes to a bank, explain how they had this amount, and then hope to get it exchanged for other (legal) currency in its place. Even business—which often carried out transactions (legally) in cash—was affected, as the demonetization made payments difficult, effectively slowing down the speed and efficiency of operations. Despite the difficulties faced by almost all segments of society, the government marketed this as a bold step to root out black money and choke terror funding. The proverbial common man, who had to stand for hours in a queue to get his own money through an ATM, was made to feel good by being told that even the high and mighty amongst business people had to stand in a queue just like him/her. Success in selling this, and the noble objectives of the step, were visible in the elections to the UP assembly (held soon after demonetization), which saw the BJP ride to power with a huge majority.

It is clear that not only did the BJP successfully overcome any negative political fallout of demonetization, but it may well have been a factor in its big success in UP. This, despite the fact that demonetization did nothing to tackle black money or counterfeit notes, with approximately 99.3 per cent of the demonetized money being deposited in the bank system and thus being converted back to legal currencies. Also, there is no evidence that it has seriously affected funding of terrorist organizations. At the same time, its negative effects on business were substantial. Overall, there is now a general consensus that demonetization was an economic disaster and that it caused much harm to the economy at a crucial time—just when there were signs of an upswing.

In retrospect, the two terms of the UPA government (2004–14) saw a stellar performance in the economic sphere, despite its political difficulties, especially from 2012. A few figures stand out: the rate of decline in poverty, 0.75 per cent per year for a decade from 1993–94, shot up to 2.32 per cent per year from 2004–05 to 2011–12, leading to a decline in the absolute number of the poor by a massive 138 million from 2004–05 to 2011–12.[69] Even more impressively, going by a different (and more comprehensive) indicator, India lifted as many as 271 million people out of multidimensional poverty between 2005–06 and 2015–16.[70]

Agricultural growth, which was 2.9 per cent during NDA-I (1998–99 to 2003–04) went up to 3.7 per cent during UPA (the ten-year period from 2004).[71] Even if the latter, as some argue, was due to the high global prices of agri-products, it should have resulted in political gain, as should the unprecedented reduction in poverty. That this economic success did not

---

[69]'Press Note on Poverty Estimates, 2011–12', *NITI Aayog*, July 2013, https://niti.gov.in/sites/default/files/2020-05/press-note-poverty-2011-12-23-08-16.pdf, accessed on 20 March 2021.

[70]'271 Million Fewer Poor People in India', *UNDP*, 20 September 2018, https://www.in.undp.org/content/india/en/home/sustainable-development/successstories/MultiDimesnionalPovertyIndex.html, accessed on 20 March 2021.

[71]'From Modi, Manmohan, Vajpayee to Rao, Here Is Who Generated the Lowest Agri-Growth', *The Financial Express*, 15 January 2018, https://www.financialexpress.com/opinion/from-modi-manmohan-vajpayee-to-rao-here-is-who-generated-the-lowest-agri-growth/1015170/, accessed on 20 March 2021.

reflect in political benefit in the 2014 election is as much a commentary on the failure of the Congress political machinery as it is on the outstanding work of the BJP's ground workers, top leaders and superior marketing skills (including, in particular, its use of social media).

Overall economic growth in the first 15 years of this century has been impressive. The GDP grew by a compounded annual growth rate of 10.5 per cent per year from 2000; comparatively, the performance of NDA-II (2014–19) has been far less impressive at 7.1 per cent.[72] Recent years have seen a marked slowdown. Undoubtedly, part of this is due to general global problems, with most economies struggling. However, the lack of bold policies to counter this, along with the combined effect of demonetization and a poorly implemented GST, has contributed to the country's inability to get to a higher growth path. Government actions in suppressing unpleasant reports and data has only made things worse, with a growing feeling that 'spin', packaging and talk are being used to cover up a dismal economic performance. The focus on religious, social and political issues, as opposed to critical economic issues related to jobs, farmer distress and revival of manufacturing, gives the impression of economic neglect and the misplaced priorities of the government.

From time to time, there have been pronouncements about doubling farmers' incomes (by 2022) and making India a $5 trillion economy (by 2024–25), especially by the prime minister. The lack of concrete plans and roadmaps, though, make these seem like campaign slogans rather than serious economic targets. Recent rates of growth, and the COVID

---

[72]"GDP (Current US$)', *The World Bank*, https://data.worldbank.org/indicator/NY.GDP.MKTP.CD?locations=IN, accessed on 20 March 2021.

pandemic, make the GDP target for 2024–25 unrealistic and unattainable. There is a school of thought that high growth rates, like China's sustained 8–10 per cent over two decades, are now a thing of the past. The new global economic climate, it is argued, makes 6–8 per cent the new 'high growth'. If so, India will have to considerably scale down its ambitions.

In any case, with the hit that the already slowing economy has taken due to COVID, India will need to reset its time horizon for economic targets. A GDP growth of 4.2 per cent in 2019–20 (the lowest in over a decade[73]) will be followed by a huge slowdown in 2020–21. In March 2020, just about three months from the early COVID cases in China, the GDP forecasts for India were already being revised substantially downwards. CRISIL, a ratings agency, had dropped its forecast for the financial year 2020–21 (FY 21) from 5.7 per cent to 5.2 per cent. A little later, analysts were predicting far larger drops. For example, on 23 March 2020, S&P Global Ratings cut its estimate for India's GDP growth for FY 21 to 5.2 per cent from its earlier estimate of 6.5 per cent, UBS reduced its forecast from 5.1 to 4 per cent, and Economist Intelligence Unit estimated a growth of 2.1 per cent.[74] How one wishes

---

[73]'GDP Growth at 3.1% in Q4 Drags Full Year FY20 Growth to 4.2 per cent', *The Economic Times*, 29 May 2020, https://economictimes.indiatimes.com/news/economy/indicators/a-better-than-expected-q4-performance-pulls-fy20-gdp-growth-to-4-2-per-cent/articleshow/76091426.cms, accessed on 20 March 2021.
[74]'Crisil Lowers FY21 Growth by 50 bps to 5.2%', *The Economic Times*, 19 March 2020, https://economictimes.indiatimes.com/news/economy/indicators/crisil-lowers-fy21-growth-by-50-bps-to-5-2/articleshow/74718482.cms?from=mdr, accessed on 20 March 2021; 'S&P Lowers India GDP Growth Forecast for FY21 to 5.2% from 6.5%', *The Statesman*, 23 March 2020, https://www.thestatesman.com/business/sp-lowers-india-gdp-growth-forecast-for-fy21-to-5-2-from-6-5-1502869047.html, accessed on 20 March 2021;

these 'low' forecasts were right! The first quarter saw the economy contract by a massive 23.9 per cent.

Estimates for GDP in 2020–21 vary, and one credible forecast for the year is −9 per cent with a strong bounceback leading to 8 per cent growth in 2021–22.[75] Even this may be difficult, and the drop even larger, given that the GDP figure for the second quarter of FY 2021 (July–September 2020) indicates a contraction of 7.5 per cent. Amongst the large economies, India's performance has been the worst, barring the UK. It is noteworthy that the GDP of China actually grew by 4.9 per cent in the same quarter.[76]

A drop and bounceback based on these figures would mean that in April 2022, GDP will be approximately where it was two years earlier ($2.9 trillion). At this stage, any predictions are fraught, but even with 8 per cent growth a year after that (at this point, a hope, rather than an expectation), the 2030 GDP will be around $5.4 trillion.

'Coronavirus Fallout: UBS Cuts India's FY21 Real GDP Growth Forecast to 4 Per Cent', *The Economic Times*, 23 March 2020, https://economictimes.indiatimes.com/news/economy/indicators/coronavirus-fallout-ubs-cuts-indias-fy21-real-gdp-growth-forecast-to-4-pc/articleshow/74774177.cms?from=mdr, accessed on 20 March 2021 and 'EIU, Moody's Slash India's Growth Forecast', *The Times of India*, 28 March 2020, https://timesofindia.indiatimes.com/business/india-business/eiu-moodys-slash-indias-growth-forecast/articleshow/74856204.cms, accessed on 20 March 2021.

[75]'ADB Expects India's Economy to Contract by 9% in FY2020-21, Sees Strong Recovery in FY22', *The Economic Times*, 15 September 2020, https://economictimes.indiatimes.com/news/economy/indicators/adb-expects-indias-economy-to-contract-by-9-in-fy2020-21-sees-strong-recovery-in-fy22/articleshow/78120768.cms, accessed on 20 March 2021.

[76]'India's Economy Contracts 7.5% in Sept Quarter, Enters Recession', *The Times of India*, 28 November 2020, India GDP Growth Rate: India's economy contracts 7.5% in Sept quarter, enters recession | India Business News—Times of India (indiatimes.com)

SIGNPOSTS OF DEVELOPMENT

Increasing awareness and sensitivity means that factors other than the GDP or purely economic metrics have become important. The excessive focus on these parameters has been at the cost of many other key indicators that more correctly depict the state of the country. These include indices related to health (for example, infant and maternal mortality rates, malnutrition, age/weight and height/weight parameters, life expectancy), gender equality (sex ratio, women's participation in the labour force, pay parity, male/female ratio in higher education), education (enrolment rates at various levels, PISA ranking, average years of schooling) and environment (pollution figures, carbon emissions, forest cover).

Amongst the economic indices, it is no longer just the GDP or per capita income that are significant signposts of development. In a developing country like India, the poverty ratio, which is the proportion of population whose incomes are below the defined poverty line, is of far greater import than per capita income. This must be tallied with actual surveys on food intake (calories and nutrition) and consumer expenditure. There is recognition of the need to go beyond this, and look at deprivation in more holistic terms—including health, education, housing, access to clean water, sanitation and electricity. The UNDP Multidimensional Poverty Index covers some of this. India stands at rank 31 of 83 developing countries in this compared to Sri Lanka at number 4 and China at 20.[77]

Another key indicator is the Gini coefficient, a measure of inequality between different income percentiles of the

---

[77] 'Global Multidimensional Poverty Index 2020: Charting Pathways out of Multidimensional Poverty—Achieving the SDGs', *UNDP*, http://hdr.undp.org/sites/default/files/2020_mpi_report_en.pdf, accessed on 20 March 2021.

population (for example, the top 1 or 5 per cent versus the bottom 20 per cent). Apart from income, wealth inequalities too need to be taken into account. With regard to economic inequality, the picture in India is hardly positive, with Oxfam International's 'Commitment to Reducing Inequality Index 2020' ranking India at 129 among 158 countries, despite (or possibly due to) years of strong overall economic growth.[78] In effect, the benefits of economic growth have disproportionately accrued to—been captured by—the upper strata of society. This has consistently been the case irrespective of the political parties in power, indicative, therefore, of similar economic ideologies and the same model of growth.

A feature of inequality in India, beyond the economic one, is social inequality. Discrimination based on caste continues, even 70 years after adoption of a Constitution that promised equality. With growing consciousness amongst the scheduled castes, scheduled tribes and 'other backward castes', they have become better organized and more assertive. The backlash from the 'upper' castes has, in some areas, led to violence, with the 'lower' castes at the receiving end. It is arguable as to whether this has got worse over time or media coverage has made it appear so. Regardless, it is evident that in large parts of the country and in many instances, social discrimination is yet rampant.

The position is very similar with regard to gender: as education and awareness amongst girls has increased, so have their aspirations, self-confidence and assertiveness. Here, too, there is a backlash from the traditionalists—both in society and

---

[78]Fighting Inequality in the time of COVID: The Commitment to Reducing Inequality Index 2020, *Oxfam*, https://oxfamilibrary.openrepository.com/bitstream/handle/10546/621061/rr-fighting-inequality-covid-19-cri-index-081020-en.pdf, accessed on 20 March 2021.

within their family. Obviously, a strongly patriarchal society is finding it difficult to adjust to a new order that includes gender equality. The strains of this change are manifesting themselves in the growing incidence of crimes against women. For a while, it seemed that a more positive outcome would be in the economic arena: an increase in the number of working women. However, there has actually been a decline—from 33.1 per cent in 2011–12 to 25.3 per cent in 2017–18.[79] Explanations range from the fact that more women are in educational/training institutions, to the possibility that the data does not reflect the actual situation and is unreliable. On the other hand, if appropriately educated and skilled women enter the workforce to even the same level as in many other countries, India would see a huge increase in economic growth. A 2018 study estimated that a 10 percentage point increase in female participation in labour force could increase India's GDP by as much as $770 billion.[80]

In this decade, factors like poverty ratio, environment/sustainability, economic inequality, unemployment rate, equal opportunity for all sections of society, gender parity, health and education indices will be as important as GDP, current account deficit or fiscal deficit. While an indicator like Gross National

---

[79] 'Data for female labour force participation rate (LFPR) for productive age group (15–59 years) taken from 'Women's Participation in Labour Market Reflects a Declining Trend', *Hindustan Times*, 8 March 2020, https://www.hindustantimes.com/india-news/women-s-participation-in-labour-market-reflects-a-declining-trend/story-5Lj9PytVpiVu6rvu9JHlZP.html, accessed on 20 March 2021.

[80] 'The Power of Parity: Advancing Women's Equality in Asia Pacific', *McKinsey Global Institute*, May 2018, https://www.mckinsey.com/~/media/McKinsey/Featured%20Insights/Gender%20Equality/The%20power%20of%20parity%20Advancing%20womens%20equality%20in%20India%202018/India%20power%20of%20parity%20report.pdf, accessed on 20 March 2021.

Happiness may remain a point of discussion and desirability, it will continue to be an elusive dream. However, measures like the ones mentioned will increasingly complement, if not supplant, growth rate and GDP.

Even so, the traditional indicators of the state of the economy will continue to be important and will determine, to a large extent, the standing of the country in the global pecking order. Concrete evidence of this is seen in the rise of China in the 1980s and that of India in the last two decades. For about three decades, till the '80s, the countries that truly mattered were the US and the Soviet Union, with Western Europe (including the UK) and Japan on the sidelines. Other countries were practically inconsequential. For two centuries before this, it was the European countries (the colonial powers) that were at the forefront. In the long-term historical context, though, all these countries were bit players till well into the 17th century. It was India and China that together accounted for the largest proportion of overall global GDP, with the two together accounting for 51.4 per cent in 1600. In the next 100 years, India's share increased from 22.4 to 24.4 per cent. However, by 1870 it was down to 12.2 per cent. Over the almost 100 years of British rule, India's share in world GDP dropped drastically to just 4.2 per cent by 1947.[81]

In this period, both India and China were very much on the decline, as colonial powers ravaged the country. Industrialization, with its huge increase in productivity, was

---

[81]Figure for 1947 from *India Unlimited*, Arvind Panagariya, Harper Collins, 2020. Figures for earlier periods (computed in 1990 dollars and in purchasing power parity terms) from 'World History by per Capita GDP', *LiveMint*, 25 August 2010 https://www.livemint.com/Opinion/Nb7KkZ3yOVSNW3vHf9K1oM/World-history-by-per-capita-GDP.html, accessed on 20 March 2021.

monopolized by European powers and the colonies were further impoverished as mere suppliers of raw material at cheap rates. It was only from the 1950s that one saw the resurgence of Asia. First, it was Japan, as it rebuilt a country and economy destroyed by the war. Then, South Korea and, later, Taiwan, Singapore and Hong Kong began to grow rapidly. China took off after major reforms in the 1980s, and created unprecedented records of economic growth.

India's high-growth phase began only in the late 1980s and ran out of steam—hopefully only temporarily—in the decade of 2010. However, it is now on the cusp of a demographic dividend, a situation in which the increase in working-age population reduces the 'dependency ratio' (that is the proportion of those below 15 or above 64 years of age, compared to the 15–64 years age group). The potential economic benefits of this, the demographic dividend, can once again put India on a high growth path for another two decades. Almost all analysts are bullish about India's medium- to long-term economic prospects, and it is generally recognized as a superpower (at least in the economic sphere) in the making. By 2030, China and India will both—as in an earlier era—be major global economic powerhouses.

As a country, India will be amongst the top three global economies in 2030. However, at the individual level, an average Indian will be way down the pecking order. Even with an assumed GDP of $5.7 trillion in 2030, the per capita income—with a projected population (in 2031) of 1,479 million—will be $3,819, compared with about $2,104 in 2019.[82]

---

[82]Population figure for 2031 from 'Population Projections for India and States 2011 -2036', *National Health Mission*, November 2019, https://nhm.gov.in/New_Updates_2018/Report_Population_Projection_2019.pdf, accessed on 20 March 2021. The GDP for 2019 is from 'GDP (Current US$);

This continues to peg India's per capita GDP far below where other countries are even today: the US is at $65,118; China at $10,262; Singapore at $65,233; South Korea at $31,762 and Switzerland at $81,994.[83]

REDEFINING DEVELOPMENT

For India, it may be more important to look at how this decade will alter the picture of poverty, hunger and deprivation in the country. Ideally, the country needs a model of economic growth in which those at the bottom of the socio-economic pyramid get a disproportionately high share of the incremental gains, reversing the present model. This will quickly eliminate hunger and poverty, improve health and reduce inequality. This could happen through a massive programme of education and skilling, which enables people to become employable or productively self-employed, and an increase in farm yields. Alternatively—or in addition—there could be substantial cash transfers directly to the poor: some form of a guaranteed basic income. The positive impact of such a programme, for the beneficiaries and for the economy, is indicated by the success of the rural employment guarantee scheme (Mahatma Gandhi National Rural Employment Guarantee Act [MGNREGA]). Despite some drawbacks, and initial criticism from many who derided it as a politically motivated 'giveaway' programme that would be disastrous for the economy, it not only sustained poor villagers in times of difficulty and drought, but it also

---

The World Bank, https://data.worldbank.org/indicator/NY.GDP.MKTP.CD, accessed 20 March 2021. The GDP for 2031 assumes GDP growth of -9 per cent in 2020 -21 and 8 per cent thereafter.

[83]"GDP per Capita (Current US$)", *The World Bank*, https://data.worldbank.org/indicator/NY.GDP.PCAP.CD, accessed on 20 March 2021.

gave a boost to the rural economy. Therefore, till such time as education/training and growth enable millions of poor to get adequate livelihoods, a direct cash transfer scheme may be an appropriate stopgap or complement, to supplement existing incomes and ensure that no one is below the poverty line. This should be a non-negotiable target for 2030, one that must have unanimous acceptance across party lines. No hunger, no poverty and ensuring a bettering of particular health and education targets specified in the UN's Sustainable Development Goals (SDGs) must be the aim of the country's economic policy. Far larger allocations for health and education will obviously be called for, but mere funding will not suffice. Structural reforms too are required in both fields if the targets are to be achieved, just as actions beyond the monetary or financial are required to reduce economic inequality.

The SDGs are—as the name makes explicit—goals in themselves. However, even for those inclined to think purely in traditional economic terms, with GDP being the single most important indicator, the SDGs are important. Better education and skills translate into higher value-add. Good health means lower work absences and higher productivity. Nothing brings home the link between the economy and health more forcefully than the COVID pandemic sweeping the world. The economic loss is already predicted to be massive and may get worse.

Though hardly anyone needs to be persuaded about the direct linkages between GDP growth on the one hand and education and health on the other, political leaders continue to neglect the latter two. Government's performance on these fronts does not become an issue even for the opposition parties. It is only in the recent 2020 Delhi elections that the AAP made this a major part of their campaign. Hopefully, this will begin a new trend with health and education, rather than emotive issues, finding their way to the top of the agenda for political parties, governments and voters.

One scenario for the 2020s would, then, be a more holistic approach to development, where health, education, inequality and poverty get as much attention as GDP growth rates. Such a human-focused development model will ensure socially sustainable growth for the country, even as it seeks to provide each individual equal opportunity to realise his/her full potential. This will, as noted earlier, facilitate higher productivity and, therefore, higher growth rates. Equally importantly, it will strengthen the foundation, providing an excellent base of continuing—possibly even accelerating—economic growth beyond 2030.

A second scenario could be one in which the goal is singularly GDP growth, and government spending on social sectors like health and education remains woefully small. It is possible that such a model may lead to high economic growth (as it did for almost two decades from the early 1990s) in the short term. However, this approach will almost certainly result in social ferment, especially given the growing awareness and the revolution of rising expectations, both of which are amplified by what is seen through the media. Increased crime would be a likely fallout, as would protests, strikes and political movements. In the medium term, such strife will seriously affect economic growth—unless it is put down strongly and ruthlessly. The implication is that an iniquitous model of development is sustainable only if it is backed by a 'strong' (near-dictatorial) government. China and Singapore (especially in the Lee Kuan Yew years of rapid growth) provide such models from our neighbourhood. In a genuinely democratic framework, large disparities will not support rapid economic growth, and a far more equitable model of development will have to be evolved. This would, then, seem to be the obvious approach; yet, there will be one or the other political party which will be tempted to take the GDP-above-all approach. It will have to get support from the disadvantaged (who would be the losers in such a model) to come to power and may do so through the route of emotional appeal (religion, nationalism) so as to override rationality. A strategy of this kind may well work, and the 2019 national elections is proof, with the BJP scoring a huge win with its ultra-nationalistic and religious campaign. At the same time, state elections indicate the limitations of the strategy, with the BJP faring poorly in many of them, relative to its huge win at the national level. This exposes the fragility of this approach, when confronted with a strong opposition. The ground reality for the poor—low income, growing inequality, fewer jobs and inadequate public services—provides sufficient ammunition to parties focused on this, if they have credibility. As those parties opposed to the BJP build their own base or come together, it is likely that the appeal that worked for the BJP in 2019 will prove ephemeral. As noted earlier, easier and widespread access to media is likely to create disaffection amongst the disadvantaged, and the abstract appeal of religious solidarity or jingoism will quickly wither in the face of the growing reality of on-the-ground economics and material needs. Yet, one can hardly discount the possibility of a model based on the assumption that high growth—even the greater inequality—will raise all boats, and the masses of poor can be kept under control through a combination of increases in income and a strong government (the China model).

Indians, though, lack the discipline of the Chinese (and East Asians in general). We like to take shortcuts wherever possible, and loathe following rules or regulations. The nearanarchy on the roads and the unwillingness to form queues are indicative of this. In the workplace too, Indians generally look for how they can do a task more easily or quickly, rather than following a laid-out procedure. This is why we have a genius for 'jugaad' (improvization) and innovation, with each individual thinking differently. Imposing 'order' top-down on such a society is well-nigh impossible.

Given these innate characteristics of Indians, the freeflowing, open-ended scenario of a raucous, somewhat chaotic democracy suits us better than an orderly, disciplined East Asian version.

In the years ahead, there is likely to be a global shift away from an excessive focus on GDP. In the economic sphere, there will be greater focus on reducing inequality, on elimination of poverty and hunger, of investments in infrastructure and services which facilitate the ease-of-living, on quality jobs and livelihoods and on providing social security, health, education and housing to all. This will suit India well because these are, in fact, its most dire needs. The over-emphasis on GDP (especially in the last three decades), on becoming an economic superpower that competes with China and the US, have diverted us from the true needs of the country. Poverty elimination and the dreams of a better life for all do need economic growth, but the gains have to accrue proportionately far greater to the 'bottom of the (economic) pyramid', in contrast to what has happened in the last few decades. This calls for a relook at not only the model of development, but at how 'development' is defined.

The growing importance of social and environmental factors, and the more widespread awareness of them, is also likely to push a shift of emphasis in the 2020s. A more human-orientated, inclusive and holistic view of development will be preferred, rather than a mechanistic, purely GDP-focused one. The fact that this also means greater freedom and a more vibrant democracy are added advantages.

By 2030, India would be well on its way on this new path. Such a view may seem optimistic, but then—as mentioned at the outset—a framework of optimism is the one we have chosen to adopt. After all, a positive view of the future is an inherent human characteristic.

6

DEMOGRAPHY

More Age-Care Homes, Fewer Anganwadis

India was the first country in the world to have announced a national programme for family planning. Launched in 1952, it was recognition of the fact that rapid growth over the already large population base may well nullify—or, at least, considerably diminish—the increase in per capita income that would come about with economic development. Being then a primarily rural economy (82.7 per cent of the population lived in rural areas in 1951,[84] and agriculture constituted 56.5 per cent of the GDP[85]), there was also concern about land fragmentation resulting in unviable farm sizes. While 'sustainability' was yet to become a popular buzzword, the constraint on the availability of natural resources was recognized. In addition, it was clear that all social services would face immense pressure and strain as a result of increased demand from a growing population.

---

[84]'eCENSUSIndia : Issue Number 3: 2001', *Census of India*, https://censusindia.gov.in/Census_Data_2001/Census_Newsletters/Newsletter_Links/eci_3.htm, accessed on 20 March 2021.
[85]'Economy', *Resurgent India*, 29 July 2019, http://new.resurgentindia.org/indian-economy-at-the-time-of-the-first-five-year-plan-1951/#prettyPhoto, accessed on 20 March 2021.

A full-fledged Department of Family Planning was set up in the Ministry of Health in 1966 and a national population policy spelt out in 1976. The programme had varying and largely limited success in different states through the 1950s and 1960s. In the 1970s, the programme began to be given specific targets. When Indira Gandhi, then the prime minister, declared Emergency in 1975, the targets were enhanced, with a strong focus on sterilization: vasectomy and tubectomy. Reportedly, the prime minister's son, Sanjay Gandhi—who wielded considerable power without any official position— was a believer in population control and a great enthusiast of the sterilization programme. One result of this, and the move to enforce very large targets, was coercive or near-forcible sterilization in certain areas (especially in north India). When Emergency was lifted and elections held (in 1977), one of the reasons attributed for Mrs Gandhi's massive loss (again, particularly in north India) was the sterilization programme.

The fallout of this was that all parties and politicians became very wary of even mentioning family planning, and the nomenclature itself changed to 'family welfare'. Instead of shifting to a programme of awareness, education and informed choice, of providing multiple alternatives through better delivery and health facilities, the whole programme was practically abandoned. This shying away from anything to do with family planning continued for many years, and it was only slowly—and much later—that it got some traction again from the government.

POPULATION THROUGH A DIFFERENT LENS

The situation is now different, as are perceptions. One change has been the comparatively low Total Fertility Rate (TFR)[86] especially in states like Kerala and Tamil Nadu. These states are amongst the 14 states that were at or below the replacement TFR of 2.1 by 2018; in fact, Kerala achieved this as far back as 1988. On the other hand, Bihar is expected to reach this milestone only in 2039.[87] This does not mean that their population stabilizes after reaching the replacement TFR; However, further growth is based only on past momentum and increasing longevity, and that the incremental increase is now beginning to taper off.

India's population is estimated to grow to 1,479 million in 2031 and to 1,522 million in 2036.[88] Sometime in the mid-2020s, it will overtake China and become the largest country. A recent (2020) study predicts that India's population will peak at 1.6 billion in 2048, and decline by as much as 32 per cent

---

[86] Total Fertility Rate (TFR), in simple terms, refers to total number of children born or likely to be born to a woman in her lifetime if she were subject to the prevailing rate of age-specific fertility in the population. The TFR of about 2.1 children per woman is called replacement-level fertility (UN, Population Division). This value represents the average number of children a woman would need to have to reproduce herself by bearing a daughter who survives to childbearing age. If replacement level fertility is sustained over a sufficiently long period, each generation will exactly replace itself without any need for the country to balance the population by international migration, (http://origin.searo.who.int/entity/health_situation_trends/data/chi/TFR/en/), accessed on 20 March 2021

[87] The TFR data and prediction is from SRS 2018 (https://www.censusindia.gov.in/2011-common/sample_registration_system.html, accessed on 20 March 2021)

[88] 'Population Projections for India and States 2011–2036', *National Health Mission*, November 2019, https://nhm.gov.in/New_Updates_2018/Report_Population_Projection_2019.pdf, accessed on 20 March 2021

by 2100 to go down to 1.09 billion.[89] This would be the level it was at about a century earlier![90]

It is in this context that the increasing emphasis on a more holistic view of family planning—as a part of better health and of informed choice based on a variety of alternative methods—is welcome. Mother and child care, reproductive health and gender equality are now in focus, as are delayed marriage and more spacing between children.

There has also been a change in how a rapidly growing population—with an ever larger number of children—is perceived. Over the last few years, concerns about 'population explosion' and 'demographic bomb' have been replaced by discussions on the benefits flowing from the 'demographic dividend'. This expression reflects the gains that emanate from a lower dependency ratio: the population of dependents (those below or above the working age range) divided by the total number in the working age group (15 to 64 years). In ageing countries like Japan (which reached its population peak as far back as 2005) and some parts of Europe, the high dependency ratio means that the large expenditures on health and pensions for the old have to come from the earnings/taxes of a proportionately smaller working age group. This casts a large burden on them, as compared to 'young' countries. India, thanks to decades of rapid population growth, already has a large working age population, which will continue to grow for some years. By 2031, this will grow to 1025 million,[91]

---

[89]"Population Shifts: Top Ten Countries by Population", *The Lancet*, https://www.thelancet.com/infographics/population-forecast, accessed on 20 March 2021.
[90]Based on Census of India, figures (2001: 1.03 billion; 2011: 1.21 billion)
[91]Calculated from "Population Projections for India and States 2011–2036", *National Health Mission*, November 2019, https://nhm.gov.in/New_Updates_2018/Report_Population_Projection_2019.pdf, accessed on 20 March

representing the largest number of workers (or potential workers) amongst all countries.

The experience of other countries—especially East and Southeast Asia, in the recent past—indicates this demographic shift results in boosting economic growth (hence the term demographic dividend). India is now poised to derive a similar gain due to its demographic age profile. One needs to be wary, though, of one essential difference: in all the 'Asian Tigers' (the countries that saw super-fast growth, especially South Korea, Taiwan, Hong Kong and Singapore), the levels of literacy and years of schooling where high, thanks to the strong emphasis on education. As a result, the young population entered the working age group with high levels of education and skills. India is not similarly placed.

The other difference is the change in technology. Now, many low-end jobs have been automated, and thus a large workforce will be an advantage only if it has the skills required to leverage the new technologies. Competition, too, has increased and countries like Bangladesh, Vietnam, Thailand, the Philippines and Indonesia now challenge India in a number of products and industries.

At the same time, technology has opened up opportunities for new products and services, based more on intellectual property, innovation and new business models, rather than merely on capital. In India, this has triggered a new entrepreneurial culture, thanks to the emphasis on—and encouragement to—start-up ventures and the maturing of a conducive ecosystem. Since innovation and entrepreneurship are seen as the domain of youth, having more young people should give a boost to such new ventures. Thus, a large population of youngsters—all fired up with ideas and willing to take risks—will mean more job creators (rather than job seekers) and higher productivity, through innovation. This is, thus, an additional bonus over and above the traditional benefits expected from the demographic dividend. However, in addition to skills and education, another key element for the benefits of the demographic dividend to be translated into economic and social gain, is health. A working population that is beset by poor health is unlikely to be very productive.

Given all the 'new' positives, the perspective on population has changed. Many now see advantages in a growing population, and family planning does not seem to require too much emphasis.

More recently, though, there is a countervailing current too, with many politicians once again (after many decades) speaking about 'population control'. Some, undoubtedly, are genuinely concerned about the growing numbers and the impact of a large population on scarce resources. However, some others have given this issue a communal angle, pointing to a growing Muslim population and an increase in their ratio in the total population. They ignore hard data that shows that religion, per se, is not a factor in population growth and the TFR is more dependent on factors like income, education level of the mother, quality of health services, etc. Thus, the TFR amongst Muslims in Kerala is 1.86 and in Tamil Nadu it is 1.74: both far lower than the TFR of Hindus in Bihar (3.29) and UP (2.7).[92]

One important aspect about demographic change over the last few decades has been largely neglected. While there has

---

[92]TFR data and prediction are from SRS 2018 (https://www.censusindia.gov.in/2011-common/sample_registration_system.html, accessed on 20 March 2021)

been strong focus on the young—their energy, dynamism and innovativeness—for their potential contribution to economic growth, the elderly have been ignored. Thanks to better healthcare, people are now living longer and the number of people over 60 is estimated to be 137 million in 2021, growing to 195 million in 2031. This represents a growth of 42 per cent, compared to an overall population growth of just 8.5 per cent. Even more striking is the growth in population of those over 80 years of age: from a mere 15 million in 2021, their population is projected to reach 23.7 million by 2031, an increase of 58 per cent.[93] This fact, of a rapidly growing population of elders, gives rise to a number of issues.

First, the health and physical well-being of the elders needs attention. At the moment, there is a strong focus on reproductive, maternal and child health. This is as it should be, but as the ratio changes between this group and those above 60 years, much greater attention must be paid to issues related to geriatric health. This needs to begin with more research and funding for it, extending to education and specialized courses, and going on to more beds and specialized centres in hospitals. Appropriate homecare and palliative facilities too are necessities. In December 2007, Parliament adopted the Maintenance and Welfare of Parents and Senior Citizens Act 2007 requiring state governments to ensure 'earmarked facilities for geriatric patients in every district hospital duly headed by a medical officer with experience in geriatric care.' However, a status report by the government to the Supreme Court indicated that, over a decade later (in April 2019) 16

---

[93]Calculated from 'Population Projections for India and States 2011–2036', *National Health Mission*, November 2019, https://nhm.gov.in/New_Updates_2018/Report_Population_Projection_2019.pdf, accessed on 20 March 2021

of the 35 states and Union Territories had not a single ward/bed dedicated to elders.

Second, psychological and social aspects—often ignored—are also important. Loneliness, neglect and even ill-treatment of elders are not uncommon, despite the cultural heritage of respect for elders, especially for parents. The changing social milieu has exacerbated this problem, with working couples in cities having no time or inclination (and limited house space) to look after ageing parents. Even their value as baby-sitters for the couple's young children is greatly diminished if they are unwell. At the extreme, passive neglect of parents is transformed into active ill-treatment, with domestic violence not being uncommon. With no one to turn to and nowhere to go to, elders have little option but to bear this. Awareness, education, societal norms and social workers are all necessary to counter this. In addition, these need to be backed by laws and their enforcement. In this, as in all other issues facing elders, civil society organizations have to play a major role. Already, some, like HelpAge India, the premier organization in this field, are doing a great deal.[94] However, given the magnitude of the problem, much more needs to be done.

Related to this aspect of social well-being is the need to evolve ways by which elders will feel wanted and involved. In doing this, the wide range of capabilities, requirements and options have to be taken into consideration. For the vast majority, the best option may be some form of engagement in the activities of the community, besides taking care of grandchildren. Building a community of elders, preferably centred on a place to meet, talk and indulge in games or group

---

[94]The work of HelpAge India was recently recognized through its being a recipient of the UN Population Award 2020 (the first Indian institution to be honoured since the establishment of the award in 1981).

activities, is a good starting point. Many who are physically fit and have the capabilities could take up activities with children, in schools or outside. Such intergenerational interaction is known to be useful to both age groups. Overall, it is important for the community as a whole to take responsibility for all the elders, but also to use them as a resource. While improving the well-being of elders and boosting their self-worth, it is also a benefit to the community.

There are examples in various countries (Vietnam, for example) of the local community taking responsibility for elders. China has formulated a '90-7-3' approach: 90 per cent of the elders are taken care of by the family, 7 per cent are looked after by the community, and 3 per cent are in elder-care or old age homes. In India, we do not have the resources to set up a massive number of old age homes, nor is this an appropriate solution in our social and cultural context. Therefore, family and community care as the means of looking after an overwhelming bulk of elders (along the lines of the Chinese model) is probably the best approach for a country like India.

Apart from community activities and involvement with schoolchildren, there are other possibilities. A substantial number—though only a small fraction—of elders are very well qualified and in good health when they retire as required by the rules. Their capabilities and vast experience is an invaluable asset that is rarely or minimally used. There is considerable scope to tap into this pool for a variety of purposes: teaching, mentoring, advising and guiding. While entrepreneurship is generally seen as something done by the young, there is no reason why elders too—with their vast experience and knowledge—cannot create start-ups. In fact, a partnership of young and old may be an optimal way of combining energy, dynamism and the latest knowledge, with experience and wisdom. Already, the corporate world is using elders on boards and advisory bodies, so as to seek the special input that they provide. Civil society organizations too can benefit from associating elders in non-executive roles. Better healthcare has meant that more and more people are physically fit for longer. In recognition of this, the government has changed the retirement age—for example, in the case of professors, directors and vice chancellors. However, it has specified upper age limits for non-executive roles too (like board membership). This age-based discrimination needs to end.

CHANGING DEMOGRAPHY, NEW IMPERATIVES

As we move into a new decade, it seems clear that a fresh approach, defined by a clear policy, is needed for the elders. They will form a large—and rapidly growing—percentage of our population. The policy must look at them as a resource: respected and now nurtured for their decades of contribution to the country, and to be utilized in ways that help their community and country, while taking proper care of their physical, social and psychological well-being. This must include a guaranteed safety net for healthcare, an adequate pension, and shelter—especially for the destitute and poor. The policy must encourage each community to take care of its elders, preferably through grants and incentives, but also by law. Dedicated geriatric wards (presently mandated, but often non-existent) in all hospitals, and special geriatric care courses for doctors, paramedics and social workers, must turn out the numbers of such professionals that are required.

The policy must also focus on ensuring ease of living in the context of the special needs of elders. Already, regulations and norms regarding people with disabilities have also helped elders—for example, access ramps and banisters or support rails, lifts, and low-floor buses. Additional facilities like special counters or queues, and help desks for elders, must be mandated in public places—like railway stations and airports, banks, hospitals and other government offices—for ticket purchase, security, enquiry, form submission and payment. Simple things like reserved seating are also helpful and show regard for the elderly.

Overall, the demographic transition to an ageing population requires reorientation of thinking, mindset and policy within government as also amongst civil society organizations. Academia needs to initiate more research and work on issues, challenges and opportunities in the context of the emerging demographic profile. While this must obviously include all health-related matters (including, as mentioned earlier, special courses and training), it should also cover other aspects—the social, psychological and economic dimensions.

It is time to begin thinking and initiating studies on the impact of new technologies on longevity. Genetics, biology and electronics are already beginning to revolutionize healthcare. Soon, organ repair and replacement (by organic or electromechanical parts) will develop to the point where, combined with predictive diagnostics, humans can live long—potentially endless lives—in good health. That this will happen is not in doubt; the only question is whether it becomes reality in a decade, or in two decades from now. Such immortality will have completely revolutionary implications on absolutely all areas of work and life. It needs discussion and debate, including on the ethical and philosophical aspects.

As far as India is concerned, while longevity is a here-and-now reality, near-immortality (given the cost of ensuring it) may be a possibility for only a handful of very rich people over the next two decades. The ethical and societal implications of this new wealth-related increase in inequity must be discussed, but for the bulk of people in the country, the more mundane issues of the elders must take priority.

For many years yet, we need a two-track policy. One part must ensure that children and youth are provided a strong foundational base through healthcare (including nutrition) and education (including skills). The second must focus on elders: ways of making sure that they live a healthy, happy and fulfilling life, even as the community and nation draw on their experience, wisdom and expertise.

For the last 20 years, much attention and funds have been devoted to the young. This is very appropriate, and must continue. At the same time, this decade is going to see a burgeoning number of elders and a big increase of their proportion in the total population. This segment of the population has so far been relatively neglected and left to fend for themselves, or are taken care of by their family. Beyond a measly pension, there are hardly any government efforts of scale and impact to either look after them, or to tap them as a resource. The pension amounts range from pitiable lows of ₹350 and ₹400 a month (Chhattisgarh, Madhya Pradesh and Bihar) to ₹2,000–2,250 (Delhi, Goa, Haryana) for those between 60 and 79 years of age.[95] The amounts for those above 80 years are a little higher. Surviving on such a miserly dole is, obviously, next to impossible.

This neglect of the elderly has to change now, for at least three good reasons. First, it is a collective moral and ethical responsibility to look after elders and ensure their well-being.

---

[95]Data courtesy HelpAge India, taken from various Government of India and state websites.

Second, a fair proportion of them can be an invaluable resource in the nation's efforts for economic growth, social development and cultural harmony. Third, from a politically pragmatic point of view, they will constitute a rapidly growing and, therefore, important voter base.

Apart from government, the private sector too has been slow in recognizing the potential of this growing number of elders. Only now does one see more products and services—and, therefore, promotion and advertising—aimed at this segment of the population. This is in contrast with the huge focus on young consumers, and even on children. Special products, accompanied by targeted marketing and advertising, are designed specifically for them. It is now time for companies to realize that elders too constitute a big and distinct market segment. Many of them—especially professionals who have retired in the last decade—have built up substantial wealth and, with no dependents now, have the capacity to spend generously.

As in other categories in India, there is huge inequity amongst elders too. On the one hand, there is a small percentage (though a large absolute number) who are wealthy. This is the group that now has both money and time, and goes on at least a couple of jaunts a year to exotic destinations (generally abroad), regularly frequents high-end restaurants, spends generously on clothes, products and housing. On the other hand, the bulk of elders are poor and have little money to spend on anything beyond the essential needs of food, shelter and clothing. For many, even essential healthcare is unaffordable, and hospitalization means financial disaster. And then there are the millions of near-destitute elders, who are dependent on their children or family or charity even for basic necessities. Despite economic growth in this decade, the scenario is unlikely to see a radical change.

Another major aspect of demographic change will be the rural-to-urban migration. Cities, as economic powerhouses, provide many avenues of employment for all levels of skills—from the unskilled labourer to the highly-educated professional. Further, because of the range of work opportunities (including entrepreneurial ones: from the street vendor to the tech start-up), they offer the dream of advancing to ever better-paying livelihoods. Naturally, then, cities are magnets for all those who want employment and desire to make their way up the economic ladder. Rural-to-urban migration has, therefore, been an ongoing factor. Hence, cities have seen high growth and it is estimated that the urban population in India will grow from 380 million in 2021 to 558 million in 2031.[96] This will severely strain the infrastructure in the cities and make far worse the already existing problems of pollution, traffic, water, sanitation and housing. Poor sanitation and dense habitations will provide a fertile ground for epidemics and health problems.

A reaction to these problems is already visible, even if in a limited way. With technology facilitating decentralization and dispersal of economic activity, there is a possibility of large-scale job-creation in rural areas. In fact, those now living in cities may choose to migrate to rural areas, contrary to the traditional pattern. There are already early indications of such a change in preference, as a result of COVID. Reports and anecdotes indicate that the intensity of the epidemic in major cities has prompted many to consider a long-term shift to smaller towns. The attractions are numerous: less traffic, minimal pollution, lower crime rate, saving in daily commute

---

[96]'Population Projections for India and States 2011–2036', *National Health Mission*, November 2019, https://nhm.gov.in/New_Updates_2018/Report_Population_Projection_2019.pdf, accessed on 20 March 2021.

time, less expensive and—with the experience of COVID and other diseases—a better health record. Already, quite a few who are 'gig-ers', working on their own, have moved base to towns in Goa or to smaller cities elsewhere. This trend began in a small way earlier, but has got a boost post–COVID and, if the governments concerned can ensure better facilities in smaller cities—especially education, healthcare, inter-city transport and electronic connectivity—there will certainly be a reverse migration. As high-income earners move to such towns, there will be a demand-driven increase in the number—and quality—of restaurants, theatres, shops and entertainment facilities. This will attract more professionals, creating a positive feedback loop, beginning with self-employed professionals, but will soon percolate to blue-collar workers, as industry decentralizes through technology enablement. With job opportunities closer to home, many from rural areas may prefer to live and work there, rather than migrating to cities. Overall, the push factor nudging well-qualified professionals away from urban problems, and the pull factor of a more serene life style with all the urban comforts, may bring about a new paradigm. This will slowly, but surely, mark the beginning of a new demographic factor. The 2020s are likely to see this seminal shift, aided by technology, thus reversing a centuries-old trend.

To summarize, the demographic scene in 2030 is likely to include the following:

i. A large population of around 1,479 million,[97] yet growing, but at a slower rate than in the past
ii. Large regional imbalances, with little or no population

---

[97]'Population Projections for India and States 2011–2036', *National Health Mission*, November 2019, https://nhm.gov.in/New_Updates_2018/Report_Population_Projection_2019.pdf, accessed on 20 March 2021

growth in the south and west, but continuing (though slackening) growth in the east and north.

iii. A huge urban population, with a few massive urban agglomerations, but a new trend of reverse migration from urban to rural areas

iv. Just like two fairly distinct regions (south/west and north/east) which exhibit substantial differences in population growth rates, there will be other dichotomous categories, based on income (rich, poor), education (minimal/primary, secondary classes and above), and location (rural, urban)

v. The world's biggest working age population, with about 1,025 million[98] in the age group of 15–64 years

vi. A very large number of elders: 195 million above 60 years, of which 23.7 million will be above 80 years[99]

DEMOGRAPHIC DYNAMICS: THE CONSEQUENCES

Each of the six major points highlighted above has considerable impact on the economy, society, culture or politics (or combinations of some of these), and an impact on the overall scenario in 2030.

The slower rate of population growth implies a smaller number of children, especially in some parts of the country (the south and west, in particular). This means a lower demand

---

[98] 'Population Projections for India and States 2011–2036', *National Health Mission*, November 2019, https://nhm.gov.in/New_Updates_2018/Report_Population_Projection_2019.pdf, accessed on 20 March 2021

[99] Figures are for 2031, based on 'Population Projections for India and States 2011–2036', *National Health Mission*, November 2019, https://nhm.gov.in/New_Updates_2018/Report_Population_Projection_2019.pdf, accessed on 20 March 2021

for goods and services catering to the young. Businesses which produce these will have to reorient their strategy and rejig their product profile. The baby products segment will face serious challenges, as will the presently thriving play schools and day-care (baby-sitting) centres. Day-care centres for infants may have to transform into care-centres for elders, as working couples look for care and engagement for their parents when they go to work. Basically, we will need more age-care homes and fewer Anganwadis.

The current boom in school education (evidenced by the large number of new schools being set up) will wane. Schools will see far lower demand, and many may have to shut down (already, states like Kerala are facing this challenge). This will be a particularly serious issue for government schools, which will face a 'double whammy': lower demand due to fewer children, and a further drop in enrolment due to the increasing preference for private schools. From overcrowded classrooms to empty ones will be quite a change!

The second impact of demographic changes (the regional imbalance) will have serious social and economic implications. With slower population growth and healthy economic progress, the south and west will see a bigger increase in per capita income. The existing inequity will be further exacerbated by the fact that economic growth in these states is likely to continue being stronger than in the north and east.

In the more prosperous areas, economic growth combined with the slowing population increase (meaning relatively fewer working age people) will give further impetus to the migration of labour from the poorer states. The regional economic imbalance and migration is certain to have both socio-cultural and political consequences. Two very different outcomes are likely: the first is a closer sense of integration, and the second (and diametrically opposite) is a backlash or reaction. An immediate example of both is the migration of people from the Northeast, in search of better education and jobs. The large influx into Delhi seems to have given old-time residents a better understanding of these people and a strong appreciation of their culture, especially their musical abilities and cuisine. On the other hand, people from the Northeast living in Bengaluru went through a harrowing time two years ago, thanks to attacks on some of them. As a result, and worsened by amplification of rumours through social media, train loads of Northeasterners fled the city in panic. Similarly, a few years ago, Biharis in Mumbai were the target of attacks, largely orchestrated by supporters of Shiv Sena, a political party that has for long been known to target 'outsiders'.

In the Northeast itself, there has been concern about outsiders. Assam for one, has been convulsed by frequent agitations on this issue, at times violent. Driven for many decades by fear of domination by Bengali culture, the agitations have been mainly directed at so-called 'Bangladeshis', assumed to be illegal migrants from across the border, though most claim to be (Indian) Bengalis long resident in Assam, or from West Bengal. The National Register of Citizens (NRC) aims to identify the illegal migrants into Assam, and the exercise of doing this (carried out in 2019) has led to much controversy, with some 1.9 million being denied citizenship on the basis of them not having the required papers. The whole process has also taken on communal overtones, with political parties quite happy to fish in the troubled waters. This has been further exacerbated by the CAA, which, in essence, would give citizenship to all refugees (migrants) from three major neighbouring countries (Afghanistan, Bangladesh, Pakistan) except Muslims. There is also a move to extend the NRC process to other states.

In this decade, as in-country migration is spurred by jobs, education and easy mobility, it would be interesting to see how the dialectic of integration versus outsider plays out. By 2030, the southern states in particular, are likely to witness a huge influx from the north, east and Northeast, as opportunities and prosperity—as also the promise of better living conditions—act as magnets for migrants. The resulting strain on the social fabric will become particularly visible if there is competition for jobs between locals and outsiders, also if there is minimal integration. Such situations are ripe for exploitation by political parties, which paint the outsiders as villains. This is giving an impetus to regional parties which claim to represent and fight for the rights of the 'sons of the soil'. Many parties in multiple states (including the national parties) are, for example, seeking reservation in jobs for 'locals'. On the other hand, as the number of migrants grows and—thanks to technology and easier processes—more of them register for voting in their new home, they will become an influential minority, able to sway election results. Some parties will, therefore, pitch their appeal to such migrants. Signs of this are already visible: in Delhi, more than one party says that they will take special care of the 'Purvanchali', mainly migrants from Bihar. In Mumbai, it is not uncommon to see the party flags of Dravida Munnetra Kazhagam (DMK) or the All India Anna Dravida Munnetra Kazhagam (AIADMK)— parties rooted in Tamil Nadu—in certain areas. By 2030, with greatly increased internal migration, such parochial parties may become more common and powerful. This will invite a backlash from parties espousing the rights of 'locals', and the resulting antagonism may well result in a reinforcement spiral with Newtonian overtones (each action giving rise to an equal and opposite reaction—in these cases, probably a greater and opposite reaction).

The major fallout of the regional divide in population growth rates will be on the political scenario. Despite migration—which will be a very small percentage of the state's population—the numbers in the eastern and northern states will increase rapidly, even as numbers in the west and south begin to head towards stability. The result will be that each MP from the populous states represents far more people than those from the slower growing states. This is because a law freezing the number of MPs from each state in the Lok Sabha was passed in 1976. This froze the number of seats at the 1971 level and was supposed to be valid till 2000. In 2001, the freeze was further extended by Parliament till the year 2026.[100] The law was first passed when there was great concern about growing population, and was seen as a means to ensure that states that did well in curbing population growth were not penalized by reducing their proportion of MPs. However, many have been arguing that this is unfair since it reduces, in effect, the value of each vote (and voter) from the populous states. For example, going by projections, in 2026 as many as 3.4 million people (on average) from Bihar, 3.2 million from Delhi and 3 million from UP will be represented by one MP, whereas only 1.8 million people from Kerala and 2 million people from Tamil Nadu will be able to send a MP to the Lok Sabha. In the case of Goa, the number will be as low as 0.8 million, even lower (0.7 million)

---

[100]'Freeze on LS Seats till 2026', *The Times of India*, 24 August 2001, https://timesofindia.indiatimes.com/india/Freeze-on-LS-seats-till-2026/articleshow/1712525869.cms, accessed on 20 March 2021.

for Sikkim and Daman and Diu.[101]

As a result of this, if the law is changed and greater parity brought to the voter–MP ratio across the country, then MPs from states like UP and Bihar may dominate the political scene even more than they now do. The big losers will be low-population-growth states like Kerala and Tamil Nadu. What will be the consequences? In 2019, there was a revival of the old controversy regarding the imposition of Hindi. A draft of the proposed NEP implied making Hindi compulsory in all schools. There was an immediate and strong reaction, especially from Tamil Nadu. The result was a new draft that changed the recommendation (about Hindi). If such controversies erupt in future, will the greater numerical domination of MPs from the Hindi heartland in Parliament (and in the government) be as sensitive to the concerns of some states (which may be represented by only a small proportion of MPs in Parliament)? If there are many such issues, what will be the repercussions? Will such repercussions be amplified by and strengthen regional parties espousing the cause of 'sons of the soil'? This may well give a fillip to centripetal forces, further abetted by a sense that they (the richer states) are subsidizing the poorer eastern and northern states, and that the latter are a drag on the more developed states. Will a post-2026 amendment that brings greater parity in terms of population per seat lead to smaller and less populous states feeling marginalized? Going down this path, one can well paint a drastic and extreme scenario, all triggered by the demographic change.

On the other hand, an optimistic outlook can be equally

---

[101]Calculated from the population projections in 'Population Projections for India and States 2011–2036', *National Health Mission*, November 2019, https://nhm.gov.in/New_Updates_2018/Report_Population_Projection_2019.pdf, accessed on 20 March 2021.

argued for, given that parties and politicians know how to handle concerns about domination, and reach compromise solutions. Possibly, a new form of the Rajya Sabha may emerge with a fixed per-state representation (akin to the US Senate).

Internal migration has long been prevalent and in good times, 'outsiders' could be looked on as people who enrich the cultural and social diversity of the country. As far as cross-border migration is concerned, the past influx from Bangladesh has been mainly driven by 'economic refugees' attracted by jobs and better economic prospects in India. However, this picture has changed considerably, despite all the politics (and communal-driven propaganda) around it. Not only is Bangladesh superior to India in many social and health indicators, but its economy has grown marginally faster than India's (7 per cent as against India's 6.8 per cent a year between 2012 and 2019). With continuing, robust economic growth, the so-called influx will reduce. In fact, the number of Bangladesh-born people in India has actually declined from 4.04 million in 1991 to 3.7 million in 2001 and further to 2.7 million in 2011. Any data in India is questionable, but the truth is that, sadly, sustained propaganda and fear-mongering seems to score over facts. Bangladeshis are the largest group of foreign-born living in India, but account for a minute 0.2 per cent of India's population.[102] Contrast this with the foreign-born in the US: immigrants were 13.7 per cent of the US population in 2018. Of this, Indians accounted for 6 per cent, that is, about 0.8 per cent of the total US population[103]—about

---

[102]'Why Bangladesh Looks More of a Magnet for Workers than India', *The Times of India*, 30 January 2020, https://timesofindia.indiatimes.com/india/why-bangladesh-looks-more-of-a-magnet-for-workers-than-india/articleshow/73777229.cms, accessed on 20 March 2021.
[103]Figures for immigrants in the US from 'Key Findings about U.S.

four times the proportion of Bangladeshis in India. Indeed, in years to come, we may well see more migration in the other direction: from India to Bangladesh!

As regards India's other big neighbour, Pakistan, the situation is uncertain. If the continuing internal strife gets worse and degenerates into anarchy, it is entirely possible that we may see a large influx of refugees from there. Of course, the border is by and large tightly controlled and monitored, making it difficult for a large number to slip across. Other, more devious, routes are sometimes used and more will, doubtless, be found, but the numbers coming through these can never be too large.

There is also the aspect of outward migration: Indians leaving for foreign shores. Historically, India has seen both, inward and outward flows. In years gone by, the country received migrants—whether refugees fleeing oppression, or traders and fortune seekers coming to make money—with open arms. That situation has changed considerably. On the outflow side too, there were a variety of emigrants: indentured labour (whose descendants are yet numerous in places as far apart as Fiji, Mauritius and Guyana), traders (particularly in East Africa) and, more recently, low-skill workers (especially in Saudi Arabia and the neighbouring Gulf countries) and professionals (now, across the world, but mainly in the US). In addition, there has for long been migration from India to the UK and to Canada, and both countries now have a substantial number of Indian-origin people. In all these countries, the migrants have greatly influenced the perception and image of India, besides adding to and affecting the local culture (many

---

Immigrants', *Pew Research Centre*, 20 August 2020, https://www.pewresearch.org/fact-tank/2020/08/20/key-findings-about-u-s-immigrants/, accessed on 20 March 2021.

say that chicken tikka masala has replaced fish and chips as Britain's national dish!). Importantly, from an economic standpoint, they remit a huge amount back to India each year—$83 billion in 2019[104]—helping to reduce the country's global trade deficit.

The global Indian diaspora, estimated to be about 20 million, is also a major factor in defining India's image and perception in each host country. Further, they are increasingly becoming important political players in their host countries—initially in countries like Fiji and Mauritius, which have a high proportion of Indian-origin people, but now also in the UK, Canada and the US. Canada has a number of them in the Cabinet; in the UK, two of the top-level positions (the ministers in charge of the treasury and of home affairs) are presently (January 2021) held by persons of Indian origin, as were a number of high-level posts in the Trump administration in the US. Now, a part-Indian person is the vice president of the US and a number of other persons of Indian origin hold senior positions in the Biden administration.

The largest number of Indians living abroad is now in United Arab Emirates, with as many as 3.42 million, followed by Saudi Arabia (2.59 million). Approximately 3 million more are in other countries in the Gulf region.[105] Though their direct participation in politics is ruled out, they are obviously a major influencer in our relationship with these countries. The new

---

[104]"Personal Remittances, Received (Current US$)', *The World Bank*, https://data.worldbank.org/indicator/BX.TRF.PWKR.CD.DT?locations=IN, accessed on 20 March 2021.

[105]According to data tabled by the Ministry of External Affairs in the Lok Sabha, quoted in 'Telling Numbers: 1.36 Crore Indians Living Abroad, One-Fourth of Them in UAE', *The Indian Express*, 10 February, 2020, https://indianexpress.com/article/explained/telling-numbers-indians-living-abroad-uae-lok-sabha-mea-6259449/, accessed on 20 March 2021.

clout of the diaspora has geopolitical and strategic implications and, by 2030, it is likely that this role—an indirect spin-off from migration and demographics—will be significant.

Overall, by 2030, migration—mainly internal, but also cross-border—is likely to be an important part, even if small, of the demographic changes that the country will witness. Despite the limited percentage of population involved, this factor will have a disproportionate impact across the board: on social, cultural and economic dimensions, and also on politics.

Clearly, India 2030 will be considerably influenced, even shaped, by two demographic factors:

- those intrinsic to the natural growth of the population and its age profile
- migration, intra-country and across borders

While one can be fairly certain about the first and its likely impact, the extent (especially of the cross-border migration) and impact of the second is far more difficult to predict. Whatever it may be, demographics is a key issue and must figure prominently in the projections and planning for India 2030.

7

SOCIETY AND SOCIAL DYNAMICS

Challenging the Status Quo

As an ancient civilization, India has seen a continuous evolution of society over its 5,000-year history. Archaeology provides some indicators and hints of what society may have been like millennia ago. Oral history, epics like the Mahabharata and the Ramayana, and more concrete archaeological research, reveal some additional details about society over the centuries. Apart from written and oral accounts, sculptures and paintings add very useful information which helps to decipher relationships within the society of the time. Since the time frame for each bit of evidence is often not directly known, research is required to deduce the particular period. This comes from scientific methods like carbon dating or inferences through diet, major calamities (earthquakes, for example) and astronomical observations which can be dated, flora and fauna (a horse in a carving sets a limit on how old it is), architectural influences, etc. More recent techniques like DNA sampling provide definite evidence about the inter-marriage or intermingling between different groups in the population who migrated into India over millennia. Though not always conclusive, these various elements of data make it possible to paint a picture of society at various times in the past.

In the last few years, exciting new findings on the formation of different population groups in various countries have resulted from research. Population geneticists now extract DNA from the bones of people who lived long ago—sometimes tens of thousands of years ago—enabling them to thereby trace when and where population groups moved. These findings, supplemented by other data from archaeology—and sometimes art and linguistics—offer fairly definitive evidence of the origins and movement of various population groups.

Many of these findings are synthesized in an excellent book, *Early Indians*, by Tony Joseph.[106] He explains how the Indian population is the result of four major migrations. The first are out-of-Africa migrants who came to India some 65,000 years ago. A second wave, around 12,000 years ago, was a population related to the early farmers of Iran, who then mixed with the earlier so-called First Indians. This mixed population catalysed the first agricultural revolution in north-western India which then developed, over thousands of years, into the Harappan civilization. Later, around 4,000 years ago, came migrants from East Asia. Soon after, between 3,500 and 4,000 years ago, pastoralists from the Central Asian steppes (Kazakhstan now) came, bringing with them Indo-European languages. Practically all population groups in India today are composed of a mixture of these four, in varying degrees.

Thus, both north and south Indians have common ancestry in the Harappans, who migrated across the country about 3,900 years ago. Marriage within their own group—the practice of endogamy—began only around 2,000 years ago. This suggests that the caste system began then (around 2,000

---

[106]*Early Indians: The Story of Our Ancestors and Where We Came From*, Tony Joseph, Juggernaut, 2018

years back) and not with the migration (of 'Arya') from Central Asia. Also, that almost every Indian—irrespective of religion, region or caste—owes 50–65 per cent of their ancestry to the First Indians.

Comparative genetic 'purity' is indicative of a separateness that must be due to either geographical isolation or societal norms, both of which would inhibit intermingling with other genetic groups. One example of such separateness in India are Parsis. This very small community has maintained its distinctiveness over centuries by retaining its cultural roots, and further ensuring its unique identity by prohibiting, through religious and social mores, marriage outside the community. As a result, and because of some outward migration, its numbers have dwindled to just 57,264 in 2011 compared to 114,890 in 1941 and 69,601 in 2001.[107]

Despite centuries of migration and shared habitations, be it villages or cities, the extent of inter-marriage amongst other groups too (from different castes, religions, ethnicities and regions) is still minimal. Even today, in the melting pot of large urban centres, such marriages continue to be rare, especially where the differences are perceived to be large (Hindu–Muslim or Dalit–Brahmin, for example). Thus, while many other barriers have crashed, inter-caste and inter-religious marriage yet remains largely unconquered.

In the years immediately after India's independence, it did appear that the country was progressing—albeit slowly—towards the idea of a casteless, secular society, with social and opportunity equality across all divides, and far greater

---

[107]'A Vanishing Race: Numbers Go against India's Parsis', *Hindustan Times*, 25 July 2016, https://www.hindustantimes.com/india-news/a-vanishing-race-numbers-go-against-india-s-parsis/story-H8hg26wO62A0DXODF9HsUN.html, accessed on 22 March 2021. Based on census data.

economic equity. However, slow economic growth, and the political attractiveness of a reservation/quota policy for jobs in government, gave rise to increasing demands for job reservation from various groups. A well-intended policy, aimed at providing opportunity and uplifting those long discriminated against—the scheduled castes and tribes—soon degenerated into political demands for reservations from various castes and groups. First, the 'other backwards classes', and then even traditionally dominant and powerful groups (for example, the Marathas in Maharashtra and the Patidars in Gujarat) agitated for quotas. Political parties have capitalized on this, and many now thrive on the support of specific caste groups. Inevitably, there are also parties who have built their success around support based on religion. What seemed like a slow but inexorable progression towards a secular and casteless society has been reversed. The ideal of a society that does not discriminate between different groups and one that assures social justice for all seems to have fallen by the wayside.

A SOCIETY IN FERMENT

The last two or three decades have seen an upsurge in identity-based politics, drawing from and fuelling a 'victim mentality' amongst different groups. Leaders and various organizations—especially political parties—have succeeded in making all groups feel discriminated against. The extreme case in point is the success of the BJP and its associated organizations in making many Hindus feel aggrieved. Typically, it is small groups ('minorities') who feel threatened or disadvantaged. Here, exceptionally, is a religious-identity defined group, comprising as much as four-fifths of the population, which buys into the narrative of being a victim! The party has succeeded in consolidating various other identities (caste, region, language) into a mega-'Hindu' identity, on the basis of creating a religion-based 'other' (the Muslim, mainly), against which Hindus need to unite.

An example of trying to build opinion against Muslims is the propaganda about 'love jihad': the claim that Muslim youth are seducing Hindu girls into marriage and converting them to Islam. This has led to vigilante groups seeking to stop any friendships across the religious divide, sometimes resorting to threats and even violence. In November 2020, UP promulgated an ordinance (Uttar Pradesh Prohibition of Unlawful Conversion of Religion) clearly aimed at deterring inter-religious marriages. Following the ordinance, in less than three months, 90 people (not surprisingly, mostly Muslims) have been booked. Many feel that this law negates rights granted in the Constitution, and directly interferes with the freedom of an adult to choose his/her partner. The controversial ordinance has not yet been sent to the Centre for examination (as is necessary for any Bills that are repugnant to central laws). Earlier, in 2008, Rajasthan (then under a BJP government) passed a similar legislation (Rajasthan Dharma Swatantraya Bill, 2008), and this is still pending with the Centre.[108] Other BJP-governed states (including Madhya Pradesh, Gujarat and Karnataka) are on the path to emulate these laws. What a change from the early years after Independence when inter-religious marriages (as also inter-caste ones) were encouraged!

Arguably then, the divisions within society have got deeper and worsened, rather than decreasing. While earlier,

---

[108]'Union Home Ministry yet to Receive U.P. Ordinance on Conversions', *The Hindu*, 30 January 2021, https://www.thehindu.com/news/national/mha-yet-to-receive-examine-up-ordinance-on-conversions/article33704410.ece, accessed on 22 March 2021

identity assertions (caste, in particular, but also region) were mainly related to jobs, and thus to economics, the latest—religious—manifestation is linked to socio-cultural factors. Thus, the focus is on the religion's customs (divorce, through talaq), food (beef eating) and dress (the cap, or a burka) as differentiators that mark religious identity and are seen as unacceptable. One can conclude that, as elsewhere, here too emotion trumps rationality. The former is aroused through socio-cultural or religious practices that are seen as not just different but negative, sometimes even in direct opposition to religious beliefs (for example, beef eating and the sacred cow). Rationality would, on the other hand, have concentrated on livelihoods and jobs: factors which, one might assume, would be predominant.

A possible interpretation is that job reservation through (non-religious) identities has run its course, with little scope for more. Yet, in the last few years, the job market has become difficult and one would, therefore, have thought that the competition for employment would outweigh all other factors. Possibly, some of the regional identity assertions (in Assam, for example) could be linked to fear of 'outsiders' usurping jobs that should go to locals. However, given that these 'outsiders' are identified (rightly or wrongly) mainly as unskilled Bangladeshis, why would educated locals see them as job competitors? Clearly, in this case, it is not jobs, but fear of socio-cultural domination or contamination that is seen as a threat. Political parties have leveraged and amplified this, either through assertion of local identity (for example, Assamese) or by cleverly identifying the outsider by religion and then converting this into a 'nationalist' issue (Bangladeshi being equal to Muslim).

Some of these socio-cultural concerns are not new (the

Assamese/Bengali issue, for one, goes back many decades). They have sometimes become strong, with an assertion of identity that seeks recognition and separateness. When a religious overtone takes over, they can become extreme (Punjab/Khalistan in the 1980s being a case in point). Even without the religious overtones, cultural and regional identities are asserted strongly, particularly when they feel threatened. Many of the separatist movements in the Northeast provide evidence of this. Small groups like the Bodos and Gorkhas, as much as larger ones like the Assamese, have at various times and with varying intensity exhibited this concern about retaining their identity. Half a century ago, attempts to impose Hindi across the country—or the perception of such an intent—triggered riots in Tamil Nadu. What followed was a strong assertion of regional-linguistic-cultural identity, verging on a near-secessionist agenda. One fallout was the rise of political parties that were based on Tamil identity. Even now, decades later, these regional parties dominate the political scenario in the state.

The manifestation of socio-cultural identity is visible across the country in the political arena. State after state has seen the rise of so-called regional parties. Some, like the Shiv Sena in Maharashtra, and some parties in the Northeast, had their genesis in an aggressive anti-outsider stance; others, like the Biju Janata Dal (BJD) in Odisha, have been born out of other concerns. As noted earlier, politics is capitalizing on the rise of socio-cultural identity, even as parties further stoke and amplify it.

For long, the generally accepted view or conventional wisdom has been that of a steady 'progressive' movement of society as a whole. This assumes a march towards a future in which all are treated equally, with no discrimination—one where there are no group biases or stereotyping. Individual interests would bring people together rather than the blind binding defined by birth: religion, caste, ethnicity or region. Instead, are we seeing a regression? Are group identities—that too, those defined by birth rather than choice—predominating over individual identities? In India, the experience of the last few decades would indicate affirmative answers. The hope that changing circumstances would lead to new viewpoints has been belied.

Research in the US (the General Social Survey, conducted every year or two since 1972 by the University of Chicago), which asks Americans their views on a wide range of topics, concludes that public opinion has grown more liberal. However, the analysis shows that this is mostly the result of generational replacement, not of changes of heart. Thus, evolving public opinion is due to younger people being more liberal and not because older people have modified their viewpoint.[109]

Conclusions from such research are obviously bound to be culture specific. Therefore, it will not be right to assume that a similar process (as in the US) is happening in India. If anything, one can argue that younger people seem to subscribe to the same biases as their elders. An indication of this is provided by the age composition in identity-based riots: it is the young who are most often at the forefront. Of course, in a country as large as India, a violent riot led by even a few thousand may represent but a minuscule proportion of the area's population; therefore, to link this to overall societal values may not be correct. Yet, despite this-but-that caveats, there is a strong case for arguing that society is at a status

---

[109]From 'Talkin' 'bout My Generation', *The Economist*, 2 November 2019, https://www.economist.com/graphic-detail/2019/10/31/societies-change-their-minds-faster-than-people-do, accessed 22 March 2021.

quo (may be even in regression) with regard to segmentation on the basis of birth identity.

The hope for any substantial change in this lies in two factors: rapid urbanization and fast economic growth. Migrants do not automatically shed their biases just because they become city dwellers. However, the hope has been that the anonymity of city life, combined with workplaces that inevitably comprise individuals with diverse backgrounds, would automatically reduce prejudice. The US study quoted earlier counters hopes of such a change of heart on a large enough scale (though the conclusions may not be equally true in India). Also, the creation of ghettos—identity-based housing clusters—minimizes non-work interaction with the 'other'. Such 'ghettoization' is, to some extent, inevitable. Migrants come at the behest of relatives or friends—almost always those who share one or more common birth identity—and stay with or near them. Even those rare individuals who migrate into a city with no known contact, look for housing near people with whom they have a bond of region, language or culture. Thus, the slums and ramshackle settlements in the city are often divided into sections clearly differentiated by the overlapping identities of caste, region, religion and language.

Ghettos of new migrants are not desirable. Governments and local bodies can help to reduce segregation between different groups and improve the quality of life for new migrants by providing ready, low-rent housing for them. This would avoid their having no choice but to stay in overcrowded and often illegal slums, with inadequate water, sanitation and electricity. Since any such housing complex would accommodate new migrants, irrespective of their origin, they will have residents from various regions and different backgrounds. This could lead to a better understanding of each other, and ultimately to a more harmonious society.

Despite the present ghettoization, there is little doubt that the worldview of an individual changes after migration to a city. Work and other daily non-work interactions expose a city dweller to a wide range of individuals with diverse backgrounds. Greater exposure to media—especially television and social media—adds a new (pan-India and, sometimes, global) dimension to the exposure that is experienced by new migrants. Together, these factors may well begin to reduce prejudice, eliminate stereotyping and change perceptions.

At the same time, some of the new windows to the world (especially through the now ubiquitous mobile phone screen) have their drawbacks too. They showcase products and lifestyles beyond the affordability of the poor or even the middle class, yet, clever marketing creates a strong desire for them. Such aspirations and the promotion of greed make for a potent combination, causing at least a few to do anything— even steal—to fulfil their new wants.

Faster economic growth could be the other driver towards a more progressive-liberal society. The expansion of employment opportunities will reduce (though not eliminate) the competition for jobs and decrease the pressure for identity-based quotas for caste or region. It could lead to a more benign view of 'others'. Also, economic growth spurs geographic mobility, as new opportunities for work and livelihood open up across the country. This will result in greater intermixing of people from different regions (and other birth identities), in work and non-work contexts, helping to nullify traditional stereotypes.

In the 2020s, rapidly increasing urbanization is a certainty, driven by both push and pull factors. The push will come from the already excessive farm 'employment' (much of which is really disguised underemployment), which will get worse with growing population and greater farm mechanization. While some of the excess farm labour will be absorbed by non-farm rural employment—food processing, micro/small enterprises, and service jobs—there will yet be a problem of surplus labour. Many of them will migrate to urban areas in search of livelihood.

The pull factor will be the growing opportunities for jobs and self-employment in cities. By all accounts, the 2020s will see faster economic growth, considerably increasing such opportunities. Despite technology-facilitated decentralization, cities will continue to be economic hubs, and will offer vast scope of livelihoods, thereby yet acting as magnets for migrants. This, and the push factor, will mean a large inflow of people into cities.

Apart from urbanization, migrants affect the social fabric in various other ways too. One is that cities become more cosmopolitan as people from different parts of the country settle there. These new residents come not only from villages in different parts of the country, but also from other cities and—a small but growing number—from other countries. While Indian cities are yet far from the extent of global heterogeneity of London or New York, they are increasingly reflecting the vast diversity of India. The overall socio-cultural impact of this is considerable. Such impact is not limited to the city or its residents. As people travel back to their original or ancestral home (village or city), they carry back ideas and experiences from their life in the city, influencing friends and relatives who have stayed behind. This makes for a multiplier effect with each returning migrant impacting dozens of others.

A second impact results from the fact that many migrants—predominantly male[110]—come without their families. These single people, without the restraints of a family, are likely to be less 'responsible', giving in more easily to various temptations. Economic pressures, hard work, frustrations and loneliness often drive people to stress relievers like alcohol and drugs. The need for money to buy these and the lure of easy money then tempts some into crime. Huge economic inequity and the flaunting of wealth by the rich, as also the cheek-by-jowl existence of the poorest slums next to great prosperity (Mumbai being an example), add to the temptation. Violence is another outcome of the potent mix mentioned above, and frustration often results in women being the target. Further, the fact that many migrants come from strongly patriarchal, inhibited and repressed backgrounds predisposes them towards crimes against women.

With more migrants and no immediate sign of a reduction in economic inequality, the conclusion must be that crime is likely to increase. Economic, psycho-sociological and cultural actions are essential if crime is not to get out of hand. Depending only on more strong-arm policing, tougher laws and better enforcement may not suffice. Policies aimed at reducing income inequality are essential, but their implementation is difficult and impact takes time. Measures that lessen exclusion and help to integrate new migrants into the community would be easier to implement and have a quicker impact.

---

[110] Though this view (of migrants being mostly male) is anecdotal and broadly held, hard data from census figures and National Sample Survey Office (NSSO) seems to contradict this. According to Census 2011, of the 78 million rural-to-urban migrants, 55 per cent were female. However, this does not detract from what follows, which has more to do with absolute numbers rather than the proportion of males.

More playing fields and team sports are possible initiatives for creation of a community and for inclusion of newcomers. Parks and gardens—though sometimes misused—are known stress-reducers. All these can help to not only reduce crime, but to have a positive impact on migrants, improving the quality of life, health and productivity.

The reality is that the 2020s pose serious risks of increased crime. Growing materialism, aspirations, inequalities and greed will be the drivers. It is essential to strengthen societal values of honesty, respect for others, gender equality and non-violence. This is a long-term project, which must start at an early age—both in school and at home—but it is necessary to begin now.

WHEN GEOGRAPHY IS HISTORY

Such public policy initiatives need to be emphasized and pursued. In the absence of these, and concerns about the crime and safety scenario getting worse, ever more communities are 'islanding' themselves. What began as common facilities for stand-by power (diesel generators) and water (tube wells), have now expanded to an array of services, particularly security. Many of these so-called gated communities have become increasingly self-sufficient, with little need to step outside for anything. They are best exemplified by the rapidly proliferating condominium complexes in Gurugram, a Delhi suburb. Lush green lawns, walking tracks, gymnasium, grocery store, vegetable shop, beauty salon, café, swimming pool, medical clinic, laundry, 24x7 support services for maintenance, clubhouse, adequate car parking, library and, of course, tight security: name it and they have it. The residents live in this bubble or island, quite cut-off from the poverty, grime and crime in the outside world. Beginning many years ago, this 'secession of the successful' has now gone a step further, courtesy technology.[111] Many residents now no longer have to negotiate the traffic outside, thanks to the ease with which high-bandwidth, electronics-enabled connectivity enables them to work from home. Video conferencing does away with the need for physical presence in meetings (and the consequent travel) just as home theatre systems—along with CDs, hard drives and video streaming—obviate the necessity of going to a cinema theatre. The widespread use of these technologies during the COVID lockdown has further reinforced the possibility and ease of living within a nearly self-sufficient bubble.

The convenience of the self-sufficient complexes is obvious, especially in the face of failure of the public services in delivering such essentials as safety, security, water and power. Given their understandable appeal, it is a foregone conclusion that such gated communities—each delivering as many services as are viable and feasible—will proliferate in the years to come. It seems, then, that we will have an even more divided city, both literally and figuratively.

Urban centres represent a melting pot into which go people with diverse backgrounds and identities, and the outcome is a 'Mumbaikar' or 'Kolkattan' or an 'Ahmedabadi'. However, it seems the melting pot might exclude the high-income segment. Their identity may not be linked to the city in which they live. Rather, their primary subidentity may be related to class or income and the 'geographical' identity defined not as living in Delhi or Bengaluru, but in cyberspace. For them, 'geography is

---

[111]See, for example, 'I, Me and Myself: Apathy of the Affluent', *The Times of India*, 18 July 2003, https://timesofindia.indiatimes.com/edit-page/LEADER-ARTICLEBRI-Me-and-Myself-Apathy-of-the-Affluent/articleshow/80922.cms, accessed on 22 March 2021.

history', and their 'neighbours' and community are defined by interest groups or work colleagues, who might well be living thousands of kilometres apart in the physical world, but next door—only microseconds away—in the e-world.

In these 'island' complexes, many do not know even their immediate neighbours. They live in a cocoon, the boundary of which is defined by the front door of their apartment. Their link with the outside world is through communication networks, rather than via roads or pathways. Can such electronic or virtual connections substitute the face-to-face interaction with friends, colleagues and neighbours? Unlike (physical) closed doors, the e-door is always open, with many people instantly responding—practically 24x7—to communication on their phones or computers.

Is such access an intrusion of privacy? While, in theory, one has the option of switching off devices or not responding immediately, in practice, there are factors that force people to not do so. One is a work-related expectation of being 'always on'. There is growing recognition that this is stressful and not conducive to a healthy work/life balance. As a result, some companies have specified 'no-communication hours', when you are not expected to respond. The second reason for the always-on mode is possible emergencies, which means that one has to look at every communication and answer every call. The third is peer pressure—the expectation of friends and work colleagues that you will be available all the time, and receive calls or respond to communication irrespective of the time of day. Finally, there is the FOMO factor: the 'fear of missing out', which pressurizes people to look instantaneously at any incoming communication. Young people, who are more active users of social media, are particularly prone to such screen fixation.

As the screen becomes one's closest companion, and much of human interaction is virtual rather than physical, what does it do to us? Psychologists say that such isolation leads to loneliness and depression. Excessive drinking and drugs are likely consequences, as is an increase in suicides. Are these the signs of an evolving society?

What are the other social consequences of these new ghettos, based on income rather than identity? Isolation, and the resulting lack of engagement with the larger community, is surely bringing about a new social dynamic. There seem to be ways of reducing segmentation, ghettos and exclusion, at the lower end of the economic pyramid. However, at the upper end of the pyramid, it is not very clear as to what policies or specific actions might bring about greater integration.

It is time to look at ways of increasing the interactions amongst different groups (and also individuals), bringing together people in ways that override the segregated sub-identities. Music, art and sport are possible ways. In all these, interest and achievement are generally not related to income, caste, region or religion. Equally importantly, identity hierarchies like caste or class, do not define the pecking order. Concerned organizations—especially civil society and government/municipal bodies—could initiate action to organize substantial activities in these areas, and draw in all segments of the population.

A NEW SOCIAL DYNAMIC

As noted in the discussion on demography (Chapter 6), a major change—which we will begin to see more visibly in the 2020s—is the growing proportion of elders (65-plus years). At the same time, the youth population (15–24 years) will grow. Based on experience, it would be fair to assume that the aged would, by and large, be cautious, conservative, cynical and resistant to change. The young, on the other hand, are expected to be rebellious, radical and idealistic. With growing numbers of both, elderly and youth, how will these very divergent mindsets affect societal values? What will be the dynamics and which school of thought would command power? Since this is not going to be a sudden transition, the process of defining—or re-defining—societal norms is likely to be evolutionary, with any change being gradual. At the same time, we have occasionally seen sudden change, with a strange mix of young and old.

Going back to the 1970s, the 'JP movement' was triggered by an elderly, greatly respected but hardly-in-the-limelight Jayaprakash Narayan. The movement, though, was driven by the youth: it was students and the young who were at the forefront of demonstrations and agitations. Of course, the political overtones became strong as the movement gathered momentum. Prime Minister Indira Gandhi clamped an Emergency in 1975, but the undercurrent of the JP movement continued gaining strength and catalysed the formation of a unified opposition party (Janata party), which swept the polls when Mrs Gandhi called an election in early 1977. The young and old worked to a common purpose; the outcome was, though, political rather than social.

A strangely similar parallel was seen in 2011. A practically unknown moral crusader, Anna Hazare, frail and elderly, initiated a campaign against corruption. Known in Maharashtra (and only to a handful country-wide) for his work in Ralegan Siddhi village, few had heard of him in Delhi. Yet, when he began his fast there in protest against corruption, and demanding a Jan Lok Pal (a people's ombudsman, to counter corruption), there was a sudden upsurge of support. Surprisingly, the massive crowds which began to gather at the site of his fast were predominantly young. A generation thought to be driven only by materialism suddenly seemed overtaken by idealism. Of course, the campaign soon took on a political colour and, as in the 1970s, the incumbent government was overthrown, suffering an ignominious defeat in the 2014 national election. Once again, the outcome of a seemingly social movement was political, reinforcing the déjà vu of young and old coming together in an idealistic movement, aimed at altering social values, but culminating only in political change.

A slower social challenge has seen young and old cast in more conventional roles. This change is the emerging agency of young women. Be it how girls dress, the freedom to go out, the choice of friends, or even the use of a mobile phone: in many places, especially in north India, deep-rooted patriarchy frowns on such 'freedom'. Yet, over the last decade or so, girls and young women have fought a continuous, though almost subterranean, battle and are clearly winning. More of them are now breaking the shackles, sometimes—yet rarely and, sadly, at high cost—even of caste. This battle has pitted the young against elders, and also men against women. Not surprisingly, the old and the men favour conservative and entrenched social norms. Despite their power, it seems that they are steadily but surely losing to determined young women.

Women's power has been on display in a different context too. Protests against the CAA and the proposed NRC have women at the forefront. Thousands of them, on protest in Shaheen Bagh in Delhi (for over three months, from December 2019, before riots and the COVID epidemic ended the sit-in), captured not just the global headlines, but the imagination of women around the country. The result was a number of similar protests in many cities across India, with determined women taking turns to make it a 24x7 affair. This, along with the change being wrought by girls and young women (noted earlier), may well mark the beginning of true empowerment of women—by women, themselves—heralding a major social change.

Elsewhere, one broad indicator of greater gender equality has been the proportion of women in the workforce. This shows how far behind India is: amongst 10 major economies, India's LFPR for women is the lowest at 24.8 per cent, compared with 61.5 per cent in China, 60.5 per cent in Singapore and 53.2 per cent in Brazil. This put it at rank 145 of 153 countries, in 2019.[112] On the other hand, India's LFPR for men is 78.8 per cent, higher than China, Singapore, the US and European countries. This means that India has the widest gender gap between the LFPR for men and women. Little wonder, then, that in the World Economic Forum's Global Gender Gap Index 2020, India ranks 112 among 153 countries.[113] In the years ahead, this has to change, and indications are that it is happening. In the process, one can predict much social ferment and tension, as centuries-old patriarchy begins to break down.

Technology, too, is triggering social change. Much of the credit for this should go to the mobile phone, for it is the device that provides access to content and communication that

---

[112]'Global Gender Gap Report 2020', *World Economic Forum*, http://www3.weforum.org/docs/WEF_GGGR_2020.pdf, accessed on 22 March 2021.

[113]From 'Gender Justice Is Key to Accomplish a Country's Goals', *LiveMint*, 17 August 2020, https://www.livemint.com/news/india/gender-justice-is-key-to-accomplish-a-country-s-goals-11597681459180.html, accessed on 22 March 2021. Based on data from International Labour Organization and World Economic Forum.

catalyses change. A great deal of this content is user generated, made easily available to all via apps on the mobile. The ease of forming groups and sharing content within them has given a huge boost to sharing of thoughts, data and videos. It is arguable as to whether the result is a widening of horizons leading to a better understanding of other cultures, or it merely serves as an echo chamber that further strengthens existing prejudices and stereotypes. It does seem that shared interest groups on WhatsApp or Instagram end up being mainly amplifiers and reinforcers of already held views. Facebook, Twitter and other social media platforms do the same. 'Fake news' has become rampant, and combined with rumours—spreading virally, thanks to social media apps on mobile phones—has sometimes even triggered riots.

The reinforcement of prejudice through the echo chamber effect adds to the segmentation of society. Religion, class and caste divisions get further exacerbated. Age may well be another axis along which division takes place. Technology, once thought of as a unifier, a tool for inclusion, democratization and harmony, is apparently playing a role that is quite the opposite. There are, though, positive aspects, too, to technology. The mobile phone is a unique and extraordinary device for access. Its widespread availability has made it a key player in a number of positive developments. It has reduced many information asymmetries, creating a level playing field between, for example, the buyer and seller. It has led to disintermediation, eliminating middlemen or minimizing their role, thus giving more power (and money) to small sellers or buyers. The Internet, accessed in most cases in India through the mobile, enables producers and creators in far-flung areas to reach buyers located anywhere. The socio-economic impact of these developments—even if slow in manifestation—is, indeed, profound.

Yet another interesting facet of technology is its impact on the young, who seem to take to it as fish to water. WhatsApp, Instagram, Facebook, Twitter and the like are tools they cannot live without. Games on the mobile are hugely popular: one called PlayerUnknown's Battlegrounds, more popular as PUBG, is reported to have had 175 million installations in India (this has been banned by the government in September 2020 for security reasons, along with other apps from China). Taking selfies and posting them for viewing by others has become an obsession for many, resulting, sometimes, in sad accidents as people try to take unique photographs in dangerous situations or locations. Easy to download, free, and easy-to-use applications like TikTok (the Twitter of video, one might say, which allows uploading of 15 seconds of video; this app was banned in India by the government in July 2020—even before PUBG—due to concerns about data privacy) are tremendously popular, both for viewing videos of others and uploading those of oneself (generally, dances and/or singing).[114] While these mobile-based apps are probably making the young more narcissistic (just watch them preening and posing, even in public spaces, as they take selfies), they are also a unifying factor, overcoming other divisions. They put the young on common platforms, unlike physical reality that is yet dominated by divisions based on identity and class. Social media stars do not count on caste or religion for popularity.

---

[114] In about a year from January 2019, TikTok was installed in 104 million mobile phones, making it the most downloaded non-gaming app worldwide. A third of the downloads were in India; see 'TikTok Is The Most Downloaded App Worldwide, and India Is Leading the Charge', Rebecca Bellan, *Forbes*, 14 February 2020, https://www.forbes.com/sites/rebeccabellan/2020/02/14/tiktok-is-the-most-downloaded-app-worldwide-and-india-is-leading-the-charge/#1898f9257266, accessed on 22 March 2021.

Technology is, therefore, in many ways a leveller, a counter to a growing tendency towards segmentation by identity.

These developments provide hope because the pace of change seems to be accelerating. Yet, there are some areas where we see only cosmetic change. One of these is feudalism. Used to emperors, kings and maharajas (occasionally queens or maharanis) for centuries, it seems difficult to alter the mindset, even after freedom and democracy. The rulers of old have been replaced in the minds of many by the leaders of today. There is willing acceptance of beacon-flashing cars, of roads being closed to let a leader pass unhindered, of inferiority and dependence. The new 'ruler' could be anyone from the prime minister to the panchayat chief, as also the police or bureaucratic head. One local example tells the story well, because it comes not from one of India's poor, backward and dependent villages, but from the glitzy full-of-educated-professionals 'millennium city', Gurugram. A newspaper reported that: 'A stretch of Cyber City...of some 2 km was cordoned off for the visit of Haryana's director general of police...who was scheduled to appear at a literature festival...heavy police deployment around the venue restricted movement of vehicles and forced people to walk long distances.'[115] This is, of course, quite commonplace and, apparently, acceptable. Such a feudalistic mindset is changing, but yet very widely prevalent. It certainly contributes to creating and sustaining an unequal society, and adds a new form of segmentation: one between the powerful and the powerless.

The 2020s, it seems, are likely to see further segmentation of society along the major birth-identity dividers (caste,

---

[115]'DGP Visits, Cyber City Sees an Evening of Snarls as Cops Cordon Off Road', *The Times of India*, 17 November 2019.

gender, religion, region, ethnicity), with class overlaid. At the same time, there are also indications of a consolidation based on one strong identity that cuts across other divides. For example, some political parties are trying to promote 'Hindu' as a consolidating identity, while others are trying to promote 'Muslim'. One day a party may come up espousing 'women' as an identity that overrides all others.

At the micro level, it does seem that the family will continue as the basic building block of any community. Interesting dynamics will be at play, though. The last few decades have seen what seemed like a slow demise of the 'joint family', comprising multi-generational households. Small living quarters and high costs meant that most migrants live alone initially, while their families continue to live in a joint family in the village. However, as their economic prospects improve, the wife and young children often join them, especially if they could find a part-time job for the wife. As a result, the village home lost its inter-generational character, and the migrant family became a 'nuclear household'. Without in-laws or household elders, and staying in a city with but a few known neighbours, meant less social support, but also more freedom, especially for women. If she went out to work, it meant not only more social space, but also a degree of economic freedom. All this has changed the family dynamic and provided a further impetus to the empowerment of women.

While such freedom is a result of breaking away from elders and living in a city, for a certain segment with higher earnings, one sees a rather different trend. Here, with the growing number of couples who both take up full-time jobs, the care of children becomes a concern. Many couples resolve this by having parents of one or the other stay with them, thus reverting, in effect, to a joint family. In many urban households, such baby-sitting grandparents are now common. This acts as a social security system and gives retired elders a new and satisfying way of spending their time. It also builds better social cohesion, since these elders—having more time on their hands than those with jobs—tend to have greater interaction with neighbours, helping thereby to create a community. Though differing values and lifestyles may well create a degree of tension within households, this near-joint-family model fosters more equal relationships. This is because of the big change from the traditional system, with parents now living with the children, in the latter's home and not vice versa. As people live longer, such a model may be appropriate for the future as it provides home care for the elders, meeting both their physical and emotional or psychological needs.

In summary, society and social dynamics through the decade of the 2020s are likely to be marked by:

i. A part of society that continues to be divided by caste, with this becoming an identity that people try to benefit from (individuals, by seeking caste-based reservations/quotas for jobs and admissions to educational institutions; political parties, by building caste-based vote blocks). At the same time, there is continuing caste-based oppression, bias and even violent atrocities.

ii. Political parties that seek to build larger vote banks by emphasizing religious affiliation that cuts across caste, and demonizing the 'other' (people professing a different religion). While this is currently seeing a lot of traction, it may well peter out over the decade and attract only a small percentage of people. If it does not, there will be increasing numbers of people who feel alienated, discriminated-against and unequal. This is a social time bomb—dry fodder that can be easily ignited by a small spark.

iii. Increasing crime, fuelled by growing economic inequality, ostentatious displays of wealth and rapidly increasing aspirations. The last will be driven by greed-inducing marketing and communication, easily accessible to all through TV or the mobile phone screen. Drug and alcohol addiction—often brought about by difficult work and living conditions, combined with lack of familial restraints amongst single migrants—compel a search for easy money, leading to crime.

iv. Division based on class, which seems poised to increase over time. Its manifestation in urban areas will be the growing number of 'gated' communities, each of which will be more and more self-sufficient, complemented by continuing growth of region, religion and caste-based 'ghettos' or slums.

v. Gender conflict, especially in rural areas and particularly between older males and younger females. This would be the result of a slow but steady evolution—cumulatively making it a revolution—in the confidence, self-esteem and independence of girls and young women. The resulting threat to traditional patriarchy is a near-guarantee for conflict, within the family as well as at community level. A corollary will be the empowerment of women, in general, and their self-assertion.

vi. A greater equality amongst the young, countering to some extent the class and other divides mentioned above. This will be the result of platforms that enable sharing, and also of fighting for common causes (youth coming together was seen in a powerful way in Delhi, following the horrific Nirbhaya rape-murder in 2012; there have subsequently been other—though less 'unanimous'—cases).

Most of the above (certainly i to iv) are divisive, exclusionary and negative. There is hope of minimizing their impact, but this calls for discussion and debate on where we might be in 2030 relative to where we want to be. We are a society in ferment, with pulls and pressures on different groups. Change is being accelerated—even driven—by technology. It is necessary to ensure that the consequent churn does not result in violence between various groups and that differences are settled amicably, avoiding unnecessary conflict. A roadmap from 2020 to a more ideal 2030 must be formulated, so as to create a more inclusive, compassionate, caring and harmonious society through appropriate policies and actions. If these are initiated now, they might make a difference in the course of the decade and the country can, in 2030, be in a far better place.

8

JOBS AND LIVELIHOODS

Will a Machine Steal Your Job?

In any country, jobs and livelihoods are crucial factors that determine well-being. Unemployment rates, where reliable, are tracked as carefully as GDP growth or stock market indices. In India, with a working-age (15–64 years) population of 916 million (2019),[116] this is both a huge challenge and a massive opportunity. The challenge lies in providing gainful jobs and/or livelihoods to such a large number, and one that will grow by an average of about 13 million every year over this decade.[117] It is also an opportunity: if productively employed, they can provide a huge boost to the economy, realizing the possibility of the 'demographic dividend' (see Chapters 5 and 6). As outlined earlier, other countries have established the benefits of the demographic dividend, with China and nations in East/Southeast Asia clocking up impressive rates of economic growth. However, that was in years gone by; today, is it yet possible to gain the same leverage from a large working age population?

---

[116]'Population Ages 15–64', *The World Bank*, https://data.worldbank.org/indicator/SP.POP.1564.TO.ZS, accessed on 22 March 2021.

[117]Calculated from 'Data Query', *World Population Prospects 2019*, https://population.un.org/wpp/DataQuery/, accessed on 22 March 2021.

In addressing this issue, it is necessary to note two facts. First, in all these countries, their education system ensured a far higher proportion of secondary-level students than in India, and with a higher quality of education (that is, a larger as well as better and more educated workforce). Second, manufacturing industries grew rapidly at the time, and were able to absorb and utilize new job entrants in very large numbers. China, for example, was able to provide employment through mass-manufacture of labour-intensive, low-value goods, in which its low wage cost (and high labour productivity) enabled it to capture global markets. It began to quickly expand its manufacturing base, both in breadth and depth, enabling it to move to higher-value goods, leveraging the scale and efficiency of production as much as its low wages. This ensured that it was able to continue providing jobs to its people even as some low-end manufacturing began to move to neighbouring low-cost countries. While it did not altogether relinquish its base of low-value manufacturing, it steadily moved up the value chain in many industries. Thus, instead of mere components and subsystems, it began to make the finished product and also market it, establishing its own brands. This enabled it to not only capture a larger part of the value-add, but also to provide more and higher-paid jobs.

Now, we are witnessing rapid automation of many a task. With technological advances, more functions are amenable to automation, and lower costs are making it economically viable to do so. While automation has some drawbacks, in routine tasks it can be more efficient and reliable than a human. Therefore, as labour costs go up—an inevitability, with economic growth and greater social support costs—and the cost of automation declines, the crossover point is being reached in an increasing number of situations.

'Industry 4.0' will use automation, robotics and AI in all aspects, including manufacturing.[118] The Internet of Things (IoT), in which billions of physical devices collect and relay data using sensors with transmitters, will provide real-time information on every possible parameter. This data will not only be collected, collated and analysed, but will be used for modelling, with machine learning helping to create ever more accurate models as more data is analysed, to predict parts or machine failure. Little or no human intervention will be required after the initial algorithm (model) is created.

Robots that work tirelessly on repetitive jobs 24x7 and never make a mistake will certainly be more efficient than humans. As costs come down, they may also be cheaper. Artificial intelligence will make them more versatile and capable of executing more complex tasks. They will instantly assimilate data from IoT devices and act on it. Given these advantages, not only the manufacturing factory of the future, but also many offices will be 'manned' by robots—or, more likely, a combination of humans and robots. Such projections are giving rise to global concern about whether machines (automation, in general) will replace humans, and whether there will at all be jobs for humans in future. Already, even in India, some manufacturing enterprises use robots. Automobile companies, for example, have robots on the shop floor in the car assembly line, replacing humans. Painting and welding are other functions where robots have replaced humans. In the services sector, automation and AI have been used far

---

[118] Apparently first used in Germany in 2011, the term Industry 4.0 was popularized by Klaus Schwab through article 'The Fourth Industrial Revolution', *Foreign Affairs*, 12 December 2015 https://www.foreignaffairs.com/articles/2015-12-12/fourth-industrial-revolution, accessed on 22 March 2021.

more extensively. This has even extended to deploying robots in restaurants as waiters—obviously, a welcome innovation in the times of COVID. These developments reinforce worries about automation taking away jobs.

In the developed countries, where automation is taking root much faster, there is serious concern. This has been one of the drivers to seriously consider schemes like a universal basic income (UBI), so that both livelihoods and demand for products are sustained. With leisure and assured income, people may indulge in travel, creative pursuits or hobbies. However, being on a permanent vacation may not be everyone's idea of heaven. Without work—its challenges, human interaction, joys and frustrations—will there be emptiness in people's life, leading to depression? Even as art and poetry flourish, will idle minds and depression mean more suicides, drugs and crime? As technology produces more capable machines, debate swirls, with extreme scenarios being painted: apart from taking away jobs, will robots or AI rule the world and turn humans into slaves? Metaphysics and philosophy too enter the picture.

Without getting into the more arcane elements of the discussion at this stage, one can note that already industry is automating. The China model of mass employment in manufacturing is, therefore, not a path that India should—or can—follow. Today's world will require a different approach to the employment issue. India will have to innovate, and evolve various alternative policies and models. In doing so, it must keep in mind the unique features of India, leveraging what it can, rather than seeking to emulate other or past (and now obsolete) models.

One important characteristic of India and Indians is that we have difficulty with a centralized, command-and-control approach. This is, in part, related to our vast and many diversities—language, religion, ethnicity, culture, cuisine, region, income, and so many more. But it also comes from a philosophy of questioning. Neither the 'obey your elders' dictum in the home, nor the 'see and listen, but do not speak' rule of the traditional classroom has been able to altogether suppress this. Therefore, whether driving on the road or working in the factory/office, we ask: why this way and not that. Further, we are prone to not just question, but to do it our way (generally, the easier way). These practices are hardly conducive to any fixed, no-deviation, assembly-line operation. Therefore, with rare exceptions, large Indian factories are not as labour-productive as those in East Asia.

India's genius is in entrepreneurship, in small and varied enterprises. It is in doing things differently, in improvising (jugaad) and innovating. The ability to think out of the box, to innovate, has become a vital factor in today's world of ever newer technologies.[119] The inherent tendency of Indians to innovate was a disadvantage, in many ways, in an era of mass production. This required performing repetitive tasks, to be done in a fixed and pre-defined manner, without thinking. However, new technologies demand innovation, doing things differently, and so open up huge new opportunities for India. While the country has not been at the forefront of invention or of new technologies, it has special expertise in creating disruptive business models. This talent, plus its ability to innovate in the utilization of new technologies, will enable it to capitalize in a world where labour is being replaced by automation, and mass manufacturing is giving way to decentralized production. Economies of scale are now being

---

[119]This has been noted in a number of publications; for example, *Crooked Minds: Creating an Innovative Society*, Kiran Karnik, Rupa Publications, 2017.

realized through centralized design and dispersed production (nearer the market): a trend being accelerated by digitization and technologies like 3D printing (additive manufacturing), IoT, automation and robotics.

These new trends augur well for India. They not only do away with the disadvantage of a generally 'indisciplined' culture, but capitalize on India's innate innovativeness. Further, the possibility of decentralized production being as, or more, efficient than large concentrated facilities, will lead to job creation on a dispersed basis. This will reduce the pressure on India's large urban agglomerations, where infrastructure has not kept pace with rapid growth, resulting in inefficiencies and poor quality-of-life.

It will make sense for India's policies to encourage and ride on these new trends, rather than trying to imitate now-outmoded paradigms for growth. What is needed are steps to encourage dispersed and decentralized production, making full use of new technologies. While the last—especially automation—may reduce the labour requirement per unit of output, it will create more jobs through higher production, based on the global competitiveness of these products.

Decentralization and dispersal of manufacturing has received a further boost due to COVID. The need for physical distancing, including in offices and on manufacturing shop floors, has resulted in a 'penalty of proximity.' Large production facilities, bringing together hundreds or thousands of workers, are no longer desirable, with distancing requirements rendering them unviable. The answer, clearly, is smaller units dispersed widely.

EMBRACING A NEW NORMAL

Clearly, fresh thinking and a new strategy are required with regard to jobs. As has been seen over the last few years, economic growth is not translating into a sufficient number of jobs. Each year, about 13 million[120] enter the potential workforce. Another recent report (August 2020) estimates that India would need to provide employment to 90 million workers who are expected to enter the non-farm job market this decade.[121] Even with accelerated economic growth, will all of them be able to get jobs?

Some argue that the metric—number of jobs—is incorrect; what is needed is adequate livelihoods. Quality jobs—those in the organized sector, with a surety of employment, along with health cover and retirement benefits—are ideal. However, these will always be a small percentage, which too may decrease further as gigging becomes the preferred route for employers (and some individuals). The bulk of jobs are in the informal and unorganized sector: contract jobs, sometimes on a daily-wage basis, with lower wages and none of the benefits available to 'regular' employees in the organized sector. Based on the Periodic Labour Force Survey 2017–18, the share of employment in the unorganized sector was as high as 86.8 per cent.[122]

---

[120] Calculated from 'Data Query', *World Population Prospects* 2019, https://population.un.org/wpp/DataQuery/, accessed on 22 March 2021.

[121] 'India's Turning Point: An Economic Agenda to Spur Growth and Jobs', McKinsey Global Institute, 26 August 2020, https://www.mckinsey.com/featured-insights/india/indias-turning-point-an-economic-agenda-to-spur-growth-and-jobs#, accessed on 22 March 2021.

[122] 'Measuring Informal Economy in India _ Indian Experience', S V Ramana Murthy, Deputy Director General, National Accounts Division, Ministry of Statistics and Programme Implementation. Accessed through IMF website https://www.imf.org/external/index.htm

A large part of employment in India is temporary, short term or seasonal: for example, in the agricultural and construction sectors. Many workers in these two high-employment sectors—a substantial number in agriculture and the bulk of workers in construction—are migrant or nomadic labour. The skew in regional development has meant that the migrants are mostly from the central and eastern parts of India, while the work is in the south, west and north. Delhi NCR, Mumbai-Pune and Bengaluru are magnets for migrant workers, as is Punjab (seasonally, for agricultural operations). Gujarat imports workers for its textile units and diamond-processing industries (especially in Surat) from Odisha, at the other end of the country. Kerala attracts migrant workers from faraway Assam and, in the holiday season, the railways operate special trains from Kerala to Guwahati. Meanwhile, Kerala itself exports labour (to the Gulf countries)!

In many cases, it is the migrant labourer who, though poorly paid, sustains the livelihood of his (sometimes her) family back in the village by saving some of his/her meagre earning and remitting it home. Many people's livelihoods, therefore, depend on the migrant labourer. How much s/he earns determines food on the plate, education for the children, healthcare and overall quality of life for the family, which often comprises not only spouse and children, but also parents and siblings. This is the reason why s/he (sometimes with spouse and children) is willing to travel to strange places in faraway states for the sake of a job. If reasonable livelihood could be assured in or near his/her home village, far fewer would migrate.

The scale and plight of migrant labour was brought home forcefully and sadly in the distressing scenes following the sudden nationwide lockdown from 25 March 2020. Most of them, eking out a living in the larger cities on a daily-wage basis, suddenly found themselves with no work and so, no money. With no trains or buses to take them back to their home villages, many started walking, mindless of the distance of hundreds of kilometres, and also fuelled by rumours of buses being available from the state border.[123] Hundreds of families—with women carrying their scanty belongings on their head and, often, children in their arms—having little food and water, could be seen trekking out of cities. Stopped by the police at state borders, they just sat on the road, not knowing what to do. Later, authorities moved them to camps and, with the help of civil society organizations and other donors, they were provided with food. These millions of people have no job security and no social security of any kind, with each day's food depending on that day's earning. Their temporary home is generally a shared room in a slum. What job or livelihood opportunities can such people hope for in an evolving economy?

When the economy is booming, they are able to get work in construction, road building or as manual labour in factories. Many work as household help; some work in restaurants or offices, and as security guards. A few, who have the skills or training, get better paid jobs in the newer sectors—working as delivery agents for food and e-commerce companies, or as drivers in taxi aggregator companies. However, they too have no job guarantees or benefits. Unemployment, for whatever reason, can mean no shelter and no food, and a single serious

---

[123]Interestingly, a somewhat different perspective on the primary reason for the migration comes from eminent sociologist, Dipankar Gupta, in his article 'The Urban Migrant and the "Ritual" Tug of Home', *The Hindu*, 6 August 2020 https://www.thehindu.com/opinion/lead/the-urban-migrant-and-the-ritual-tug-of-home/article32279861.ece, accessed on 22 March 2021. He argues that 'What disturbs him [the migrant] profoundly at such times is the fear of dying alone with nobody to perform the rites for him.'

illness in the family can result in wiping out any meagre saving and getting into deep debt.

The challenge, then, is to create livelihood opportunities for not only the millions entering the workforce, but also for the surplus of agricultural workers. The latter surplus (often disguised as 'under-employed') will grow with mechanization. The farm economy itself could potentially provide work for many if more grading, sorting and processing of produce is done at the village or taluka/district level. In addition, new jobs will be created for operating and maintaining agricultural machinery. As technologies like IoT, drones and solar pumps begin to proliferate in the agricultural sector, they will need installation and maintenance. All these will be higher paid jobs, but will require skills and education of a level that are presently scarce in rural India. However, persons with secondary class education can be quite easily trained in a few months to handle much of the installation and first-level maintenance. Many of these tasks can be done by village entrepreneurs, and such self-employment may well be the way of the future. This opens the door for them to expand their service offerings into new areas and possibly provide employment to a few more people.

Companies selling equipment in rural areas may welcome such a model, and provide the necessary training to the village entrepreneur who would then be their 'authorized service agent.' Today, the village mechanic—capable of simple repairs to a two-wheeler, for example—is inevitably self-taught or learnt the basics by being an apprentice to an experienced repair person. This informal, often inadequate, learning could be supplemented by a structured and proven course delivered by the equipment-maker. To encourage entrepreneurship, such a course must also include the basics on handling finance, savings and investment. At some point, the entrepreneur may go beyond maintenance and begin to market products, so a smattering of sales and marketing in the course will help.

Agriculture, as the dominant sector in rural India, may offer considerable scope for new job functions, even as it sheds many jobs in more traditional work roles (sowing, nurturing, harvesting). However, digitization and emerging technologies will create a whole host of new opportunities in other sectors too in rural India. Amongst these, health and education will open many opportunities, as will the basic infrastructure of ICT.

All aspects of healthcare are being rapidly digitized: patient data and storage, diagnostic equipment, treatment, after-care, epidemiology, clinic and hospital management. Data analytics, machine learning and AI are being increasingly used for accurate diagnosis and also for deciding person-specific medication. Computers and software are also playing an important role in drug discovery, cutting down the time required for this as also for testing and proving new drugs.

In rural areas, even a simple innovation like reminders through SMS (for regular medication, for vaccinations, or for a periodic check-up) seem to have had a perceptible impact on improved health. Tablets (computers) given to Anganwadi and Accredited Social Health Activist (ASHA) workers have helped to improve mother and child healthcare, including that of pre-school children.

An example of digital technologies for healthcare is the work of the Tata group. A major transformation was brought about in AIIMS in Delhi just by putting in new systems and adding a few trained people so as to streamline patient movement. The average waiting time for patients became two hours instead of six, and 80 per cent of them came with appointments instead of just 20 per cent earlier. Building on this, Tata took up a project in Kolar district in Karnataka, again creating a new class of 'bridgital workers', who facilitated things and reduced the unnecessary administrative workload of doctors. This project set up a call centre, with doctors and nurses taking calls from patients, resulting in saving travel, time and money for all those in far-flung villages across the district.[124] Projects like these show how, with minimal incremental investment, one can bring about considerable improvement in health services. They leverage technology, but also create new jobs.

There is great scope for such jobs, which bridge the gap between new technologies and the lay-person user. Within healthcare itself, there are myriad functions where such 'bridging' roles are required and can take the benefits of technology across the last mile. As in the case of technology use and maintenance in agriculture, here too training will be necessary. If this can be done, millions of new livelihood opportunities will open up across the country, of which many will be in the rural areas, enabling local employment.

Healthcare is certainly going to be one of the boom sectors worldwide in years to come. In India, as healthcare expands—as it must—for all, and there are the added needs of a growing population of elders (see Chapter 6, on demography), the demand for healthcare professionals will multiply. In addition, there will be global demand too, given the rapidly aging populations in Europe and Japan. This will include doctors, specialists and para-medical staff. With many elders living on their own, there will also be need for home-care staff, with basic medical training. If we can create the necessary training and education infrastructure, India will be well placed to tap

---

[124]This description is drawn from *Bridgital Nation: Solving Technology's People Problem*, N. Chandrasekaran and Roopa Purushothaman, Penguin Allen Lane, 2019. The book also provides many other examples of new 'bridgital' jobs.

into this large source of jobs.

The availability of online education and training courses will open up new avenues for entrepreneurship. Creation of mini-'classrooms' with Internet-connected computers and projection facilities, and 'laboratories' or simulated workshops for hands-on training guided by a video course, are examples of such entrepreneurial opportunities at the village level. Conducting face-to-face tutorials, as part or extension of online courses, will provide a job opportunity to university (or even high school) graduates. As more of those who are highly educated or qualified begin to live in the villages, they may help to create other transformations that will give a boost to the rural economy and generate more jobs.

Content creation for online courses will be another source for jobs. Quite apart from courses for schools or colleges, there is a substantial appetite for courses of all kinds: on cooking, gardening, yoga, fitness, art, dance, music and a wide range of other areas. This opens up livelihood opportunities for people with various diverse interests and capabilities, including those who are not academically inclined and may have dropped out of school or college.

Many of these possibilities require structured training and may see fruition only within the framework of a conducive ecosystem, a task best undertaken by the government since it has to be at scale. Ongoing programmes that invest heavily in the rural areas (including the Pradhan Mantri Awas Yojana for housing, the rural roads programme, MGNREGA and Swachh Bharat) need basic skills like masonry, plumbing, electric wiring and carpentry. The demand for these could fuel entrepreneur-led local training at the block/taluka level, resulting in immediate jobs to the trainees. Some would move up to higher-paying opportunities through further training (electric wiring to repair of pumps, or simple carpentry to furniture-making, for example), organized at the district level. A similar approach could be adopted for healthcare, with basic training making people employable for simple jobs, and then providing deeper training for higher-level functions.

Will initiatives like these help to provide livelihoods for the millions who join the workforce each year? As evidenced from recent years, fast economic growth alone does not automatically generate the quantity of jobs that are needed. A combination of a new model of development and economic growth may possibly be the answer.

In this context, an important point of concern is the low LFPR of women, which is amongst the lowest in the world. Of greater concern is the fall in LFPR for women: from 31.8 per cent in 2005 to 20.5 per cent in 2019[125] (though another report puts this figure at 24.8 per cent,[126] both indicate a substantial drop). Explanations for this vary, from more women being in educational institutions (and, therefore, not considered as being available in the labour force) to greater prosperity (and, hence, no necessity for women to work—given many areas where women are allowed to take up jobs only out of economic need). Whatever the reason, the low LFPR for women is indicative of a serious gender issue. It also holds back the contribution of women to economic growth (especially as more of them are now better educated and skilled). From the point of view of jobs, as more women do enter the workforce, it means a greater need for new jobs.

---

[125]'Labor Force Participation Rate, Female (% of Female Population Ages 15+), *The World Bank*, https://data.worldbank.org/indicator/SL.TLF.CACT.FE.ZS, accessed on 22 March 2021.
[126]'Global Gender Gap Report 2020', *World Economic Forum*, http://www3.weforum.org/docs/WEF_GGGR_2020.pdf, accessed on 22 March 2021.

THE FUTURE OF WORK

The concerns about technology consuming jobs through automation have been discussed. Yet, as noted, tech also creates new jobs. One area is the growing number of livelihood opportunities in the 'platform' or online world. This is part of the 'gig' economy, and ranges from sophisticated work (often for foreign clients) in developing software, website designing, translation and editing, to food delivery. Estimates indicate that the number of food delivery agents in just one company (Zomato) in India is over 230,000[127] and the number of drivers in one taxi-app service (Ola) was estimated at 2.5 million in 2018.[128] China's more developed market has at least 5.7 million delivery personnel in its two main players (Meituan Dianping, backed by Tencent Holdings, and Ele.me, a part of the Alibaba Group).[129] In India, these gig workers have no social security safety net. In Brazil, though (where over 600,000 drivers work for Uber alone), then-president Dilma Rousseff made it mandatory for employers to sign a contract with domestic help, guaranteeing a fixed salary, holidays and other benefits.[130] India needs to think of how to deal with the

---

[127]'Zomato Claims to Disburse Rs 216 Crore Every Month to 230,000 Riders', *Entracker*, 6 September 2020, https://entrackr.com/2019/09/zomato-claims-to-disburse-rs-216-crore-every-month-to-230000-riders/, accessed on 22 March 2021.
[128]'Uber Claims Top Spot in Indian Ride-Hailing Market', *TechCrunch*, 8 February 2020, https://techcrunch.com/2020/02/08/uber-claims-top-spot-in-indian-ride-hailing-market/, accessed on 22 March 2021.
[129]According to the Nikkei Asian Review, quoted in 'A Race to Keep China's Food Delivery Business Bustling', *The Hindu*, 21 December 2019, https://www.thehindu.com/news/international/a-race-to-keep-chinas-food-delivery-business-bustling/article30368209.ece, accessed on 22 March 2021.
[130]'The Rush to Informal Jobs', *The Hindu*, 8 February 2020, https://www.thehindu.com/news/international/the-rush-to-informal-jobs/article30771497.ece, accessed on 22 March 2021.

issue as the number of gig workers soars. The new labour code includes some degree of social security for such workers.

Amidst all the technological churn, the global pandemic caused by the COVID virus has drastically changed many things. Some aspects, like the worldwide economic downturn (expected by many to be amongst the worst ever), may be a short-term phenomenon, which will have a severe impact on present jobs, and a dampening effect on the creation of any new jobs. However, it will also have long-lasting consequences. One will be the result of work-from-home (WFH): a necessity during the lockdown, its possibilities and advantages have now been savoured. Some individuals, and many companies, will see this as an ideal way of working. Individuals may like the flexibility it offers and the possibility of becoming gig workers, self-employed 'contractors' who work (from their own premises) part time and/or for multiple clients. Persons who are home-bound, particularly the vast number of educated women, would see WFH as a means of getting part-time work, doing it from their home at a time that is convenient, keeping occupied even as they earn an income.

Companies will see WFH as a way of reducing pressure on their space requirements, saving money on real estate and overheads like electricity, air conditioning, etc. Besides, it may enable them to move to more gig work, enabling direct savings on the compensation expenses that go with 'regular' employment (medical expenses and retirement costs, for example), and the flexibility of scaling human resources up or down, as required.

Already, a very large Indian services company has announced an ambitious 25x25 model: by 2025, only 25 per cent of its employees will need to work from office, and they too will work there only 25 per cent of the time.[131] Doubtless, many others too will plan for similar changes. Even today, some companies do not have dedicated office space for all their staff. Whenever someone needs to be physically present in office s/he 'books' a seat.

Amongst the most effective ways of being safe from the COVID virus is physical distancing. Ensuring this in the work environment—in office, shop, or factory—is not going to be easy. It will certainly require a thinning out, a reduction in density. Thus, the savings that could have accrued as a result of WFH (fewer people in office, less real estate needed) may be neutralized by the requirement for lower people-density. Moreover, there will be costs associated with testing and safeguarding those who are required to come to work. This penalty of proximity is a factor that, aided by technology, will push decentralization and may disperse many jobs to smaller towns and rural areas.

Another, and rather different outcome, resulting from concerns about the pandemic (and human carriers), is that organizations may find automation an attractive alternative. After all, robots are not affected by the pandemic and do not have to be quarantined, nor does one have to worry about distancing or wearing of masks! Changing costs—increasing for humans, and decreasing for machines—tilt the trade-off even further. One example is from a recent news report that carried

---

[131]"TCS "Work from Home" Policy: Only One-Fourth of Workers to Come to Office; CEO Explains Vision 25×25', *Financial Express*, 27 May 2020, https://www.financialexpress.com/industry/tcs-work-from-home-policy-only-one-fourth-of-workers-to-come-to-office-ceo-explains-vision-25x25/1971995/#:~:text=Explaining%20the%20company%27s%-2025%C3%97,of%20their%20time%20at%20work, accessed on 22 March 2021.

the story of a gas and oil company (Cairn Oil).[132] Its Barmer plant (in Rajasthan) was managed by over 7,500 personnel on-site in the months before the COVID pandemic. After the lockdown was announced, this number dipped to just over 1,500. Despite this, the company recovered 1.6 lakh barrels of oil every day, compared with 1.8 lakh barrels earlier. This marginal dip, too, was due to lower demand. Its production was maintained only due to its investment in automation and digitization over the last two years. With this experience, one can be almost certain that the company—and others like it—will further increase the investment in automation and look at ways of reducing human-power.

AND THE WINNER IS...

On the one hand, then, is the push for automation, the use of machines to replace humans; on the other, there are the new jobs that technology itself opens up. Will technology complement or supplement humans? Only time will provide an answer. It does seem, though, that the response to this question may vary from sector to sector and situation to situation. Also, most importantly, it will depend upon the ingenuity and innovation of humans, and our design of the overall systems within which we use technology.

Concern about new technologies leading to a loss of jobs is not new. It is said that in 1589 when William Lee went to the English court, seeking a patent for his invention, a

---

[132]What follows about Cairn is from 'Automation Key to Post-Pandemic Production', *The Economic Times*, 27 April 2020, https://economictimes.indiatimes.com/news/company/corporate-trends/automation-key-to-post-pandemic-production/articleshow/75395665.cms, accessed on 22 March 2021.

knitting machine, Queen Elizabeth I turned down the request. She felt it would 'assuredly bring to them (her subjects) ruin by depriving them of employment.'[133] Despite this, history establishes that new technologies have been net job creators: while some jobs are lost, many more new ones are created. The problem is that the skill sets required for new job roles are different than those that were required for earlier jobs. Thus, those displaced by technology from certain functions or tasks are not the ones who can automatically fit into the newly emerging job roles. Net gains in employment hide the pain of those who lose jobs and do not have the capability to do the new ones. This is, of course, the traditional development dilemma: net gain, but also who loses and who benefits?

Training and re-skilling of the existing workforce is one part of the solution; another is a robust and universal social security system that provides for unemployment benefits and/ or a UBI. The first requires widespread infrastructure and a system that can provide relevant and quality training on a large scale. Leaving this to individual companies is not a feasible solution, given that the overwhelming majority are Micro, Small and Medium Enterprises (MSMEs) with practically no capability to organize and carry out such training, even if content is provided. It will, therefore, have to be an effort done by large entities—probably best done jointly by industry and government, working also with academia, in a public–private partnership (PPP) mode. The already existing Sector Skills Councils could be the nucleus of this large-scale and ongoing re-skilling effort. Yet, even with a successful re-skilling programme, there will be many who will not have

---

[133]From 'Robots May Well Take Your Job—Eventually', *The Economist*, January 2020, https://www.economist.com/books-and-arts/2020/01/23/robots-may-well-take-your-job-eventually, accessed on 22 March 2021.

the capabilities required for the new jobs. Also, there will be a continuous churn of older functions being automated or becoming redundant (and displacing workers), and ever new jobs being created. Hence, the absolute necessity for the social security safety net/UBI.

The extent of job churn will vary, depending upon sector and context. In India, the speed and spread of automation over the next decade will yet be limited. Major labour-intensive sectors, including construction, garments and textiles, retail and logistics, are unlikely to see a great deal of human-displacing automation. The slower speed of such displacement provides a window to rapidly ramp up training and to ensure a better educated workforce, enabling a shift to new jobs, quality employment and entrepreneurship.

Despite this, providing gainful livelihoods to millions of minimally educated and largely unskilled surplus agricultural labour, as also those displaced from employment, will be a major challenge in the coming years. It is imperative to aggressively promote sectors that have the potential to create a large number of jobs at various levels, especially those that can absorb the mass of unskilled people. One such sector is tourism, and India needs to push hard on this—attracting both domestic and foreign tourists—to create jobs on a large scale at various levels of skill, in hospitality and travel. The generation of jobs on a massive scale in the services sector must be a vital part of the agenda for India in the 2020s. Even as the country pushes education—ensuring more years of schooling for all—and tries to generate more high-productivity, 'quality' jobs (those that ensure regular employment and social security benefits), it will have to also focus on providing livelihoods for the huge number who are minimally educated and unskilled. By 2030, this number should decrease considerably, as past efforts on improving skill and education levels begin to make an increasing impact. Meanwhile, technology-triggered jobs would begin to increase. Between these two factors, the employment scene should look far better.

Further, there is also the possibility of quickly evolving a suitable human-plus-machine model, which will minimize disruption even as it creates new jobs. This phygital or bridgital approach, which seeks to build bridges connecting the physical (human) with the digital (technology), is of particular relevance and interest to India, given the large population and the growing workforce. It will also raise the value-add, making possible better paid jobs. Of course, this too will require the development of new capabilities, necessitating an extensive skill development programme to retrain existing workers. It will also need changes in the curriculum for various courses in the universities, and a flexible or agile system that facilitates continuous changes as ever newer technologies emerge. Close collaboration between industry and academia—a long-standing goal that has become a cliché—will be essential, to ensure ongoing relevance of educational content.

In the longer run, therefore, as the man/machine story continues to play out, it is more likely to have a man-*plus*-machine ending. To the technophobe, this may sound like sheer optimism; we think not. Such a view is based on hard evidence. For example, a project using deep learning for breast cancer diagnoses conducted by a team from Harvard Medical School found that the clinical pathology error is 3.9 per cent. With AI, the algorithm had a 2.5 per cent error rate. But when AI and clinical diagnosis were combined, the error rate decreased to 0.5 percent. This makes a compelling case for how AI, used in conjunction with traditional diagnostic criteria, provides the best results.[134]

Creating appropriate human-plus-machine/AI models will certainly take a high degree of creativity and innovation, not only in technology, but more so in designing organizational systems and business models. However, a combination of uniquely human qualities, married to the advantages of machines, will be the final winner. This will ensure a growing number of jobs, absorbing most, if not all, the workforce. The rest, a small minority, will be going through re-skilling and training, with livelihoods protected by social security and UBI (a model not too dissimilar to the 'bench strength' model of IT companies, in which a proportion of employees is in training or skill building).

The suggestions so far have not touched on labour reform, by which most people mean a freer labour market, with minimal restrictions on working hours, overtime, etc., of workers, but most of all, permitting companies to hire and fire. Many feel that such reforms will promote employment. Recently, soon after the 'unlock' phase of the COVID-related restrictions began, a few state governments did, in fact, relax some of the regulations safeguarding workers' rights. The reality is that relaxations ('reforms') of this type will do little when the bulk of employment (close to 90 per cent) is in the informal or unorganized sector where, in any case, these restrictions do not apply. They will neither change the conditions in which these employees work, nor will they have any impact on the enterprises. The best way of ensuring their growth may well be to have common labour laws, applicable to all enterprises, along with an universal system of unemployment insurance and social security for all workers.

---

[134]'Why Health Care CIOs Can't Delay on Embracing AI', *Harvard T.H. Chan School of Public Health*, https://www.hsph.harvard.edu/ecpe/why-health-care-cios-embrace-ai/, accessed on 22 March 2021.

In summary, in the 2020s, India needs to take the following actions to promote jobs and livelihood:

i. Provide universal and free school education, healthcare and social security to all, supplemented by a universal basic income; this is an essential element to support people in the unorganized sector and in the growing gig economy.
ii. Redesign structures and processes to decentralize and ensure efficient delivery of services at points closest to the user (for example, upgraded primary health centres and primary schools), thereby reducing the need, time and cost of accessing more distant facilities.
iii. Evolve a model of decentralized development; create scale, where required, through virtual (electronic) integration.
iv. Promote local entrepreneurship, by providing facilities, finance, training and skills.
v. Create an ecosystem for training, skilling and local livelihood opportunities in rural India, especially related to new technologies.
vi. Through high-quality education and training, position India as a global talent source; export service capabilities, either by delivering from India or people going abroad.
vii. Build new human-mediated user-to-technology (machine) links, even as the country leverages to the maximum extent the capability of emerging technologies.
viii. Promote innovation, design-led manufacturing and efficient global service delivery, rather than focusing only on low-value (and increasingly automated) mass manufacturing.

ix. Give an impetus to people-intensive services like education, health and tourism (for both, Indians and foreigners); position India as a global hub for these. This would also require high investment in sectors like construction and infrastructure, which would add to employment.
x. Evolve and promote human-plus-machine/AI models that fully leverage new technologies, even as they create new jobs.

Given the size of India's population and its growth (soon to make it the most populous country), jobs and livelihoods will be amongst the biggest challenges facing us in the decades to come. Many fear that technology will greatly amplify the problem, through growing automation. Millions of unemployed youth can lead to a crisis, given their volatility, and result in the breakdown of social order. On the other hand, the demographic dividend of a large number of young reduces the dependency ratio and can provide substantial economic gain. This requires, though, that they be productively employed, despite automation and the consequent evaporation of low-end mass-production jobs.

It is for India to leverage its vast human resource and also high technological prowess to lead the way in ensuring jobs and livelihoods by creating new models (including the 'man-plus-machine' approach) of development. Education, skilling and innovations in technology, organization and business models will be the key. 'Quality livelihoods for all' should be the focus of the country in the 2020s. Well-conceived and effectively implemented plans can help achieve this goal. By 2030, we predict, India will do so, creating a new development model for itself and a path for others to follow.

9

TECHNOLOGY

Every Breath You Take: Pervasive Tech

In preceding chapters, the role and impact of technology on various key areas has already been covered, either explicitly or implicitly. Yet, given the major impact of technology, it is worth looking in greater detail at its role, especially on how it may contribute to shaping India in this decade and beyond. This chapter, therefore, focuses on technology.

Technology has now become the ubiquitous underpinning of not only the economy, but also of much that we do for leisure or at home. It permeates across social sectors and activities, and is often an intermediary even in person-to-person communication. It can help us to learn more about ourselves, our world and beyond; to take us to adventures and explorations below the oceans or in deep space. At the same time, it can be the cause for our self-destruction, through nuclear weapons, climate change, or biological warfare; ironically, it is tech itself that may provide solutions to many of these problems.

The many ways in which technology has facilitated work and made life easier are well known. Over the centuries, and especially in the last few decades, technology has helped to increase productivity and create wealth. Agri-tech, through new seeds, inputs, farming techniques and crop/food preservation technologies, has banished famine from practically all countries (wherever it exists, lack of purchasing power—poverty—rather than shortage of food is the prime cause). In industry, technology has led to new products, more efficient production and increased productivity. In daily life, devices like the TV set, computer and the near-ubiquitous mobile phone have radically changed what we know and how we communicate, besides redefining our routine and use of leisure time. Also, these devices are not only contributing to, but creating social change. While technology has sometimes had negative side-effects (pollution being one) and even helped to forge more deadly weapons of war capable of devastating the world, it has reduced drudgery and made life generally better. Yet, many worry about the disparities it amplifies, or even creates, in an already unequal society.

Left to itself, technology does have a tendency to add to existing inequities. This is because it often requires money (to own a device like a smartphone or computer), education and training to be able to access services. Therefore, those who are socio-economically disadvantaged tend to get left behind. For example, there is a treasure trove of courses and learning material available online, but accessing these needs a device and connectivity. During the COVID lockdown, a large number of schools and universities have moved to online classes. Many are unable to 'attend', though, due to lack of a computer (or even a smartphone) or poor Internet connectivity. Interesting—and sometimes heartbreaking—stories have emerged about the efforts of students to somehow join the classes. Photographs of children on house roofs or tree-tops to seek Internet connectivity tell their own story.

Like education, healthcare through telemedicine, remote training and e-commerce is constrained by availability of a device and connectivity. The benefits of these services are, therefore, available only to the better-off, thus widening an already existing gap.

In a country with huge inequities—particularly economic and social—it is vital that all possible means be used to reduce the gaps. Technology has the potential to bridge the chasms, provided it is embedded into systems that consciously seek to do this. Already, the rural-urban information gap has narrowed, with the proliferation of TV (especially DTH) and mobile phones, which are now seen even in very remote areas. New technologies must now be deployed to close the gap in education, health and training. This requires communication reach, inexpensive data and cheaper devices. Community access points, content in the local language and apps that are user-friendly (WhatsApp is a good example) are also essential. Inclusivity—in addition to access, affordability and availability—must be the mantra for all services.

India has a history of using technology to try and bridge the gap. When television first came to India in the 1950s, TV sets were placed in classrooms for the benefit of all students. The path-breaking Satellite Instructional Television Experiment (SITE) in 1975–76 took development and education programmes to villages in remote and backward parts of the country even before TV covered many major metropolises. In more recent times, government services and many other facilities have been made accessible to villagers, via computers and the Internet, through public-access Common Service Centres (CSC). There are now 400,000 CSCs and they are planning to provide additional services, including 'digital doctor', 'digital banker' and 'digital teacher'. Also, each CSC will have five 'digital cadets' to take services to the doorstep of villagers.[135] In his 2020 Independence Day address, the prime minister announced that broadband would be provided to 600,000 villages in 1,000 days, and this should take digital services to all.

Apart from concerns about amplification of inequities, another broad worry is with regard to jobs: will technology take away jobs? This question has become even more relevant in the wake of the COVID pandemic. Earlier, automation of certain tasks was seen as being a possibility; now, it has become an attractive way of reducing dependence on humans. With the need for physical distancing and concerns about the spread of the virus, many offices and factories are actively looking at how they can replace employees with technology. Advances in AI, data analytics and robotics have made it possible for machines to replace humans in a growing range of jobs. This has, in fact, already begun to happen. The worry about job loss is, therefore, not unfounded. Yet, as has been argued in the chapter on jobs, there is a possibility of quickly evolving a suitable human-plus-machine model. Also, historical experience shows that new technologies, in fact, create more jobs. There are two problems, though: a period of disruption, between the loss of jobs and the creation of new ones and the different (generally higher) skills required for new jobs. The first may well result in a drop in employment for a few years, causing difficulty and pain. The second requires a massive programme of re-skilling through updating and upgrading capabilities.

---

[135]Inputs on CSC from Dr Dinesh Tyagi, CEO, and Rishikesh Patankar, COO, Common Service Centres, e-Governance Services India Limited, Government of India.

LEVERAGING TECHNOLOGY

In the new education scenario, technology will not only be the content, but also the means of education. Already beginning to be a part of the education system through MOOCs, online education has gained greater importance and traction because of the COVID pandemic and the consequent lockdown. Even when getting back into classrooms becomes possible, online may be a large part of the new blended form of education.

Technology also provides other avenues of facilitating, even enhancing, conventional education. Augmented and virtual reality have become excellent means for creating virtual laboratories, and for training. Simulators for training pilots have long been in use, and the proliferation of such simulation facilities can be foreseen, especially as costs decrease.

Through the 2020s, the use of technology in education at all levels will see a big upsurge. An even bigger use of technology will be for training. Millions who enter the workforce, and equally large numbers who need to be re-trained, will go to institutions which use technology to provide high-quality, near-real-life training in an efficient and easily scalable manner. India's future, linked as it is to the human resource capabilities that it can build, will crucially depend on how well it uses technology for education and training. Success in this will ensure, possibly, the biggest pool of intellectual capital in the world by 2030. This base of a workforce of hundreds of millions of highly skilled and highly educated people—larger than of any other country—will enable India to move to a higher orbit of economic growth. It will also be the driving force for India to be amongst the world leaders, intellectually and economically, by 2050.

A key element of this, and other uses of technology, will

be the development of new technologies. This requires large investments in R&D on an ongoing basis. India's track record in this respect has been dismal, as bad as its meagre budgets for health and education. This will have to change, quickly and radically, if the country is to realize its potential. The 2020s, it is hoped, will be a time of transition, with rapidly increasing investments in the related areas of R&D and education. Also, apart from money, both fields require reform: in the case of R&D, how it is organized and managed; in the case of education, doing away with the excessive, rigid and centralized regulatory framework.

In terms of leveraging technology, the 'downstream' area of techno-entrepreneurship and innovation has witnessed considerable government support in recent times. Policies and funding have facilitated the setting up of start-up companies. This has given a considerable boost to technology-based entrepreneurship. Most often, the technology itself is an already existing one. However, the specific application or business model may be new, at least in India. This is fast creating a 'technology sector' in industry—one which spans across diverse areas (from electronics to genetics), but shares the commonality of technology being at the core of the business. New technologies, especially in AI, robotics, data analytics and IoT, as also in genetics, bioscience and medical technology (especially after COVID), will spur an even faster growth in the tech sector. In these areas, both manufacturing and services hold great promise of rapid development. The 2020s are certain to see a boom in this tech sector.

As 5G becomes the communication standard in this decade, its speed and low latency will facilitate a wide range of new applications. In industry, IoT devices will proliferate. Combining sensors and transmission capability, they will collect data and send it to other devices or to computers. This will enable analysis or immediate corrective action. AI platforms can process the data for predictive analysis, ensuring timely preventive maintenance or shutdown of equipment. High bandwidth connectivity will enable rapid transmission of large amounts of data. This could be used for sending design details to various manufacturing facilities where automated machines can convert the design to physical form, for example, cloth to clothes. Additive manufacturing using 3D printers or other machines can convert raw material into ready-to-sell products. Designs can be changed quickly and cheaply, not only for seasonal variations but also for customization. Each product can be made unique at minimal additional cost or time.

Software-driven design and production will enable decentralization and remove any advantages of economy-of-scale. An additional driver of decentralization will be the 'proximity penalty': a cost which COVID has brought to the fore due to the need for physical distancing. This means that it is no longer wise to have a large number of people working in a limited area: be it factory shop floor or office. New developments make it technologically feasible, economically viable and socially desirable to disperse manufacturing facilities and offices. Production can, thus, be dispersed (for example, to various rural areas, or to customer locations) across the country, in some ways emulating the proven success of global supply chains. New business models will emerge out of this. It may lead to demographic changes in the country, since people-concentration will be unnecessary and cities will no longer be the only hubs for economic activity. A lot of it—and hence jobs and people—will move to smaller towns and even villages. Such movement will be further facilitated by other technologies that make life in rural areas as easy and comfortable as in cities. Physical infrastructure like roads, transport, water supply and sanitation will have to be upgraded in a major way, and technology can help in doing this quickly and efficiently. In areas like education and healthcare, apart from schools and health centres or hospitals, online courses and telemedicine will play a big role, ensuring quality which is as good as that in cities. As a result, technology could create jobs for villagers nearer their home. It is also possible that many city-dwellers may migrate to jobs in rural areas. Thus, technology may well create a reversal of a historical trend.

Another fall-out of COVID is that fears of other such devastating global pandemics hitting us at regular intervals will mean the death of tourism. Few, it is felt, would want to take the risks inherent in travel or the outside chance of being stranded—possibly in a different country—if there is a sudden lockdown. A contrary view is that memory is short and, in a year or so, most people will once again be travelling and holidaying. Time will tell which view prevails but, meanwhile, 'virtual tourism' has got a big boost. This involves the use of virtual reality technology to enable people to 'see' all the sites that they want to, 'visit' museums and art galleries, or just 'walk' on the streets of a faraway city. You can even 'sit' in a café in Paris or in a restaurant in New York—though, unfortunately, you cannot yet savour the coffee, food or wine! Of course, augmented reality—combining the real and the virtual—can almost do that: while you relax at home with your own cup of coffee or wine and food, you will be 'virtually' in Paris or New York. Such uses of new technologies are already proliferating and their ongoing development will begin to blur the lines between virtual and real.

'DRIVING' THE FUTURE

This decade is likely to see a major change in transportation. Petrol or diesel and the internal combustion engine, dominant for a century, are likely to be increasingly replaced by electric mobility. Requiring but a fraction of the number of components necessary for the traditional engine, electric vehicles have an inherent attraction in manufacturing and, potentially, in cost. At present, the batteries are expensive; however, their cost is decreasing and a technological breakthrough in storage is overdue. One can expect that, by 2030, electric vehicles (both two and four wheelers) will cost less than the conventional ones. The necessary infrastructure of battery charging stations (or battery exchange locations) will develop rapidly, if there is a policy push. Meanwhile, technologies for faster charging will ease this constraint. For India, one concern is the raw material: present storage devices require imported raw material, which will create a new dependence (as we have today on oil).

In this area, the agenda for the 2020s for India is clear: invest heavily in R&D on storage (batteries), encourage a phased switchover to electric vehicles, and develop the ecosystem for them, including extensive infrastructure for charging and battery exchange. At the same time, there is need to incentivize cycling and walking. Both contribute to better health, lower pollution and lower imports. While incentives could include no tax for bicycles (or even a subsidy), the best one is likely to be physical infrastructure: better pavements and walkways, safe and dedicated cycling tracks. Today, even in the few places these exist (in parts of Delhi, for example) they have been taken over not only by motorized two- and three-wheelers, but sometimes cars too.

The use of hydrogen as a fuel has long been discussed, even proven. However, despite its no-pollution advantage (the waste product is water), it is yet expensive, inconvenient and suffers from safety concerns. While it seems unlikely to be common place by 2030, this may change quickly. One driver would be the launch of a 'Hydrogen Energy Mission', mentioned as part of the Union Budget in February 2021 (following its announcement by the prime minister in November 2020). Additional acceleration could come from a major Indian conglomerate (well known for scale and speed of execution), which is reported to have already initiated serious work to soon make hydrogen a commonly-useable fuel.

For intercity travel, high-speed trains are likely to be an important means of transportation in future. While these do not involve any radically new technologies, and are extensively used in some countries, the infrastructure for them—including signalling, safety, communication and track security—will need sophisticated systems. Such trains, especially if run from and to city-centres, can efficiently replace a great deal of short-haul air and road traffic. High-traffic corridors between nearby pairs of cities (like Mumbai–Ahmedabad, Pune–Mumbai, Chennai–Bengaluru, Delhi–Chandigarh) could greatly benefit from high-speed trains. India's capability in this field is yet limited and, in the short and medium term, it will have to depend on imports. However, given the legacy of Indian Railways and the cumulative experience and expertise built up over the decades, the development of these technologies should not pose much of a challenge.

Helping the country to master these technologies will be the India–Japan agreement for the equivalent of a 'bullet train', high-speed train corridor from Ahmedabad to Mumbai. Preliminary work has already begun. However, unconfirmed reports indicate that the numerous problems besetting it mean that the intended deadline of 2022–23 will not be met, and that a delay of a few years is likely. In February 2021, the government indicated its plan to create a few more high-speed train corridors.

The biggest obstacles to an efficient roll-out of such links are likely to be mainly non-technological. Apart from acquisition of land for the tracks and ensuring no trespassing by humans, animals or vehicles, there are other nitty-gritty problems. One would be stations. Even today, for many people, the biggest deterrent to train travel is the station experience: first, getting there through chaotic traffic conditions; and then, the general disorder, crowds, dirt and sense of disorganization that prevails at the station. Added to this are continuous and loud but often incomprehensible announcements of delays, change in the arrival/departure platform for trains, etc. Technology, even in simple things like better audio systems and displays, are helping to improve things, but a lot more needs to be done in the non-tech area.

Economics of high-speed trains is another challenge. Costs, including that of land acquisition, are high. Other forms of transport—both low-cost airlines and buses or taxis—offer fares that may be cheaper. Countering these will not only require fares that are competitive, but a better overall experience. This must include safety, comfort and punctuality; quick and easy access to transport to and from the station, including taxis, buses and metro/local trains and reasonable fares for last-mile travel.

Despite these issues, given its size and population, India is badly in need of an efficient and fast long-distance mass transportation system. As new technologies emerge and costs come down, the country must take a leap in this area, along the lines of what it has done for intra-city transport through metro systems in the last two decades. Developing technological capability in this area, and simultaneously creating the industrial base for domestic manufacturing, is crucial. With appropriate policies, this will happen through the 2020s, so that by 2030 the country is a frontrunner in the field of high-speed trains.

In this, India could take a leaf out of China's book. That country has built the world's largest high-speed rail (HSR) network, adding 35,000 km in just the last decade, a total which exceeds the combined length of rest of the world. Japan, a pioneer in HSR, has just 3,041 km and the US a mere 735 km. The maximum speed of trains in China's HSR is 350 km per hour—the fastest in the world.[136] China's development and manufacturing capabilities now enable it to be an exporter in this field too.

China has also long worked on new transportation technologies like magnetic levitation. It has had an operational high-speed Maglev train service (over 400 km/hour) between Longyang Road station and Shanghai Pudong International Airport station from April 2004.[137] This technology is probably not economically viable yet for train services, despite the advantages of comfort and speed. It has other applications too, including in the defence sector. It is, therefore, important for India to keep abreast of such technologies.

Hyperloop is a newer concept, and one that is yet to be

---

[136]Details about China's HSR network taken from 'From Nobody to Somebody: China's High-Speed Rail in Numbers', *China Global Television Network*, 1 October 2020.

[137]'The Shanghai Maglev Route', Union Workshop, https://cdn.cloudflare. steamstatic.com/steam/apps/376933/manuals/Shanghai_Maglev_Manual_ English.pdf?t=1549296809, accessed on 23 March 2021.

operationally established. It is based on pods/trains moving through a sealed low-air-pressure tube, which enables supersonic speed due to minimum air resistance. Elon Musk (its creator, and founder of Tesla and SpaceX) sees this as the future of mass rapid transportation. Combined with his drive for high-tech tunnelling (through his Boring Company), the hyperloop could reach the central hub of cities, with no disruption to onground traffic. India is amongst the countries that have shown interest in this technology, and a Mumbai–Pune hyperloop service was being discussed,[138] though it may now be shelved.[139]

In general, transportation technologies—whether e-vehicles, hydrogen fuel, high-speed trains or hyperloop—are going to be an important area for R&D and a vital part of the economy, through both manufacturing and provision of services. While air services will continue to grow, substantially new technologies for aircraft are unlikely in this decade. The situation is likely to be similar as far as water transport is concerned. In both areas, there will certainly be increases in automation, higher efficiencies in fuel consumption and a decrease in pollution, but radical changes are unlikely.

The Smart Cities programme could, potentially, be a big user of technology. Many of the newer technologies could find immediate use. IoT, data analytics and AI have already

---

[138] 'Mumbai to Pune Hyperloop Project Likely to Begin in 2020', *The Hindu*, 18 October 2019, https://www.thehindu.com/news/cities/mumbai/mumbai-to-pune-hyperloop-project-likely-to-begin-in-2020/article29729306.ece, accessed on 23 March 2021.

[139] 'Mumbai–Pune Hyperloop Travel in 25 Minutes! How the Concept of 1,220 kmph Technology Came about; Top Facts', *Financial Express*, 22 February 2020, https://www.financialexpress.com/infrastructure/mumbai-pune-hyperloop-travel-in-25-minutes-how-the-concept-of-1220-kmph-technology-came-about-top-facts/1875183/, accessed on 23 March 2021.

well-established use cases in areas like traffic management, power conservation, bus routing and bus schedule updates. Blockchain has use in property registration and other applications. Drones are being used in India for crowd surveillance and management. They have also been deployed for spraying disinfectants, monitoring lockdowns and making announcements in the context of COVID.

Elsewhere, drones are being used for delivery of food or packages in urban areas. However, they are particularly useful in inaccessible areas or during calamities (floods, cyclones, earthquakes) when road transport is not possible. Surveillance along the border is done by drones; an unfortunate extension of this is the delivery of arms, across the border, to terrorists. Many other applications are being operationalized as new technology enhances the capability of drones.

NEW FRONTIERS IN HEALTH

Amongst the most exciting areas of technological development—and one of great relevance to India—is healthcare. This often combines the latest in genetics and biological sciences with electronics, data analytics and AI/ML (machine learning). Its potential for diagnosis is tremendous. Without doubt, in some cases it can do as well as, and sometimes better and faster than, a doctor. Already, in analysing X-rays, complete digitization of the process and automated diagnosis is possible. Massive data sets are the input for machine learning and, combined with AI, will soon take us to personalized medicine. In some ways, this will combine the role of the general practitioner of yore, who knew your personal medical history and your body responses, with that of the super-specialist, so as to prescribe a treatment specific and more suitable for you. The importance and feasibility of this is already being established in the field of oncology, where individual responses to treatment and drugs vary considerably.

Many of these new tools are based on non-invasive tests, sometimes using simple inputs like saliva, sweat or tear drops as a basis for diagnosis. This obviously facilitates quicker and cheaper testing—both of crucial importance to India, and particularly so in the case of epidemics. Linking such diagnostic equipment to transmitters embedded in them, or to mobile phones, will enable transmission of the data to a central facility. This will facilitate further analysis or confirmation by a specialist, and a collation of data for further epidemiological or other analysis. Advanced technology may even make possible near-instantaneous results. Imagine what a non-invasive, simple, immediate-diagnosis test can do in a COVID-like situation.

Progress in biosciences is heading towards the creation of organs (from stem cells, for example) or their within-body, in-situ, repair. Organ transplants using artificially developed ones will soon become a standard procedure. In future, bio-electronic organs seem a distinct possibility. India has a good base of expertise in biology, electronics and IT, and this could be leveraged for taking forward work in this area. This would complement India's capability in pharmaceuticals and medicine.

India's pharmaceutical industry has been growing and is becoming an important global player. It started and thrived on efficiently and cheaply manufacturing drugs, whose patents had just expired. It won international acclaim when it supplied drugs to counter the HIV contagion in Africa at a fraction of the cost being quoted by Western firms.[140] Today, it produces more than half the global output of vaccines.[141] Over the years, investments in R&D have begun to pay off and India has slowly moved up the value chain to create active pharmaceutical ingredients (APIs) and drugs though, even now, a lot of APIs are imported (mainly from China). The combination of technical expertise with low cost and at scale manufacturing has the potential to make India a major global source of pharmaceuticals.

In the context of COVID, the world is looking at India's manufacturing capabilities to not only mass produce hundreds of millions of vaccine doses for itself, but for other countries too. At the same time, a number of Indian companies are also developing vaccines. Such a combination of development and manufacturing capability bodes well for the future.

This science and technology (S&T)-based industry is bound to see an ongoing boom as health becomes increasingly important to individuals and governments across the world. In this decade, India can convert its potential into reality with greater investments in R&D in this field, as also by

---

[140] Compared to the normal price of the AIDS cocktail in the West of $10,000 to $15,000 a year, an Indian firm (Cipla) offered to supply the triple-therapy drug 'cocktails' for $350 a year per patient to a doctors' group working in Africa. From 'Indian Company Offers to Supply AIDS Drugs at Low Cost in Africa', *The New York Times*, 7 February 2001, https://www.nytimes.com/2001/02/07/world/indian-company-offers-to-supply-aids-drugs-at-low-cost-in-africa.html#:~:text=In%20a%20move%20that%20could,The%20Indian%20company%2C%20Cipla%20Ltd, accessed on 23 March 2021.

[141] India produces 60 per cent of the world's vaccines according to 'How India Can Be a World Leader in Making Covid Vaccine and Keeping It Cheap Too', *The Print*, 6 May 2020, https://theprint.in/india/how-india-can-be-a-world-leader-in-making-covid-vaccine-and-keeping-it-cheap-too/414701/, accessed on 23 March 2021.

inducting the latest manufacturing technologies. Building on its past success and credibility, India is now exporting the Covishield vaccine (developed by Oxford University and AstraZeneca, manufactured by the Serum Institute of India) to a number of countries—from next-door neighbours to distant Brazil. Soon, another COVID vaccine, Covaxin—developed and manufactured indigenously by Bharat Biotech—is also expected to be widely exported. This may well position us, by 2030, to become the 'pharmacy to the world'.

'MAKE HIGH-TECH IN INDIA'

India has long harboured the hope of becoming a big manufacturer of electronics hardware. Fifty years ago, it began with producing TV sets and later moved to even more sophisticated items like telephone exchanges and computers. State-of-the-art satellite communication hardware and DTH TV reception equipment was developed by ISRO and made by Indian industry as far back as the 1970s. Somewhere, though, it missed the bus in fast-evolving technologies and moved to 'screwdriver technology', involving import of all sub-assemblies and merely putting them together in India. With liberalization and freer, low-tariff imports, even this was not necessary; products, especially consumer goods, were imported in ready-for-sale form. Realizing the high impact of tech imports on India's balance of trade (one estimate, made in 2009, predicted that import of electronic goods alone would exceed that of oil by 2020[142]), and the potential

---

[142]'Report of Task Force to Suggest Measures to Stimulate the Growth of IT, ITES and Electronics Hardware Manufacturing Industry in India', *Ministry of Electronics and Information Technology, Government of India*, 2009, https://www.meity.gov.in/writereaddata/files/Task_Force_Report-

for local manufacture, new policies have been formulated to incentivize local production. This has had an impact, and a fair amount of electronic goods (especially high-demand items like mobile phones and TV sets) are now assembled in the country. However, despite the production incentives and the large (and rapidly growing) domestic market for these products, India is unattractive as a base for component manufacturing. As a result, in many cases, the country is back to the assembly-and-packaging-only stage, with minimal value addition and negligible component manufacturing. There is, though, a slow movement towards some backward integration.

Increasingly, manufacturing is based on global supply chains, with various components of the system being made in different countries, based on competitive advantage. Where any component is made depends upon a variety of complex factors, including talent, cost, tax laws, labour laws, logistics, availability and cost of land, water and power, safety and security. India does not make the cut, today, for most electronic components. While the overall government policy is of strong encouragement, there are many obstacles on the ground. Given the importance of electronics—for job creation, its range of applications, export potential and strategic importance—India must remove the numerous obstacles and ensure a facilitative ecosystem for the growth of a large indigenous electronics industry. This must be a priority in the 2020s. A window of opportunity has now opened. Thanks to the US–China trade stand-off, and other geopolitical reasons, there is a move to diversify production beyond China. As a potential alternative

---

new_21211%282%29.pdf, accessed on 23 March 2021 and 'Making India Atmanirbhar in Electronics', *Financial Express*, 27 August 2020 https://www.financialexpress.com/opinion/making-india-atmanirbhar-in-electronics/2066551/, accessed on 23 March 2021.

destination, India could now attract a larger part of the product value-chain for electronics. The Production Linked Incentive scheme, announced in October 2020, could help to accelerate this.[143]

India can well emulate its success in IT software through a similar success in hardware if it plays its cards correctly and intelligently. The present signs and trends are positive, and by 2030 India should become a major exporter of electronic goods.

India set up facilities for aircraft manufacturing almost seven decades ago. In partnership with foreign suppliers, production of some parts, assembling and maintenance were done in India at Hindustan Aeronautics Ltd in Bengaluru. With a large base of technical talent and an engineering industry, combined with potentially high demand, one would have expected India to become a manufacturer—if not also a designer—of aircraft. However, India's capability in this field is still very limited. Not only in aircraft, but in the whole gamut of high-tech defence equipment, India continues to be one of the world's biggest importers, with little indigenous production capability. Recent events (in mid-2020) on the border with China portend—and will necessitate—a big increase in defence spending. While immediate needs will have to be met by imports, this is an opportunity to develop a large and tech-based defence production industry in the country. There is now a renewed commitment and thrust to this, evidenced by large orders being placed for local production of equipment, including procurement of a very substantial number of the indigenously developed Light Combat Aircraft (Tejas).

---

[143]'Production Linked Incentive Scheme (PLI) for Large Scale Electronics Manufacturing', *Ministry of Electronics and Information Technology, Government of India*, October 2020.

While we have been slow in the local production of defence equipment, the country has done better in two other high-tech and strategic sectors: space and nuclear technology. In both, there is a fairly strong base of domestic R&D as well as manufacturing expertise. However, the limited domestic orders, and constraints regarding exports, have inhibited the growth of manufacturing capacity. A more aggressive domestic programme—for nuclear power plants or launch vehicles, for example—would help. An export push, with appropriate ways of bypassing the international constraints, would be an additional demand generator. Without these, India's capability in these two high-tech sectors is resulting in minimal gain from an industrial viewpoint. Recent government initiatives to open up the space sector for participation by private industry may help to tap the large global market, especially for small satellites and launch vehicles. This should give a boost to the capability for manufacturing space hardware.

Tech entrepreneurs, creating new start-up enterprises, have recently brought a lot of dynamism to the aerospace sector, especially in space and unmanned aerial vehicles (particularly drones). A number of companies have come up, some of whom have begun to tap the global market. They, along with other companies, have also begun to change the scenario with regard to products for defence, with greater indigenous production.

While it is a long way off (though always seeming to be just at the near horizon), nuclear fusion could be the future of energy, promising boundless and 'clean' power at minimal cost. India must stay abreast of this technology, as it has tried to do in the case of nuclear fission and fast breeder reactors. Its involvement in the international programme for fusion (the international thermo-nuclear energy reactor [ITER]) should provide invaluable experience and data. Energy is at the very base of all development, and staying abreast of new technologies in this area is critical.

Another area—literally, more down-to-earth—is agri-tech. Blessed with abundant rainfall and a very large arable land mass, India is now an exporter of foodgrain. However, its productivity is still low compared to many other countries, and better yields could turn it into a granary. In this context, development of new seeds and practices can provide a big boost. Genetically modified foods are yet controversial, and India has been very wary of permitting these. However, research to develop better seeds, which can also provide more nutritious crops with added vitamins and minerals, is a necessity. In some areas, one or a few MNCs have a virtual monopoly on seeds for high-yield and/or pest-resistant crops. To counter this, India needs to develop indigenous capability in this area.

Apart from seeds and farming techniques, agri-tech includes soil assessment (in-situ or remotely), early detection of water stress or disease in crops, precision farming, crop-yield prediction, water management and general automation of farm operations. Advice to farmers, price and other market information are also important. All these involve a host of technologies: sensors, IoT devices, communication links, drones and satellites, backed up by computers, data analytics, robotics and AI. Platforms (accessible via mobile phone apps) for sharing/hiring of farm equipment on a pay-per-use basis, crop and input prices, and financial loans are also needed.

Many of these technologies and applications are already in place; they need to be taken further, and others developed. Overall, agri-tech in all its various facets is an important area for R&D and tech deployment. In fact, agriculture, one of the oldest 'technologies' developed by humans, may be amongst the prime users of the newest technologies. India has had a very active programme of research in agriculture for many decades. This needs to be rejuvenated and expanded to include the whole gamut of technologies relevant to agriculture. Such an effort can help to capitalize on India's natural endowment of soil, land, water and weather, and bring prosperity to rural India through greater productivity.

Increased productivity, though, should not be measured merely in terms of output value (revenue), but in terms of output per unit input. The present system encourages production maximization without worrying about input usage, since major inputs—water, electricity and fertilizer—are available free or at subsidized rates. Bank financing, too, is subsidized (and loans sometimes written off). This induces wasteful use of these inputs, with high exogenous or long-term consequences (land degradation, water-table depletion, etc.). At the same time, a minimum support price (MSP) makes for an assured return. Attempts to reform the system and make it more market-based (including doing away with the monopoly of the agricultural produce market committee [APMCs]) have been resisted, as it is feared that this will mean the end of the MSP. The latest agricultural reform laws, passed by Parliament in September 2020, have led to a major agitation by farmers. Beginning in Punjab, this spread first to adjoining states, and then more widely. While there are good arguments on both sides, there is clearly need to bring far greater efficiency to the value chain. The input chain works reasonably well, but the forward integration (from farm to consumer) is inefficient. Sorting, grading, storing, transporting (including cold stores and cold chains) and processing of farm produce could certainly be vastly improved through appropriate technologies. There is urgent need to do so, especially for high-value perishables like fruits, vegetables, animal husbandry (milk, meats, etc.), fish and other marine products. In this, as in a number of other areas of the overall agricultural sector, agri-tech is poised to play as important a role as fin-tech has in banking and finance.

In the coming years, many other technologies will be of importance and use to India. Basic research in foundational areas like biology, mathematics, physics, chemistry and material sciences, must be complemented by that in applied fields of special relevance to India. Energy is one such area. Environment and sustainability is another. Computers and information science/technology will drive work in a lot of other areas and are important fields in themselves. A programme on high-performance computing was launched a few years ago. More sustained work on these is needed, as also in emerging fields like quantum technology. In February 2020, the Union Budget for 2020–21 did include an outlay of ₹8,000 crore over a period of five years for the National Mission on Quantum Technologies and Applications. This welcome proposal needs to be vigorously executed.

Beginning right from Independence, over seven decades ago, India has built up a big network of research laboratories. This includes a large chain of laboratories of the CSIR, which cover a very wide range of disciplines; and institutions dedicated to research for defence needs, space and atomic energy. In addition, there are others focused on agriculture, bio-science and medicine. This infrastructure, plus a growing focus on research in the universities and in industry, should speed up India's journey on the road of technological advancement.

From time to time, various schemes have been created to allow scientists and technologists from the R&D institutions and academic institutions to set up enterprises. There is need for a greater thrust on this, through schemes that would encourage those so inclined to convert their research work into commercial products. The government should allow selected persons (technologists/professors) from the R&D sphere to take special leave—on a full pay basis for a year and half-pay for another year—to pursue an entrepreneurial idea, with free use of their own research/IP/patent. In addition, they should be given a grant of ₹1 crore for investment in their enterprise, if they can find a co-investor willing to invest a similar amount. To start with, 20 such 'entrepreneur-fellowships' may be given to those selected as having the most promising proposals. The number could go up to 100 in a few years if the idea is seen to be working well. Such a scheme, going well beyond the present limited ones, may lead to a lot of flow of technology from labs to industry to market, leveraging and utilizing the capabilities built over decades in the country's research infrastructure.

THE NEXT SILICON VALLEY?

Technology has been playing a growing role in the economy and, as detailed earlier, in various facets of daily life. As a result of continuing invention and innovation, technology is fast becoming ubiquitous and is transforming industry and business. Digitization is the new watch-word, with enterprises across sectors, as also the government itself, adopting digital technologies in a big way (all the more so after the start of the COVID epidemic, which brought home forcefully the utility and need for ICT for everything from WFH and learning, to shopping and entertainment). India's IT capabilities have played a big role and have particularly been crucial in keeping the economy ticking.

India's IT software and services sector now clocks up revenues of about $200 billion a year. Given its nature and people-intensity, a large proportion of this is gross value add (GVA) for the economy. Its contribution to the economy is, therefore, between 5–7 per cent. Since the size of this sector was minuscule in the early 1990s, it has, in effect, added about 5 per cent to the GDP within 30 years. Even as this sector continues to grow, can some other new technology now help the country to add a similar increment to economic growth in the coming years? Given the accelerating pace of technology advancement and use, it is possible to speculate that a still-nascent technology could add a chunk of the order of 5 per cent to the economy over the next 10–15 years. What would be that technology? Since a definite answer to this question may not be possible, the best that can be done is to follow the model of the IT success story. This means facilitative government policies, creation of a conducive ecosystem, minimal regulation at the early stages, and encouragement to entrepreneurs and innovation. This may give birth to many technologies and enterprises, out of which may come the next 'IT story', contributing hugely to economic growth.

With its existing base of talent and capabilities, India could be a major global force in technology. It could also become a model for how technology is used to narrow the gaps and schisms in society. These goals require a big ramp-up in funding for R&D, supportive policies and structures, and the development of a nurturing ecosystem, including close collaboration between industry, academia and government.

A few countries, especially China, Israel and South Korea, have demonstrated how funding and focused attention can result in big pay-offs in technology. India has been a laggard in this. Government investment on R&D continues to hover at (in fact, generally below) 0.75 per cent of GDP for over two decades and more. We would do well to learn from leaders, and use the 2020s to invest substantially in building technological capabilities, with the aim of being a frontrunner in at least a few key areas.

Investments in tech, though, do not provide an immediate return: harvesting fruit from the seeds sown takes some years. In the meantime, it is wise to look for quicker means of accessing the latest. One way of doing so is by acquiring technology from abroad, and the best route may be the acquisition of companies that have developed it (the additional advantage being that it comes along with the experts who did so, opening the possibility of continuous upgrades and new development). While the private sector could do this, the risk involved may be a deterrent, especially for key strategic technologies that may have only a limited commercial market. One could, therefore, consider government funding for this. However, given that it may be good for the government to stay at arm's length from such foreign acquisitions in hi-tech areas, it would be better for it to create a 'fund of funds' which will invest in privately-run funds dedicated only to such acquisitions. The latter, with a matching investment at stake, will ensure that the acquired foreign company gets well connected into the Indian industry ecosystem. It will also make sure that there is a thorough due diligence on all aspects of the foreign company: its technology, promoters, management, financials, etc.

These steps could help propel India into a position of leadership in selected technologies. While technology has strategic and economic dimensions, the country must also use its technological capabilities to meet the needs and challenges of systems that are designed to reduce societal gaps. Technologies must be developed or adapted so as to be suitable for decentralized and rural use, facilitating dispersal of industry and economic activity. Those meant for public use must be simple and easy to use, with all complexities at the back-end; user devices must be low-cost, with more expensive ones being of community-use design, and they must be accessible and useful for the disadvantaged, including especially the growing number of elders and those who are otherwise-abled. Technology must also help in reducing drudgery, find solutions for mechanized cleaning of drains and sewage pits, and facilitate ease of living. India must marshal its innovation and tech talent so as to be the global leader in such models that leverage technology for inclusive development and an improved quality of life for all.

This could be a priority for technology for the decade, so that, by 2030, inequities of income, knowledge and opportunity are vastly reduced. Unfortunately, not all inequities will go away—certainly not in a decade—but the negative trend can be reversed, bringing hope and a better life to millions.

The next 10 years can be the 'techade' which focuses on 'closing the gap'.

Epilogue

INDIA 2030+

Creating a Happy Country

Earlier chapters have outlined the trajectory that India may follow in key areas in the 2020s, and where it may reach in 2030. This section summarizes the main points, and then integrates them to present a holistic picture of India in 2030. It also attempts to peep further ahead, beyond 2030: what might India look like when it celebrates a century as a republic in 2050?

At India's independence in 1947, there were more than a few who doubted its ability to survive for long as one nation. Many felt that it was only British rule that had held it together and, before that, in differing geographical forms, the Mughal emperors. India had never been one country earlier. Even at Independence, it was a hodgepodge of British-governed areas, 'princely States' with varying degrees of freedom and some 'ungoverned' areas. The tragic riots, killings and mass migration due to the partition of the country reinforced the view that India was not ready for independence. Over and above this, the decision to be a democracy with universal adult franchise seemed foolhardy to many. For, how many examples were there of a huge country, with mass illiteracy, voting to elect its leaders?

Each time there was a crisis—language riots in Tamil Nadu, the India–China war in 1962, food shortages in the 1960s—doubts about the country's integrity and survival would surface. It was only some two decades after Independence that questions about India's survival slowly faded away. The India–Pakistan war of 1971 finally put paid to any doubts on this count, and the aftermath of Emergency (1975–77) reinforced India's standing as a resilient democracy.

The economic front saw similar, though slower, transition. India was at one time considered a 'basket case', surviving on imported (often gifted) food and living a 'ship to lip' existence. The derogatory phrases were supplemented by an image of India with a begging bowl, seeking aid from rich nations. Now, certainly for the last quarter century, India is a much feted and sought-after economic partner. It is the country with the maximum number of poor, and destitution is still widespread, but its large middle class makes it an attractive market, and its projected growth indicates bright future prospects.

India's size, growing economic strength and its significant military power gives it an important place in the global arena. This has been supplemented by its strength as a moral force amidst selfish countries (though some would say this has waned in recent years, with its poor record on human rights and social harmony). Its technological prowess in key areas, including missile and nuclear technology, and its rich sci-tech talent give it added weightage. Amongst developing countries, these facets of India, as also its traditional non-alignment or independence from the superpowers, are widely respected, putting it into a position of leadership. In global fora, many developing countries are known to blindly vote with India. Evolving global power dynamics are beginning to change some of this, but India continues to carry a lot of weight. In recent years, diplomatic outreach has further strengthened India's position with regard to many countries (though, arguably, it has lost its preponderant position in the immediate neighbourhood).

In recent times, China has become a major contender in terms of global influence. As the US becomes more inward-looking and protectionist, it is China that is seen as a globalizer, reaching out to other countries with generous economic aid and assistance. Its ambitious Belt and Road Initiative (BRI) seeks to project its lead role right into the heart of Europe. Thanks to China's infrastructure projects in various countries, trains from its industrial heartland now carry goods all the way to Germany, saving a great deal of time and money as compared to traditional transportation by ship. Barring India, practically every country that China approached has signed on to the BRI. While there is now some concern in most countries about the huge debt this involves, it is seen as a big step towards their economic betterment. Supplemented by additional bilateral arrangements—like the ambitious China–Pakistan Economic Corridor—this has given China tremendous diplomatic leverage in a large number of countries, adding to its image as a leading global power.

In contrast, India is constrained not only by its much smaller economy (as compared to China) but also by its inability to take bold and imaginative initiatives. Yet, the traditional goodwill towards India and the popularity of Indian culture—especially movies, music and yoga—could provide India a springboard to reignite traditional bonds. This is especially true of countries in Southeast Asia, Africa, Central Asia and the Gulf.

In the 2020s, if India can ensure sustained economic growth and makes a special effort to build cultural, political and economic ties, it can propel itself to a major global role. For a variety of reasons, both China and the US are actively disliked in many countries, whereas India tends to be looked upon favourably (except, unfortunately, in our immediate neighbourhood). While China and the US will continue to be the dominant powers globally in 2030, India could play a major role if it cleverly leverages its soft power. A critical element of this is its reputation as a democratic, secular country that respects minorities, and promotes social harmony and inclusive growth.

Apart from China, India may face challenges from 'middle powers' too. For example, one area that is likely to see intense competition for influence in this decade is Central Asia. It has a vast and under-populated land area, is rich in natural resources and is of strategic importance to its neighbours. China, Turkey, Iran, Russia and India will all be contenders in the game, with each having good reasons to keep the others out. Of course, this does not altogether rule out the possibility of partnerships amongst some of them, possibly separate ones for different countries in the region. For example, India and Iran—and Russia, to an extent—are working together with regard to Afghanistan. On the other hand, the US and India, both speaking of a strategic partnership between them, are not quite on the same page with regard to Afghanistan.

In an evolving strategic scenario, with the growing power and reach of China, and some emerging middle powers, India will have to leverage its full repertoire of capabilities. Given the power asymmetry with China (and the US), its best bet will be to pick and work with suitable partners. It is well-placed to do so, with countries like Japan, Australia and Vietnam quite happy to partner India.

Even as it seeks to counter China, India will need to try and build a positive and cooperative relationship. The economic relationship—despite the huge skew causing an adverse trade balance for India—is important: intermediate goods and components from China drive crucial parts of Indian industry (pharmaceuticals and electronics, in particular), and cheap consumer goods benefit the mass market. Also, on some global issues—climate change, for example—both are on the same side. Completely antagonizing China and fully aligning with the US is not in India's interest. India's goal must be strategic autonomy, and this requires clever manoeuvring, on a case-by-case basis, between the two superpowers of this decade. In some ways, it has to be a reinvented non-alignment.

A key necessity for India to begin playing a global role is to liberate itself from being tied up by Pakistan and China. One possibility that has been suggested here (spelt out in the chapter on security) is for a tripartite agreement with China and Pakistan, based on a vision of the future, which could bring peace to the border and an end to cross-border terrorist forays or support to them. Crafting such an agreement, without compromising national interests, would have to be a key agenda for India in the 2020s. An agreement—even a tentative one—will be truly transformative, enabling India to truly move to the world stage and also accelerate its development.

MAKING INDIA A WINNER

In the economic arena, the COVID pandemic and consequent restrictions have seriously affected an economy that was already faltering. GDP growth in 2019–20 is estimated at 4.2 per cent (the lowest in over a decade),[144] and the estimate is of

---

[144]'GDP Growth at 3.1% in Q4 Drags Full Year FY20 Growth to 4.2 per cent', *The Economic Times*, 29 May 2020, https://economictimes.indiatimes.com/

a disastrous minus 7.7 per cent in 2020–21.[145] Even a V-shaped (or sharp) recovery in the following year, which is being projected (GDP may bounce up to 10–10.5 per cent growth in 2021–22[146]), will mean two lost years of growth. The outlook beyond that, though, is positive. The remaining years of the decade could see high growth, comparable to that seen in the first decade or so of the century. While the rate of growth and extent of iniquity will determine the size and depth of the Indian market, it is certain to be large. Despite the slowdown and COVID, India will have a middle class—depending, of course, on the criteria for defining this category—of around 500 million consumers. This, and the overall size of the economy (which could be around $5.4 trillion by 2030), will give India clout. Its absolute size will make it the third largest economy in the world and, in the 2020s, its growth rate is likely to surpass that of China. Pharmaceuticals, healthcare, education, electronics and technology will be high-growth drivers of the economy. Each has a large and rapidly growing domestic market, plus great export potential. By the end of this decade, India will be a major global force in all these sectors.

---

news/economy/indicators/a-better-than-expected-q4-performance-pulls-fy20-gdp-growth-to-4-2-per-cent/articleshow/76091426.cms, accessed on 23 March 2021.

[145]'First Advance Estimates of National Income, 2020–21', *Ministry of Statistics & Programme Implementation*, 7 January 2021, https://pib.gov.in/PressReleasePage.aspx?PRID=1686824#:~:text=The growth in real GDP,a contraction of 7.2 percent, accessed on 23 March 2021.

[146]According to Shaktikanta Das, the Reserve Bank of India governor, quoted in 'Economic Growth Will Only Move Upwards: Shaktikanta Das', *The Economic Times*, 5 February 2021, https://economictimes.indiatimes.com/news/economy/policy/rbi-projects-gdp-growth-rate-of-10-5-for-fy22/articleshow/80702345.cms, accessed on 23 March 2021.

Yet, India will continue to be a country where poverty is rife, even if destitution is rare. Despite much progress, the shame of being home to the maximum number of poor people is likely to continue for some years. One had hoped that the early 2020s would see a considerable reduction in the proportion of poor in the country. However, the COVID pandemic has had a huge negative effect, pushing tens of millions back into poverty.

Hopefully, this will be a short-term impact: in a year, as the COVID epidemic reduces and more people get vaccinated, the economy could be on track again. This could mean that poverty, though not altogether banished, will be much reduced. Poverty reduction, and better livelihoods for those at the bottom of the economic pyramid, can be accelerated by reducing economic inequity. A surge of sympathy, with some degree of genuine empathy, was seen in the country as images of jobless daily wage workers trekking home with families and meagre belongings, flashed across TV and mobile phone screens. This may well lead to a more equitable society by 2030, as organizations and government make efforts to change the present exploitative and vastly iniquitous employment arrangements. India could create new paradigms of development, which combine equity and economic growth with jobs and decentralization. Technology will facilitate decentralized production, innovative business models will promote a human-plus-machine approach, and a major skills upgradation programme will help in massive job creation. These, in turn, will further reduce iniquity and poverty.

With this, by 2030, India will not be a prosperous country, but it would have eradicated extreme poverty and a large proportion of its population will have a reasonably comfortable material life. Food, shelter, clothing and livelihood will not be an issue, nor will safe water and sanitation. Education and healthcare will be easily and freely available to all, and quality standards will be ensured. Pollution is unlikely to go away, but the air and water will certainly be cleaner. Mass public transport will continue to be crowded (physical distancing will neither be required, nor feasible), but will be affordable and available. Individual non-polluting modes of transport, especially bicycles, will be incentivized, and better pedestrian facilities will be assured, encouraging walking and a resurgence in cycling. High bandwidth and reliable electronic connectivity across the country will ensure easy and cheap access to information, education, healthcare and entertainment, through affordable devices.

This connectivity, along with other new technologies and a philosophy of Gandhian (or frugal) engineering[147] will also facilitate the decentralization of work, making it possible for many tasks and millions of jobs to move to rural areas. Taking work to people—rather than taking people to work—will be the new mantra, as Arthur Clarke's dictum 'communicate, don't commute' becomes the work philosophy (practised extensively, out of necessity, during the COVID lockdown).

Demographic trends indicate that India will, in a few years, be the world's most populous country. It will continue to grow, with the population reaching a peak of 1.6 billion in 2048 (by 2100, it is projected to decline to 1.09 billion).[148] Despite

---

[147]'Innovation's Holy Grail', C.K. Prahalad and R.A. Mashelkar, *Harvard Business Review*, July—August 2010, https://hbr.org/2010/07/innovations-holy-grail, accessed on 23 March 2021.

[148]'Fertility, Mortality, Migration, and Population Scenarios for 195 Countries and Territories from 2017 to 2100: A Forecasting Analysis for the Global Burden of Disease Study', *The Lancet*, 14 July 2020, https://www.thelancet.com/action/showPdf?pii=S0140-6736%2820%2930677-2, accessed on 23 March 2021.

falling fertility, it will continue to be a young country for many years, and the large working-age population will result in an ongoing 'demographic dividend' by ensuring a low dependency ratio. However, the absolute number of elders will see a rapid increase. This will mean that serious effort must be made to ensure a healthy and fulfilling life for them. The regional skew in birth rates and proportionately lower population in more prosperous states will lead to greater migration and possible social tensions. As noted in Chapter 6, it could also have political repercussions if seats in Parliament are linked to population, which would give states like UP and Bihar even greater representation. This will need to be addressed before 2026, when the present freeze on seats is due to end. This could potentially be an explosive situation, even threatening national integrity. Fortunately, past experience gives reasons for optimism, through finding suitable and acceptable solutions.

India has long been a fractured society with deep divides—mainly of caste, but also of religion, ethnicity, region and language. The economic divide is overlaid on these, often reinforcing them. Gender discrimination too is a huge additional burden, as are old age and disability. While some of these seemed to be decreasing with progress, development and modernity, it often seems that this is but an illusion. The last few years have seen an upsurge in some of these divisions. A part of this may be perception, based on greater awareness and media exposure. However, it is likely that there is, in fact, an increase in discrimination and this is often manifested in violent form, particularly with regard to gender, religion and caste. In the latter part of the 2010s, the situation seems to have worsened.

One view is that we are at the peak; things will begin to settle down and social harmony will return. It is widely acknowledged that such harmony is essential for development; it is also an attribute that has greatly contributed to India's moral force in the global arena. Social harmony, and integration of communities that have felt excluded and marginalized, will ensure that terrorists have no safe havens. Without these, they will find it difficult to plan and execute any action and terrorism will find it hard to survive in a hostile ambience, nor will terrorist seeds take root in non-conducive soil. Our assessment is that in recognition of these factors, the country will see increasing social harmony through the 2020s.

Social cohesion, economic well-being (including jobs) and greater devolution of power to states and local bodies: together, these will vastly reduce, if not eliminate, the sense of alienation currently felt by some regions and groups. As a result, insurrections of the type seen in central India ('Left-wing extremism'), as also the separatism in parts of the Northeast and in Kashmir, will have few adherents. The decrease in violence and community involvement will facilitate development, creating a positive feedback loop between the two (decreased violence and development).

On another crucial front, India will accelerate its progress towards becoming an important R&D centre, where intellectual property is developed at scale. This will be backed up by an education system which, through major reforms in the early 2020s, will deliver high-quality education, comparable to the best anywhere. Turning knowledge into wealth will be millions of entrepreneurs, helped by proactive government policies and India's demographic profile (with the massive numbers of young, who are innovative and willing to take the risk of being self-employed). Already known for 'frugal innovation', India's increasing investment in R&D will help it to add discovery and invention to its abilities to improvise and innovate.

Work and jobs are a major worldwide concern. Thanks, in part, to well-intended policies with unintended consequences, an overwhelming proportion (certainly over 80 per cent, though estimates vary) of India's workforce is in the unorganized sector or on contract employment, with no job security or social security benefits. So-called 'gig work' has vastly increased following the growth of the 'shared/platform economy', with, for example, taxi aggregators (like Ola and Uber) treating drivers as 'independent contractors' and not employees. The same holds true for delivery executives of companies like Amazon, Flipkart or Zomato. The gig economy is here to stay, but, for this to be sustainable, it needs a robust social security net, to take care of education and health of the family, old age pension, and periods of unemployment. India is just beginning to address this issue, and the 2020s must see the quick evolution of an appropriate framework to provide the necessary safety net. It would then help gig workers who prefer this lifestyle, contract workers and daily wage labour, as also companies that desire flexibility in the means of getting work done through part-time, full-time, or contract workers.

Another challenge to jobs and livelihoods is technology. Automation threatens to replace humans in a growing range of tasks. In India, this process will be slower than in developed countries, given the lower wages. Also, increased entrepreneurship across the country will mean more job creators and less job seekers. In addition, if India can create the right human-*plus*-machine model—rather than human *or* machine—it will, in fact, result in an increase in jobs. There will yet be the problem of redeployment and suitability for the new jobs, in terms of knowledge and skills. The answer will be a massive programme of training, updating and upgrading for existing employees, and suitable courses of education and skills for those entering the workforce. This will be a major agenda for the nation in the 2020s, to take the economy forward by moving it to a high value-add orbit, as also to ensure quality livelihoods for the large number of youth who enter the workforce during the decade. Many of them may choose to work abroad, where opportunities abound, particularly in the numerous countries that will face a shortage of talent and human power. Success in mass-scale skilling will enable India to fully reap the demographic dividend and give it the springboard for continued robust growth beyond 2030.

In many key areas including health, education, agriculture, labour and land policies, it is the states that are decision-makers. In these and other areas, action and implementation too will depend upon the states. Good governance—effective, sensitive and accountable—at all levels is, therefore, a crucial element of the projected scenario for 2030. In areas like health, community involvement is a necessary ingredient. The COVID pandemic has highlighted this, as also the need for strong mutual trust between the authorities and the people. Strengthening democracy, especially at the grass roots, is essential, so is decentralization and the devolution of power—not just from the Centre to the states, but also to the level of local bodies (panchayats and urban municipalities). The Constitution explicitly provides for this, and it is time to fully implement the provisions. Technology now makes this easier, through communication links, cloud technology and commonly accessible databases. It can ensure the efficiency of governance in a rural panchayat, even in a remote area. With this, governance and democracy in the 2020s can take a new shape and aid in the rapid, citizen-centric, citizen-driven and inclusive development of the country.

Fears of a 'surveillance State' have been stoked by the

worldwide trend in recent years toward strong, authoritarian leaders and centralized, ultra-nationalistic governments. Technology has made possible direct surveillance, as also the collection and analysis of data about citizens, on a scale never imagined before. Even in deeply democratic societies, such data collection and surveillance has become commonplace, justified and largely accepted as being necessary from a security viewpoint. Now, following the COVID pandemic, many (probably most) people are willing to trade-off privacy against health too, providing further justification for government to collect a great deal more data about individuals. It seems 1984 (Orwell's dystopian prediction of the future) is finally here.[149]

Decentralization and devolution of power could considerably obviate concerns about an overbearing, 'Big Brother'. India could well lead the world in this, creating a model and setting an example for not merely electoral, but participatory democracy. India's unique 3D advantage—demography, diversity and democracy—has been noted.[150] The 2020s provide the opportunity to add another special 3D combination: democracy, decentralization and devolution. Together, these can make India a winner.

In taking this positive path, what we do in the coming years will be crucial. For India, this is indeed the decisive decade.

---

[149] *1984*, George Orwell, Secker & Warburg, June 1949.
[150] "Incubating Innovation in India", Kiran Karnik, *The Economic Times*, 8 December 2009, https://economictimes.indiatimes.com/opinion/et-commentary/incubating-innovation-in-india/articleshow/5312461.cms, accessed on 23 March 2021.

A SHARED VISION FOR INDIA 2050: A HAPPY COUNTRY

Thus far, we have looked at the present context in a few areas in some detail, and made projections for how things may be in 2030. In the process, there are assumptions, or suggestions, of the path to be followed in the 2020s that will lead to the predicted outcomes. This section seeks to look further ahead: what might India be in 2050, as it celebrates a century as a republic?

Making long-term predictions is difficult. The impact of seemingly small changes results in very different outcomes due to compounding. If India's GDP were to grow at 6 per cent a year from an assumed $5.4 trillion in 2030, it would increase to $17 trillion in 2050. However, if it were to grow at 8 per cent, it would reach $25 trillion. While this is impressive, it is sobering to take a comparative look at China. Any comparison and a projection (uncertainties, PPP, exchange rate, etc.) necessarily has its own limitations. Despite these caveats, it is interesting to see that even if China grows at only half the rate of India (assumed at an optimistic 8 per cent a year till 2050), it will reach $44.6 trillion—almost double India's $25 trillion.[151]

Speed is not the only issue; at worst, one will reach the defined end-point later or earlier than anticipated. Direction is also important; small differences in direction could lead to very different destinations. A slow but steady decline in freedom could be a slippery slope, leading to a totalitarian, theocratic and aggressive State (as in the dystopian scenario in

---

[151] Based on China's GDP of USD 14.3 trillion in 2019 as stated in 'GDP (Current US$)', *The World Bank*, https://data.worldbank.org/indicator/NY.GDP.MKTP.CD?locations=CN, accessed on 23 March 2021. The projection assumes that, like India, the economy is at the same level (as 2019) in 2021

the chapter on democracy). On the other hand, the projection made earlier in this chapter could lead to very different and positive outcomes. In view of the uncertainties inherent over a 30-year period, any forecast for 2050 must necessarily be viewed with a pinch of salt, and some scepticism. Yet, it is a useful exercise: if nothing else, it could stir a debate on where we want to reach. This, in fact, should be the main purpose: to create a debate and dialogue, which could result in evolving a shared vision of our goals.

An analytical or detailed forecast of India in 2050 is not being attempted here (it deserves a separate book); instead, the next few paragraphs only aim to paint a very broad-brush scenario—and an extremely brief one—of what the country could be.

By 2050, all Indians, even the poorest, will be well fed; live in a house with safe water, electricity and a toilet; be assured of free, high-quality healthcare and education; adults will have a livelihood (job or entrepreneurial activity), re-skilling opportunities, unemployment insurance and a pension. Every community, in rural or urban areas, will have an adequate number of parks, playgrounds and sports facilities, as also museums, art galleries and theatres. City forests will complement the long planned for 33 per cent forest cover across the country. This, and minimally polluting industry and transport, will ensure clean air even in large urban agglomerations.

New policies, aided by technology, will disperse industries and workplaces across the country. They will also ensure the best facilities and infrastructure everywhere, including geographically difficult rural areas. As a result, people will stay wherever they prefer, and cities will become far less congested. High-speed trains and excellent highways connecting all parts of the country will make travel fast, easy and cheap, even as the airline networks become far more extensive. Most people would choose to walk or bicycle for short distances, and use electric mass transport systems for longer commutes. Motorized individual transport (cars, two-wheelers) and taxis will operate on batteries or hydrogen fuel, ensuring minimal pollution.

India will lead the world in the near-complete changeover to renewable energy (wind, solar and hydro), and be on the front-ranks of power storage technologies (batteries). Work on nuclear fusion reactors will be coming to fruition, and the first such commercial plants will begin operation. Having more than met its global commitments towards a reduction in carbon and greenhouse gas emission, India will help other countries to emulate its success and reverse the adverse effects of climate change.

Ubiquitous broadband connectivity will be so cheap that it will be provided free to every household, with companies garnering their revenue from content and applications. This will be a major driver of the dispersal and decentralization of all work, reducing the pressure on cities. It will also enable telemedicine and learning or working from home for those so inclined, or forced by circumstances to do so.

Caste, religion, region and other divides will long be forgotten. People will take pride in the distinctiveness of their culture, language, cuisine, couture, ethnicity and other special characteristics, but this will be as a celebration of India's diversity, rather than as exclusionary or divisive factors. Social harmony will be marked and promoted through sharing, affection and empathy, creating community bonds that cannot be broken.

Technology and innovation will add strength to India's traditional soft power. The competition between China, India, the US and a resurgent Europe will be played out more in the realm of development, technology, ideas and art, rather than militarily. Yet, India will be strong enough to have full strategic autonomy, and to assert itself when necessary—including in the new realms of cyber and outer space.

India's image is currently of a large, lumbering elephant. It threatens to become a hippopotamus: an aggressive, loud, slow creature, which is the world's deadliest large land mammal. In our positive scenario, these images will be replaced by that of a gazelle: agile, smart, adaptive, fast (capable of short bursts of extreme speed and sustained periods of moderate speed) friendly and likeable.[152] Indians will cease being aggressive jaguars and touchy porcupines: the 'angry Indian'[153] will be replaced by the friendly, compassionate and wise one.

Is this brief summary of a rosy future merely a wish, a dream? In many ways it is. Yet, there is no reason why it cannot be actually realized. Already, even today, almost every one of the elements of it is in evidence in one or the other part of India itself. All that needs to be done is to adapt and scale these positive examples.

India may or may not be the world leader in some of the areas mentioned, it may or may not be a true superpower; it may or may not eventually overtake the US and China, and be the richest country. By 2050, we may or may not achieve these ambitions. But there is one prize that we should aim for: that of being the happiest country.

That would, indeed, be a worthwhile goal.

---

[152]Description of hippopotamus and gazelle from LiveScience and National Geographic websites.
[153]'Do We Really Want a Superpower India Populated by Angry Indians?', Kiran Karnik, *The Economic Times*, 7 August 2012, https://economictimes.indiatimes.com/opinion/et-commentary/do-we-really-want-a-superpower-india-populated-by-angry-indians/articleshow/15382725.cms, accessed on 23 March 2021.

INDEX

Aadhaar, 4
Aam Aadmi Party (AAP), 11, 27–28, 70, 140
  Delhi election 2020, 140
  'mohalla' (locality) clinics, 70
Active pharmaceutical ingredients (APIs), 234
Agricultural produce market committee (APMCs), 240
Agricultural reform laws, 240
AI-based chatbots, 115
Alexa, 115
Alexander the Great, 2
Alibaba Group, 209
All India Anna Dravida Munnetra Kazhagam (AIADMK), 162
All India Council for Technical Education (AICTE), 102–3, 117
Al-Qaeda, 38
Amazon, 256
Anganwadi and Accredited Social Health Activist (ASHA) workers, 205
Anganwadi programme, 121
Anti-CAA protest, 26–27
Anti-corruption movement, 126
Anti-defection law, 6
Arabian Sea, cyclones in, 61
Arab–Israeli conflict, 38
Armed Forces Special Powers Act (AFSPA), 43–44

Artificial intelligence (AI), 104, 197
Ashoka University, 101
Asian Tigers, 148
Aspect of outward migration, 166
Association for Democratic Reforms (ADR), 5
AstraZeneca, 235. *See also* COVID
Astronomical observations, 169
Asymmetric warfare, 60
Automation, 113–15, 196–200, 209, 211–12, 214, 218, 222, 231, 239, 356
Ayushman Bharat Yojna, 69

Balakot bombing, 24, 41. *See also* Pulwama killings
Balance of trade, 235
Bangladesh, adult literacy rate, 90
Bay of Bengal, cyclones in, 61
Behavioural science, 73–77
  importance of, 77
Belt and Road Initiative (BRI), 44, 248
Bharat Biotech, 235
Bharatiya Janta Party (BJP), 8–9, 11, 13, 16, 22–28, 32, 125–28, 130, 141, 172–73
  Bihar assembly election, 24
  Delhi assembly election, 11
  ground workers, 130

national election (2014, 2019), 9, 11, 27–28
'nationalistic' space from, 26
nationalist agenda, 16
strategy of election campaigner, 23
ultra-nationalistic and religious campaign (2019), 141
UP assembly election, 128
Biju Janata Dal (BJD), 175
Bio weapons, 59
Biological warfare, 50, 60, 78, 219
Biological weapons, 78–79
Biological Weapons Convention, 78
Birla Institute of Technology and Science (BITS), 101
Black swan, 55–56, 58
Bottom of the (economic) pyramid, 142
Brazil, LFPR for women, 187
Broadband connectivity, 261
Bullet train, Japan agreement for, 228
Byjus, 107

Cairn Oil, 212
Canada, Indian-origin people, 167
Cases pendency in High Courts, 14
Cash-for-question scam, 8
Central Bureau of Investigation (CBI), 22
Child malnutrition, 75
China
 aggressive stance, along the Line of Actual Control (LAC), 46
 ahead of India in both economic and military terms, 38
 ascent of, 38
 Belt and Road Initiative (BRI), 44
 –Bhutan agreement, 52
 'factory of the world', 122
 GDP growth, 131–32
 growing power and reach of, 249
 healthcare expenditure, 67–68
 high-speed rail (HSR), 230
 implications for India, 38
 –India rivalry, 56
 India's second-largest trading partner, 38
 infrastructure projects, 248
 LFPR for women, 187
 military expenditure, 45
 model of mass employment, 198
 '90-7-3' approach for elderly care, 152
 –Pakistan Economic Corridor, 248
 per capita GDP, 138
 population, 146
 R&D expenditure, 111
 rapid growth models, 140
 re-education centres, 31
 –Russia ties, 45
 strong support of Pakistan, 46
 top player in AI, 111
 UNDP Multidimensional Poverty Index, 133
China–Pakistan attack, possibility of, 64
Citizenship (Amendment) Act (CAA), 25–27, 161, 186
City forests, 260
Civil war, 37, 40–41
Clarke, Arthur, 253
'Clean' power sources, 63
Cleaning robot, 114
Climate change, 38, 60–62, 219, 250, 261

Coal-based thermal power, 63
Coercive 'donation', 5
Coercive measures, 7
Common Service Centres (CSC), 221
Communal hatred, 32
Comptroller and Auditor General (CAG), 126
Constitutional rights of citizens, 16
Council for Scientific and Industrial Research (CSIR), 118
Coursera (online education platform), 105
COVID
    collateral economic impact, 85
    consequences of, 81
    consequent restrictions, 250
    Covishield vaccine, 235
    cross-national exchange of data, 80
    decentralization and dispersal of manufacturing, 200
    disruption in global supply chains, 80
    disruption in livelihoods, 82
    economic loss, 139
    illness and mortality due to, 85
    importance of agility, 86
    jobless and penniless migrant-labour families, 82
    lockdown, 81, 108, 220
    media coverage, 71
    online classes, 220
    personal protective equipment (PPE), 70
    shortage of hospital beds, 81
    testing kits, 71
    trauma of, 85
    unlock phase of restrictions, 216
    use of technologies during lockdown, 182
    vaccine nationalism, 80
    V-shaped economic recovery, 251
    wake-up call, 82
    work-from-home (WFH), 210
    See also Health
Crimes against women, 63, 135, 180
Criminal conspiracy charges against former MPs, 8
Criminal justice system, 14–23
CRISIL, 131
Cross-border firing, 41, 51–52, 58
Cross-border terrorism, 38
Cyber-attacks, 49–50, 63, 78
Cyber warfare, 60
Cyber weapons, 59
Cybersecurity, 58, 111

Data analytics, 115, 119, 205, 222, 224, 231–32, 239
Data mining, 105–6
Day-care centres for infants, 160
Debt-repayment obligations, 125
Decentralization, 35, 55, 86, 116, 157, 179, 200, 211, 225, 252–53, 257–258, 261
Defections, 7
Defence expenditure, 48
Delhi Assembly elections (2020), 11. *See also* Aam Aadmi Party (AAP)
Democracy
    earliest instances of, 2
    government is an important element of, 15
    meaning of, 1

pitfalls of, 6–13
rights of minorities, 9
Demographic dividend, 137, 147–49, 195, 218, 254, 257
Demographic trends, 253
Demography, 144, 153, 184, 206, 258
   communal angle, 149
   communal-driven propaganda, 165
   consequences, 159–68
   'demographic bomb', 147
   'demographic dividend', 147
   demographic scene in 2030, 158–59
   demographic transition, 154
   estimated population, 146
   'family welfare', 145
   impact of new technologies on longevity, 154
   in-country migration, 162
   internal migration, 165
   job opportunities closer to home, 158
   migration, 160, 168
   new imperatives, 153–59
   'population explosion', 147
   regional divide in population growth rates, 163
   regional economic imbalance, 160
   regional imbalance, 160
   rural-to-urban migration, 157
   slower rate of population growth, 159
   total fertility rate (TFR), 146
   two-track policy, 155
Demonetization, 127–30
   negative political fallout of, 128

Department of Family Planning, 145
Dependency ratio, 137, 147, 218, 254
Devolution of power, 255, 257–58
Digitization, 200, 205, 212, 232, 242
Direct cash transfer scheme, 139
Direct military confrontation, 58, 60
Discrimination based on caste, 134
DNA sampling, 169
Dog whistle, 23
Domestic violence, 76, 151
Double whammy, 160
Dravida Munnetra Kazhagam (DMK), 162
Drinking and drugs, 184
Dubey, Vikas, 18n16

Early Indians (Joesph), 170
Ease of Doing Business (EoDB), 62, 127
East India Company, 124
ECA quota, 100
eCENSUSIndia, 144n84
Economic divide, 254
Economic inequality, 134, 135, 139, 180, 193
Economic mobility for employment, 106
Economic revival package, 71
Economic well-being, 255
Economy
   agricultural growth, 129
   demonetization, 127
   ease-of-living, 142
   effect of demonetization, 130
   estimates for GDP (2020-21), 132
   foreign exchange crisis, 125

GDP growth, 130–31
high-growth drivers of, 251
high-growth phase, 137
human-focused development model, 140
introduction of Goods and Services Tax (GST), 127
medium- to long-term prospects, 137
per capita GDP, 138
poorly implemented GST, 130
pronouncements about doubling farmers' incomes, 130
rate of decline in poverty, 129
redefining development, 138–43
signposts of development, 133–38
traditional indicators, 136
Education
academic or intellectual knowledge, 113
action plan, 116–22
adult literacy rate, 90–91
central universities and institutes, 97
creation of a Coordination Forum, 98
diversity and flexibility, 116
dropouts, 95
enrolment at the primary school stage, 91
extent of literacy, 90
foreign universities to operate in India, 103
government efforts to raise quality, 101
gross enrolment ratio, 95
importance of finance, 88
importance of human capital, 89
inclusion and diversity in admissions, 118
Industrial Training Institutes (ITIs), 93
'institutes of eminence', 102
lack of skill education, 92
'lowest common denominator' approach, 98
'marks inflation', 92
online courses, 108
online learning, 105
paucity of quality educational institutions, 103
present structure of higher education, 96
private engineering colleges, 100
quality and relevance of learning, 95
quality of education, 91–92, 116
R&D (major driver), 110
rapid expansion of, 96
right to education (RTE) Act, 91
simultaneous automation, 114
state-of-the-art laboratories, 97
structural flaws, 95–107
technology (driver of education), 105
neglect of the, 155
loneliness, neglect and even ill-treatment of, 151
Election Commission of India (ECI), 3–6, 105
bulwark of a smoothly functioning democracy, 3
independence and objectivity of the, 6
introduction of EVMs, 3–4
powers, 3
process and the role of, 5

steps taken by, 6
voter awareness and education programmes, 4
voter verifiable paper audit trail (VVPAT), 4
Electoral arithmetic, 23
Electoral bonds, 5
Electoral procedure, 2–7
double voting, 4
money power in elections, 4
successes and ills of, 2–6
Electric vehicles, 63, 227
phased switchover to, 227
use of hydrogen as a fuel, 228
Emergency (1975), 28, 32, 145, 185, 247
Employment
actions to promote jobs and livelihood, 217
agriculture–dominant sector, 205
'bridgital workers', 206
close collaboration between industry and academia, 215
command- and-control approach, 198
concern about new technologies, 212
COVID virus, 210
design-led manufacturing, 217
digital technologies for healthcare, 205
economic mobility for, 106
ecosystem for training, 217
effect of booming economy, 203
entrepreneurship, 199
evolve and promote human-plus-machine/AI models, 218
future of work, 209–12
gig workers, 209
global service delivery, 217
in healthcare, 206
high-productivity, 'quality' jobs, 214
high-quality education and training, 217
human-mediated user-to-technology links, 217
human-plus-machine model, 215
impetus to people-intensive services, 218
innovation, 217
local entrepreneurship, 217
model of decentralized development, 217
net gains in employment, 213
online education and training courses, 207
quality jobs, 201
'quality livelihoods for all', 218
redesign structures and processes to decentralize, 217
scale and plight of migrant labour, 202
social security safety net, necessity for, 214
surety of employment, 201
temporary, short term or seasonal, 202
training and re-skilling, 213
universal and free school education, 217
work-from-home (WFH), 210
Encounter killings, 17, 19, 21–22
Energy security, 62–63
Enforcement Directorate (ED), 21–22
Entrepreneur-fellowships, 242

Entrepreneurial activity, 260
Equal opportunity for all, 135

Fake news, 188
Family planning, 69, 73, 75, 144, 145, 147, 149
Farm mechanization, 179
Farmers' agitation (2020), 33
Fear-based self-censorship, atmosphere of, 28
Female labour force participation rate (LFPR), 135
Fiji, proportion of Indian-origin people, 167
Financial Action Task Force (FATF), 42
Financial warfare, 60
First Indians, 170–71
First-past-the-post electoral system, 10–11
   pitfalls of, 11
Flipkart, 256
Food security, 50, 60, 63
Food shortages (1960s), 247
Foreign Contribution (Regulation) Act (FCRA), 22–23
Foreign direct investment (FDI), 123
Fractal analytics, 77
Frugal innovation, 255
Fund of funds, 244

Galwan, clash in, 46
Gandhi, Indira, 30, 124, 145, 185
Gandhi, Rahul, 126
Gandhi, Rajiv, 124
Gandhi, Sanjay, 145
Gandhian (or frugal) engineering, 253

Gated communities, 181–82, 193
Gautam Buddha, 2
GDP growth, 131, 139–40, 195, 250
Gender discrimination, 254
Genetically modified foods, 239
Geographic mobility, 106, 178
Germany, reunification of, 36
Ghettoization, 177–78
Gig economy, 209, 217, 256
Gig work, 209–10, 256
Gini coefficient, 133
Girl children, neglect of, 76
Global power dynamics, 247
Goods and Services Tax (GST) (2017), 127, 130
Goswami, Arnab, 15n14
Gross National Happiness, 135
Gross value add (GVA), 243

Harappan civilization, 170
Harvard Medical School, 215
Harvard University, 106
Hate speech, 3
Hate-based campaign in 2019, success of, 25
Hate-mongering leaders, 29
Hazare, Anna, 126, 185
Health
   accredited social health assistants (ASHAs), 68
   Ayushman Bharat Yojna (2018), 69
   behavioural science, 73–77
   child malnutrition, 75
   component of national security, 78–83
   comprehensive national nutrition survey, 66

high mortality is poor nutrition, 75
inadequacies in basic healthcare, 69
is happiness, 83–87
key indicators, 65
life expectancy at birth, 67
maternal mortality ratio (MMR), 66–67
'mohalla' (locality) clinics, 70
poor nutrition and bad health, 67
primary health centres (PHCs), 68
private spending, 67
public expenditure on health, 67
total healthcare expenditure, 67
HelpAge India, 151
Higher Education Commission of India (HECI), 103, 105
Higher Education Promotion Commission (HEPC), 117–20
  compensation for staff and faculty, 119
  criteria for recognition, 119
  fixed grant for research, 119
  safeguard the interests of students, 120
High-speed rail (HSR), 111, 228–31
Hindustan Aeronautics Ltd, 237
HIV-AIDS epidemic, 84
Hong Kong, economic growth, 137, 148
Hum Log, 75
Human Development Index, 65, 89
Human-plus-machine model, 215–16, 218, 222, 252, 256
Human-replacing devices, 114
Hydrogen Energy Mission, 228
Hyperloop, 230–31

Identity-based riots, 176
IIMs Common Admission Test, 99
IIT Joint Entrance Examination, 99
Imported crude oil and gas, dependence on, 62
Income Tax Department, 21
India shining, 125
India–China military confrontation, 45
India–China relationship, 37, 51
India–China war in 1962, 247
Indian Institutes of Science Education and Research (IISERs), 102
Indian School of Business (ISB), 101
Indian Space Research Organisation (ISRO), 74
India–Pakistan rivalry, 51, 56
Indo-US nuclear deal, 57
Industry 4.0, 197
Insolvency and Bankruptcy Code (2016), 127
Interactive voice response system (IVRS), 115
Internal insurgencies, 42, 47, 49, 54–55, 59–60
  Khalistan movement, 42
  'Left-wing extremism' (LWE), 43
  militancy in Kashmir, 42
  Naxalbari in West Bengal, 43
International thermo-nuclear energy reactor (ITER), 238
Internet connectivity, 109, 220
Internet of Things (IoT), 197, 200, 204, 224, 231, 239
Islamic Caliphate, 39
Islamic State of Iraq and Syria (ISIS), 39, 55
IT software and services sector, 242

Jamia Millia, police action, 15, 26
Jan Lok Pal, 185
Jawaharlal Nehru University (JNU), 20, 25, 28, 100, 118
  police action in, 15, 26
Jingoism, 9, 141
Joseph, Tony, 170
JP movement, 185
Judicial system, long delays in, 17, 20

Kendriya Vidyalayas, 121
Khalistan, 32, 42, 44, 175
Korea, R&D expenditure, 111

'Lab created' virus. *See* COVID
Ladakh, clashes with China, 58
Lady Shri Ram College (LSR) for Women, 99–100
Language riots in Tamil Nadu, 247
Law Commission, 19
Lee, William, 212
Left Front government, 13
Left-wing extremism (LWE), 43–44, 54, 60, 255
'Liberals' ('Lutyens' elites' or 'Khan Market gang'), 24–25
Light Combat Aircraft (Tejas), 237
Love jihad, 173

Machine learning, 197, 205, 232
Mahabharata, 169
Mahajanapadas, 2
Mahatma Gandhi National Rural Employment Guarantee Act [MGNREGA], 138, 207
Main Kuch Bhi Kar Sakti Hoon, 75
Maintenance and Welfare of Parents and Senior Citizens Act (2007), 150
Majoritarian approach, 9
Majoritarianism, 8, 10, 23
Male child, preference for, 76
Male progeny, historical preference for, 77
Mass migration, 246
Massive Open Online Courses (MOOCs), 105–6, 223
  element of, 106
  India as a major consumer, 106
Mauritius, proportion of Indian-origin people, 167
Medical tourism, 84–85
Military expenditure, 44
Minimum support price (MSP), 240
Ministry for Human Resource Development (HRD), 98
Minority appeasement, 9
Mobile-based apps, 189
Modi, Narendra, 24, 126–27
Mohalla clinics, 27. *See also* Aam Aadmi Party (AAP); Health
Money inducements, 7
Moral policing, 21
Motorized individual transport, 261
Multi-candidate election, 11
Multi-party system, 10
Musk, Elon, 231
Muslim appeasement, 24

Nalanda, 104
Narayan, Jayaprakash, 185
Narcotics Control Board (NCB), 22
National Democratic Alliance (NDA), 125
National Education Policy (NEP 2020), 102–3, 105, 116, 121–22, 164

National Investigation Agency (NIA), 21–22
National Mission on Quantum Technologies and Applications, 241
National programme for family planning, 144
National Register of Citizens (NRC), 25–26, 161–62, 186
National Sample Survey Office (NSSO), 180n110
Naxalites, 25
Nehru, Jawaharlal
  aggressive forward policy, 54
  tryst with destiny speech, 123
New political formations, 34
Next-generation nuclear power, development of, 63
'9/11', September 11, 38
No-communication hours, 183
Non-farm rural employment, 179
No-support-to-terrorists clauses, 53
Note-based democracy, 6
Nuclear power plants, 57, 238

Online coding-classes start-up, 106
Online courses, 105–8, 117, 207, 226
  content creation for, 207
Open defecation, 76
Organisation for Economic Co-operation and Development (OECD), 110
Outward migration, aspect of, 166
Oxfam International, 134

Paid news, 4
Pakistan
  attempted invasion of Kashmir in 1947, 41
  cross-border firing, 41
  Kargil incursion in 1999, 41
Partisanship of the police, 20
Partition in 1947, 32
Patents or intellectual property rights (IPRs), 111
Penalty of proximity, 200
People-focused development, 59
Periodic Labour Force Survey (2017–18), 201
Personal security and safety, 63
Pharmaceutical industry, 233
Plausible deniability, 78
Policy paralysis, 9, 126
Politicization of the police, 21
Pollution, 27, 62, 70, 133, 157, 220, 227–28, 231, 253, 261
Population control, 145, 149
Post-election combination, 7
Poverty ratio, 133, 135
Poverty reduction, 252
Pradhan Mantri Awas Yojana, 207
Pre-election alliances, 7
Prenatal sex determination, 77. *See also* Health
Prevention of Torture Bill (2010), 19
Princely States, 246
Production linked incentive scheme, 237
Professional police force, 21
Programme for International Student Assessment (PISA), 110
Proxy wars, 49
Psychological warfare, 50
PUBG, 189
Public health. *See* Health

Public opinion, 12–13, 176
Public–private partnership (PPP) mode, 213
Pulwama killings, 24

Quantum technology, 241
Queen Elizabeth I, 213

Rajasthan Dharma Swatantraya Bill (2008), 173
Rajya Sabha, seat in the, 7
Ram temple in Ayodhya, foundation-stone-laying ceremony, 30
Ramayana, 169
Rao, Narasimha, 125
Religious-identity defined group, 172
Renewable energy programme, 62
Research and Development (R&D)
   government investment on, 243
   on hydrogen, nuclear fusion, 63
   quickly operationalize electric vehicles, 63
Re-skilling opportunities, 260
Right of Children to Free and Compulsory Education Act (2009), 91
Right to recall, 6
Rights to employment, food and shelter, 59
Robots, 58, 114–15, 197–98, 211
Rousseff, Dilma, 209
Run-off system, 11

S&P Global Ratings, 131
Sabarimala temple, 13
Sample Registration System (SRS), 67
Satellite Instructional Television Experiment (SITE), 74, 221
Saudi Arabia, Indian-origin people, 167
Schemes for subsidized cooking fuel, 76
Screwdriver technology, 235
Second independence. *See* Economy
Second World War, 37
Sector Skills Councils, 213
Secularism, Constitutional principle of, 25
Sedition, law on, 22
Self-employment, 179, 204
Seshan, T.N., 3. *See also* Election Commission of India (ECI)
70 years of misrule, 24, 34
Shah, Amit, 24
Shaheen Bagh, 26–28, 33, 186. *See also* CAA
Shared vision for India 2050, 259–63
Shared/platform economy, 256
Shifting alliances, 7
'Ship to lip' existence, 247
Shiv Sena, 161, 175
Singapore
   economic growth, 137
   LFPR for women, 187
   per capita GDP, 138
   rapid growth models, 140
   super-fast growth, 148
Singh, Birender, 7
Singh, Manmohan, 43, 57, 123, 125–26
Slowdown, 130–31, 251
Smart Cities programme, 231
Social cohesion, 192, 255

Social harmony, 34, 53, 56, 247, 249, 254, 255, 261
Social media platforms, 188–89
Society and social dynamics
  birth-identity dividers, 190–91
  caste-based reservations/quotas for jobs, 192
  division based on class, 193
  drug and alcohol addiction, 193
  equality amongst the young, 193
  FOMO factor: the 'fear of missing out', 183
  gender conflict, 193
  genetic 'purity', 171
  geographical isolation, 171
  inter-marriages, 171
  job reservation through identities, 174
  new social dynamic, 184–94
  'nuclear household', 191
  political attractiveness of a reservation/quota policy, 172
  public policy initiatives, 181
  regional-linguistic-cultural identity, 175
  reinforcement of prejudice, 188
  slow demise of the 'joint family', 191
  social consequences, 184
  socio-cultural factors, 174–75
Socio-cultural agenda, 9
South Asian Association for Regional Cooperation (SAARC), 53
South Korea
  clandestine biological weapons programme, 79
  economic growth, 137
  per capita GDP, 138
  super-fast growth, 148
Soviet Union, disintegration (1991), 37
SpaceX, 231
Sri Lanka
  adult literacy rate, 90
  UNDP Multidimensional Poverty Index, 133
Start-up ventures, 148
STEM (science, technology, engineering, mathematics), 104, 111–13
Subsidized bank financing, 240
Supreme Court, 13–16, 21, 150
  backlog of pending cases, 14
Surveillance State, 257
Sustainable Development Goals (SDGs), 139
Swachh Bharat, 72, 207
Switzerland, per capita GDP, 138
Symbiosis International (deemed university), 101

Tahrir Square, Cairo, 26
Taiwan
  economic growth, 137
  super-fast growth, 148
Taksim Square, Istanbul, 26
Taliban-ruled Afghanistan, 56
Taxi-app service (Ola & Uber), 209, 256
Tech entrepreneurs, 238
Technology
  advances in AI, 222
  agri-tech, 220, 239
  artificial intelligence (AI), 224, 231
  blockchain, 232

data analytics, 222, 224, 231
development of new
  technologies, 224
'driving' the Future, 227–32
in education, 223
5G, 224
farming techniques, 239
human-plus-machine model, 222
impact of, 219
importance of electronics, 236
investments in, 244
IoT, 224, 231, 239
leveraging technology, 223–26
'make high-tech in India', 235–42
new frontiers in health, 232–35
next Silicon Valley, 242–45
online courses and telemedicine, 226
policies and funding, 224
position of leadership, 244
priority for, 245
progress in biosciences, 233
proliferation of TV (especially DTH), 221
robotics, 222, 224
science and technology (S&T)-based industry, 234
side-effects, 220
software-driven design and production, 225
transportation technologies, 231
'virtual tourism', 226
Terrorism, 22–23, 38, 40, 42–44, 49, 51, 53, 59–60, 63, 255
  acknowledged as a global problem, 42
  growth of, 40
  requires local support for logistics, 42
Tesla, 231
Third-degree methods, 19–20
Third World, 37
TikTok, 189n114
Total Fertility Rate (TFR), 146n86, 149
Transistor bomb incident, 30
Triple-therapy drug 'cocktails', 234n140
Tuberculosis (TB), 72
Tukde-tukde gang, 25
Two-front war, 44, 47

Ultra-nationalism, 9, 32
Under-employed, 204
Undertrials, 16–17
UNDP Human Development Index, 65
UNDP Multidimensional Poverty Index, 133
Unemployment insurance, 216, 260
Unemployment rate, 135, 195
Unilateralism, trap of, 61
United Arab Emirates, Indian-origin people, 167
United Kingdom (UK)
  healthcare expenditure, 68
  Indian-origin people, 167
United Nations 'Convention against Torture and Other Cruel, Inhuman or Degrading Treatment or Punishment' (UNCAT), 19
United Progressive Alliance (UPA), 9, 126–27, 129
  policy paralysis, 126
  scams and the anticorruption protests, 126

United State of America (USA)
  allegations of corruption and
    scams, 9
  –China trade stand-off, 236
  healthcare expenditure, 68
  Indian-origin people, 167
  per capita GDP, 138
Universal basic income (UBI), 198
University Grants Commission
  (UGC), 102–3, 117
Urbanization, 177–79
Uttar Pradesh Prohibition of
  Unlawful Conversion of Religion
  ordinance, 173

Vajpayee, Atal Bihari, 125
Ven Conmigo, 75
Victim mentality, 172
Vote-bank politics, 11
Voter ID cards, 4

Voter–MP ratio, 164

WhatsApp, 188–89, 221
WhiteHat Jr, 107
Women-dominated protests, 27
Work from home (WFH), 182,
  210–11, 242. *See also* COVID
World Economic Forum's Global
  Gender Gap Index, 187
World Health Organization
  (WHO), 61
World Trade Organization (WTO),
  61

Xenophobia, 9

Yeltsin, Boris, 79

Zomato, 209, 256